Freiherr de La Motte-Froque

Romantic fiction

Freiherr de La Motte-Froque
Romantic fiction
ISBN/EAN: 9783337104641
Printed in Europe, USA, Canada, Australia, Japan
Cover: Foto ©ninafisch / pixelio.de

More available books at **www.hansebooks.com**

FRONTISPIECE.

ROMANTIC FICTION

BY

DE LA MOTTE FOUQUÉ

ILLUSTRATED

London and New York:
GEORGE ROUTLEDGE AND SONS
1876

CONTENTS.

	PAGE
The Eagle and the Lion	3
The Vow	33
The Unknown Patient	39
The Victor's Wreath	63
Berthold	75
Rose	91
Eugenia	113
The Privy-Councillor	141
The Lantern in the Castle-Yard	163
The Prince's Sword	169
The Siege of Algiers	187
Head-Master Rhenfried	293

The Eagle and the Lion.

HERE was once a fair maiden called Alfhilda. She dwelt on the high Norwegian mountains, near to the sea, in an old castle known far and wide, on account of strange apparitions which were seen there. Alfhilda was the fairest and wisest of all maidens. When any one was so favoured as to be allowed to gaze on the heavenly blue of her eyes and the noble features of her fair face, shaded by dark locks, he received, as it were, new life. Minstrels were inspired to lofty strains; warriors to victorious deeds. But all who had hitherto vied for the love of the beauteous lady had been rejected with a dignity and majesty which for ever forbade their return. Already was it said that Alfhilda, too exalted for earthly love, and guarded by the spirit-ancestors of her wonderful race, neither could nor would give herself to mortal man.

Then it came to pass that a young Swedish hero, of great renown and graceful presence, landed on the coast of Norway. His name was Sywald; and he was but now returning to his northern home from a glorious expedition in the south. Now, also, he heard of the beauty of Alfhilda, and pondered how he could obtain a sight of the far-famed maiden.

"What will it avail you?" said the old warrior-minstrel Wehrmund, of whom he had asked counsel. "You can as little win her love as any other mortal. And if the wonderful majesty of the maiden pierce through you heart and soul, and you sail forth again into the wide world full of keen sorrow, you can only reproach yourself for having perversely pierced your heart with your own spear."

"Ah, Wehrmund, so skilled in song," sighed the knight, " how very, very old you have become since you invented your sweet lays on the banks of the Rhine! Oh, I pray you, noble skald, call back to your remembrance how it then was with you, and whether you could have chanted such glorious songs, or done such valiant deeds with your sword, had it not been for those sweet pangs of love which filled your heart so softly with a pure joy and a pure sorrow for a noble lady who was then far distant from you, and has remained far distant all your life long! Did not your heart beat higher than the hearts of other men, only because you thought in song and war on a lovely approving smile? Yes, you must know it, must know it far better than I can,—the highest boon that can be granted to a hero is, to have in his heart the image of a bright noble woman. Of the rest let the weird-women dispose!"

The old skald bent his head in assent; a slight tinge of shame passed over his face.

"You have spoken better than I did, young man," said he; " and I will gladly do my best to guide you up to the rocky castle of the wondrously fair maiden. Only you must know, that now, when winter-storms howl through woods and valleys, and the solemn yule-feast is near at hand, is no favourable time to visit the fortress of Alf-hilda. At all times it is encompassed by wonderful apparitions; but in this month they throng there so strangely, that even the minds of heroes have been bewildered and distracted in sudden terror. If, then, I may counsel you, young hero, wait for spring-tide, whose joyful gales are most favourable to the enterprises of such as you. But, anyhow, you must let the approaching yule-feast pass over."

"*Must* I?" cried the youth, kindling with anger, his eyes flashing fire. "Truly, my good master, of *must* I know nothing! And unless you can and will shew me some better way of reaching the castle of the lady, I will at once spring on my dappled grey steed, and ride up the mountain, through snow and over rocks, the nearest way. Then I will knock at the lofty castle-door; and my bold deed itself shall proclaim me a dauntless knight."

Old Wehrmund smiled, and answered: "Well, well! thou needst not fancy that thou canst frighten me with thine impatient gestures, young sir. Do that which thou canst not help doing. I have done what is befitting me as a wise minstrel and an experienced man."

He was going forth from the hall where they had been drinking together, but Sywald seized his hand, and spoke with a gentle voice: "Nay, dear master, you should not either be so very severe towards a youth as to leave him for good, and all on account of a hasty word. You know well that I am one who keeps his word; and I do not fear the perilous ride I just now spoke of. But to have displeased and turned away from me a minstrel and hero like you,—that lies as a heavy burden on my heart. I pray you, do not give me this pain."

The old man looked at him very kindly, sat down again at the stone table, and spoke the following words: "Since this ride is, then, decided on in thy gallant heart, thou wilt do best to undertake it either at noontide or just at midnight. It is true, that at such times the ghosts are let loose in their most frightful forms; but then, a bold eye is always desirous to see distinctly and clearly into the combat, wishing to know the whole amount of the danger. The uncertain twilight, on the other hand, of dark glimpses and half-spoken warnings, chills and bewilders often the bravest heroes."

"Yes, I will ride off at midnight," said the knight, well pleased.

"Thou must take the road along the sea-shore, which leads up to the castle-rock," continued the old man. "I know well that neither thou nor thy grey are prone to dizziness."

"Least of all," answered Sywald, "when the sea glances below me with its white-crested waves."

"So is it with me also," said Wehrmund. "I am much more likely to be dashed to pieces amongst inland rocky precipices. Whatever apparitions may pass before thee, dear son, let them go their way unquestioned and unchallenged. It may be that one amongst them will have a hideous serpent on his head, but yet be fair, almost noble, to look upon. Then shalt thou draw thy good sword from its sheath, and pass a stroke from east to west, and one from north to south, with all thy strength, through this phantom of the air. The vile thing will appear afterwards somewhat hideous, and indeed terrifying; but thou must not mind that. Only ride on undismayed; for by this thou wilt render Alfhilda a great service."

"Ay? Then the monster may have three serpents on

his head, instead of one!" cried Sywald. "If it pleases Alfhilda, I can all night long keep up the sport, and hew through the phantom."

"Beware, beware!" warned the skald very earnestly, "lest thou think far too lightly of such things. It may be that he of whom thou speakest so freely shall become thine enemy most to be dreaded on earth. But now, if thou comest to the castle, thou wilt find a silver horn hanging before the outer door; thou must softly and carefully unfasten it from its chain, and blow in it gently. Wert thou to blow too loud a blast, it might, in spite of the cold winter, raise a wild storm of thunder and lightning through our northern mountains. But thou art an understanding knight, and wilt never call such wild assistants out of the old night. Oh! by all the gods of Asgard, I feel now as if thou wouldst most gloriously achieve this adventure."

"Listen!" said the knight; and he sprang up, for then sang a warder from a neighbouring watch-tower:—

"Let him who fears the midnight ghost
   Speed back to house and home;
For the stars shine out, a heavenly host,
   From the ancient sea,
   In mute majesty:
Ye wanderers, cease to roam."

"It is high time!" cried Sywald. He hastened to the stables, and began to saddle his steed. Master Wehrmund had followed, and looked on, well pleased, as the youth laid the costly trappings on his grey, the while speaking very kindly to the noble animal.

"Dear horse," said he, among other things, "this ride may perchance be the most glorious and joyful that we have ever taken together. But then, also, you must not start—do you hear? I know very well that you are not soon frightened at dangers; but hideous figures may meet us. Only press on, my beautiful steed, press on with your light tread. You have already seen on the burning strands of Africa many hateful twisted snakes and other venomous reptiles; and though you trembled at them a little, still you carried me swiftly and surely on the right way. So also you will do to-night: is it not true?"

And, as if it understood its master, the gallant horse looked at him with a sharp, friendly glance, joyfully struck the pavement with its hoofs, and neighed loudly three times. Then the young hero threw himself into his saddle, greeted yet again kindly the old skald, and galloped forth lightly into the starry night.

The sea heaved and swelled before the stormy night-wind; the white foamy wreaths of the waves rose and vanished, and returned to dash against the stony shore. The beech-woods, which sloped down towards it, looked stiff and glittering with frost; high above them rose the rocky point and the towers of Alfhilda's castle.

As now Sywald quickly passed through the solitary forest, his longing desire to see his beautiful unknown mistress grew more strangely strong in his beating heart. It seemed to him that the bright fair form, with her dark tresses, hovered before him in cloud and mist; and he joyfully turned his horse out of the beaten track, which led to the inhabited country, and spurred him up the narrow rocky path, which kept close to the shore of the roaring sea.

Before long, there met him one like a tall warrior, from whose helmet a light was flashing upwards. Sywald forthwith thought that it was the phantom which he was to strike with a double blow, and he held himself ready for the decisive stroke. His horse snorted and foamed under him. But as the appearance came nearer, it proved to be no warrior, and indeed no man, but rather a gigantic wolf: it walked on its hind-legs, and shewed its teeth fiercely at the knight, and what shot upwards from its head was red blood out of a deep wound. But Sywald rode on in silence, according to the direction of the minstrel, till his startled horse had passed the monster.

As he turned a corner, he saw what appeared to him a massive arch, which sprang from the sea-shore, stretching high over the path, till it joined a jutting corner of the rock; but, on a nearer approach, he perceived that an enormous serpent had lifted itself out of the sea, and, overarching the road, had laid its head upon the rock. It had turned its hideous face sideways, and put out its tongue in horrible likeness of a human being, as if mocking and grinning upon the knight as he passed beneath. The noble steed reared wildly, and made as if he would rather plunge into the waves below him than pass under that dreadful arch. But Sywald gave his war-cry, and then the gallant animal deemed that the foe was awaiting them beyond, and, with a joyous neighing, he dashed under the fearful apparition.

And now the rocky path became more and more wild, and steep, and rugged, and narrow. At one of the narrowest parts there sat a veiled woman, like a beggar, who, with wild gestures, stretched out her arms towards the knight, almost closing up the dizzy path. He was about to rein in, and give her an alms, but the minstrel's warning flashed upon him. He quickly urged on his horse, and it was only a phantom-like cloud, through which he passed. But a horrible voice sang behind him—

" Right well escaped, thou daring knight:
 Hadst thou bestow'd that gift on me,
In halls of everlasting night
 I should have prison'd thee.
No beggar I: behold a queen divine!
Though but a dreary realm of gloom is mine."

The horror with which this strange song filled the heart and mind of Sywald soon vanished, for he was now near the summit; and the castle of Alfhilda glanced brightly above the craggy points of the rocks. Then the grey steed galloped so lightly and joyfully over the now more level road, that the little silver bells which adorned his saddle and trappings, and even the knight's great golden shield, resounded sweetly as a merry song of clear young voices.

"Good luck to this honourably achieved adventure!" said a solemn voice; and, looking round, Sywald saw the noble figure of a man: he was leaning, as it seemed, in deep, sad thought, against the rock; but he then stood up, and putting his hand into a cleft, he drew out a drinking-horn, which he offered to the knight.

"I know that you are weary, very weary," said the stranger, with a kindly greeting; "and you need not for that take shame to yourself: you have accomplished more in this ride, far more, than falls to the lot of most heroes. Now the goal is reached — now you may take breath and rest. Seat yourself on this jutting rock, and let us pledge each other."

Sywald had already laid his hand on the mane of his horse to throw himself off, when it struck him that it did not become an honourable knight to stop even an inch short of the appointed goal. He said courteously, "Thanks for your hospitality, my kind unknown friend; but this time I must refuse it, however welcome a good drink would have been to me." And he spurred on his grey without suspicion. But the stranger muttered sounds of displeasure behind him; and Sywald, that he might not appear to be alarmed at them, drew in his gold-embroidered reins, and fixed his bright calm eyes again on the man, while the horse advanced very slowly. Ah! then he suddenly recognised the phantom-warrior with the snake on his head, of whom Wehrmund had forewarned him. "I defy you, in the name of the fair Alfhilda; and now, you bold complainer, stand fast to your arms!" So cried the joyful Sywald: his gallant horse was quickly turned round, and a powerful stroke of his sword whizzed in lightning-like rapidity from east to west, and north to south, through the spectre enemy: it horribly lost its human form, and slowly sank, roaring, from the rock into the depths of the sea. It was as if many voices howled dismally over the fall of the conquered enemy.

But, descending from the summit of the rock, there came down towards the knight many-coloured little lights, — some formed in the air flowery wreaths and crowns, others danced along the ground in ranks. And Sywald, drawing nearer to them, perceived that they were brilliant transparent spirits, in the shape of surpassingly lovely children; some, like maidens in gay waving garments; others, boys carrying shining weapons, and riding on little steeds of a strange colour, now light-green, now red like a rose. Sywald would willingly have spoken to these beautiful little creatures, who greeted him very kindly; but, thinking on Wehrmund's warning, he hastened on, only returning their greeting in silence. He knew well that these were the friendly little elves who, in Iceland, are called " the good people."

He had now reached the level summit of the rock, which, even in the sharp frost of a winter midnight, was still a fair garden; for, as if representing a stately hall, the northern beeches had entwined their high branches, glittering with frost, till they formed a vaulted roof, under which the knight rode as in a crystal palace; and here and there shone what appeared in the starlight like floors of bright silver, but were really round ponds, covered with the most transparent hardest ice. Huge black eagles, roosting among the branches, looked down upon the knight with fiery eyes; but they either returned to their nest again, or flew upwards with heavy wings into the night sky.

The knight was yet thinking whether he dared awaken the lady of the castle, or whether it might not be better to linger in this magic garden until the early sun should be reflected in the crystal ice, when he found himself, through an unexpected turn of the vaulted walk, immediately before the castle-gate. And near him swung on its delicate silver chain the richly ornamented horn, as if beckoning and inviting him to rouse its tones by his breath. There was no longer reason to fear that he should disturb the slumber of the lady: already shone through all the gaily painted shutters of the building a bright light, almost like that of day; and the parapet of the highest tower looked like one brilliant row of torches. And in the midst of these dazzling torches, who stood so tall and queen-like in white waving robes? her dark tresses floating over her noble brow, her earnest unearthly look raised towards heaven!

As the melody of flutes and harps, the name of "Alfhilda" rang softly through Sywald's heart. He dared hardly loosen the horn from its silver chain; and—this time he had not needed the minstrel's warning—gentle and noiseless as a sigh, he breathed into it the notice of his arrival. The sound was wafted in low echoes through the passages of the castle. The lady, indeed, wrapt in solemn thought, seemed not to have heard it; but a maiden forthwith hurried to give her notice; and a hardly perceptible, yet kind bend of her head said, "Yes." The castle-gates flew open before the knight, and two richly dressed pages held his horse.

As he now stood before her in her dazzling hall—she on a throne supported by two lions, moulded out of pure gold; he in deep reverence, almost kneeling, while he leant on his shining sword—there began between them the following discourse. Alfhilda spoke first. She chanted—

ALFHILDA.

Thou wanderer bold, thou venturous knight,
Thou daring youth,—dost thou come here
At the feast of yule? And didst thou speed
Up the mountain-side thy bounding steed,
Through the form of each opposing sprite,
Nor hostile ghost nor spectre fear?

SYWALD.

Thou lady fair, thou beauty bright,
Thou softest beam of radiant light!
No trembling heart is his who kneels,
And dares to woo thee, lovely star!
He is a fearless child of war,
His breast a victor's daring feels,
He owns a conqueror's might.

ALFHILDA.

Who speaks of wooing? who of love?
Bold hero, thou art much to blame.
Say, Sywald (for I know thy name),
What valour canst thou prove?
Hast thou beheld that form of dread,
Him with the snake around his head?

SYWALD.

From east to west I smote him once,
And cleft his hideous crown;
From north to south I smote again,
And struck the monster down.

ALFHILDA.

Hero of heroes, thou hast done
Great deeds of might for me!

SYWALD.

Lady, if so, I then have won
The claim to fight for thee,
The right to woo thee with my sword,
And win a favouring glance and word.

ALFHILDA.

Not so, bold knight; no deed of thine
  Can ever win my hand;
That hope, poor youth, thou must resign,
  For barriers 'twixt us stand:
Yet what doth part us I will now reveal,
Nor, noblest one, from thee the truth conceal.

Then she made a sign with her snowy, beautifully formed hand; and two maidens brought in a seat, on which the knight was to place himself opposite to the lady's throne. Then two other maidens brought him rich wine in a tall silver beaker; and when he had emptied it, the lady dismissed all her attendants. She then began to speak as follows:—

"You cannot be ignorant, my noble hero, how in our mysterious northern lands many strange transformations take place; and they all happen through a solemn charm, and the power of a brave strong spirit: the utmost that less noble minds can do, is to take the form of wolves or raging bears; but *my* ancestors, in their lofty thoughts, aimed at something far better."

"That did mine also," answered Sywald. "They had obtained a wonderful robe of feathers from an old enchanter, and when they drew it on, they became eagles of great strength; in memory of this, I bear an eagle on my shield."

"Have you never put on this robe of feathers, sir knight?"

"Not that, fair lady. I would rather ride forth on my horse to knightly deeds, or guide my bark through the foamy waves. But command only, and to-morrow morning you shall see me flying as an eagle above your battlements, and waging victorious warfare with my winged relations, as many of them as are here roosting on your rocks."

"Lord Sywald, methinks you would ride into the jaws of the most horrible death, could you thereby accomplish your will!"

"Not so, fairest lady; but to fulfil *your* will, most readily."

"Nay, Sywald, I dread these disguises, and I command you never to put on the like."

"The gods be praised! Now you have shewn yourself to be my mistress, and now am I your knight."

"You shall truly be my knight, but my bridegroom never. For know, there was no creature on earth royal enough for my race to change forms with but the lion alone, whose fearful majesty my ancestors had learnt in their voyages to the south. So they oft-times trod our northern forests in the strange noble form of lions, till my father, rich in all hidden lore, laid a ban on the fearfully great gift, that neither he nor his descendants might ever again use it. But he spake thus to me on his death-bed: 'Alfhilda, thy brave brothers are yet lions, by their noble pride, and unconquerable courage, and princely manners. And whilst they traverse distant kingdoms, and spread over the world far and wide the glory of our lion-race, I will leave to thee my mysterious knowledge. It will bring much horror upon thee; but it will give thee many glorious sights. Rest satisfied therewith, and renounce all that man calls joy on earth; for thou art far above holding intercourse with those of another race, much more above marrying with such. Thou art the child of the lion-heroes; think well on that.'"

"And I am the son of the eagle-heroes!" cried the indignant Sywald; "and if your father were a true lion-hero, he must have added some condition through the fulfilment of which a brave northern warrior may shew himself worthy to become your husband."

As if almost startled, the royal lady looked upon him, and said: "You are a bold, impetuous man, but you are also a gentle, noble knight; and you shall hear what the exploit is which my father has appointed to be my suitor's trial. He shall not only take alive, but tame to the obedience of a hound, and bring here into the far north, one of the wildest, most savage lions which the distant land of Africa brings forth in its burning deserts; proving by this wonderful deed that he has the right of king and lord over the noblest and fearfullest beasts of the earth. Then first will it be allowed him to ask of the daughter of the lion-race, 'Lady, wilt thou grant me thy love?'"

"Soon shall I dare say to thee, 'Lady, wilt thou grant me thy love?' Meanwhile may all the gods protect thee!"

So spake Sywald; and gravely greeting her, he left the room.

Alfhilda had well nigh called him back—for, as it were, a light cloud of loving fear swept over her clear brow—but, maiden-like, wrapping herself in her veil, she was silent. And the knight halted, at break of day, before the hall of the minstrel.

"I have learnt all in my dreams," said Wehrmund, as he came forth. "Oh, my son, how dangerous a task is thine, and yet how blessed! The rays of the sun, giving glorious promises, shine round thee like a golden wreath. Now does it behove thee to keep true, and pure, and strong."

"Of that no man can doubt, I trust," said the proud youth.

But then words of solemn warning broke from the lips of the minstrel.

"Dost thou, then, know, my Sywald, whom thy sword struck last night? It was the evil Loki,[1] the enemy of all the gods of Asgard, though once he was himself one of them. And those who met thee before were his bad children—the wolf Fenris, the serpent Midgard, and Hela the queen of the pale ghosts who died without renown."

"But how can this be?" asked Sywald. "Have not

[1] In the mythology of the northern nations the supreme god and creator of the world was Odin; his wife was Freya; and their son Baldur the Good. There were inferior gods and goddesses, who inhabited the palace called Walhalla, in the city Asgard, which was likewise the abode of all those warriors who died gloriously in battle. Loki was the bad spirit, who had, for his pride, been driven from the Walhalla, where he once sat with the good gods, and who had since been the implacable enemy of the gods of Asgard and of all virtuous men. Loki effected by treachery the death of the good Baldur, and confined him in the gloomy halls of his daughter Hela, or Death; but Baldur was to be freed at the last day, and to reign for ever with his father Odin. The other children of Loki—Fenris the Wolf, and Midgard the Serpent—helped their father in all his treacherous attempts upon mankind, though their power was limited. It can easily be perceived from what truths these fables had their origin.

the gods bound Loki to a rock? Are not chains, that cannot be broken, about Fenris? Is not the serpent Midgard in the deep circling the earth? And dare Hela venture up from her pale land of the dead?"

"She dares not indeed, my son; and all is as thou hast said. But the shadows of these evil beings pass through the world in a wonderful way, and try to allure the children of men; and if they succeed, these fearful phantoms rejoice very horribly. But when a blow of a sword such as thine strikes the deceiving father of this hateful progeny, —him who has the power to put on an almost hero-form, —then all the evil spirits moan and howl; and for months not one of them dares come again into light. Alfhilda may now pass the spirit-haunted days of the yule in undisturbed joy with the little glittering fairies, or with other friendly elves. But the evil Loki and his wicked house are wroth with thee. By the time thou reachest the African shores, they will be again free to work their crafty devices; and then beware of them, my Sywald! beware of them!"

Earnestly thanking him, the youth pressed the hand of his warning friend, and hastened to prepare the ship for his voyage to the south.

On the early dawn of the third day he set sail, defying the storms of winter; and he himself, sitting at the helm, guided the vessel through the boundless ocean. Old Wehrmund stood on the shore, thoughtfully giving him a last greeting.

After landing on several coasts, and there shortening the necessary delay by many brave and noble deeds, also after many fights in open sea with pirate-robbers, Sywald, in the first days of spring, anchored before that high Spanish rock which has since been called Gibraltar; and from thence he gazed in deep reflection on the level coast of Africa, which lay opposite.

What troubled him in some degree was, the thought of his good steed. For it seemed to him that the horse would be a hindrance to him in the strange adventure that he was about to undertake; and yet, till the present moment, he had never trusted him to the care of any one but himself.

The noble horse stood by him as if he shared his trouble, and caressed him so softly and quietly, laying his beautiful head on his master's shoulder, as if he knew what his thoughts must be, that at last Sywald called out resolutely: "No; come what may, my dear faithful grey, you shall go with me."

Then the good horse neighed joyfully, and pranced around the knight, and allowed himself to be embarked much more patiently than usual, seeming to take pleasure in the voyage.

The name and the resolute character of the northmen were already well known to the people who inhabited these coasts. It therefore came into no man's head to hinder such a knight on his journey; on the contrary, they were well pleased when, of his own accord, he went on his way in peace and quiet. So, after some days' journey, Sywald reached the borders of the wide, infinite tract of sand which is called the Desert of Sahara. He had never before penetrated so far; and he looked in some wonder on the lifeless, boundless extent. His horse snorted and stood still even before he drew in the bridle. The attendants held behind their leader, shuddering. Then he turned to these faithful men, and said: "This adventure henceforth is for me and for my grey alone. Load him with as much food and drink as he can carry, especially with fodder for himself. I shall walk by his side." He sprang from his saddle; and his men obeyed him in silence.

When all was ready, he shook each of them by the hand, saying: "You must pitch a tent for yourselves in this place, and here wait for me during three hundred nights. When they are passed, and you have not seen me again, you must set up in the very place where I now stand a runic stone, and inscribe on it that I honourably lost my life in the service of the noble lady Alfhilda. I need no higher praise; for this is dearer to me than any other earthly thing. Then you must take ship and go home, and relate to the old minstrel Wehrmund what has happened. But he will have learned all beforehand, through his wonderful dreams. And so good-night!"

The stars were just beginning to shine out of the clear cloudless heaven, and their light was reflected in the quiet tears of many a brave man's eye. But Sywald went forth into the desert in a joyous mood, murmuring low to himself a song upon Alfhilda's majesty and sweetness,— his faithful horse, a little startled and surprised, but yet fresh and courageous, following him.

Soon the cool night-wind raised a cloud of sand between the knight and the troop he had left behind him; and the brave men, who had thought to follow their master with their keen eyes far into the vast plain, lost him suddenly out of their sight: even his footsteps, and those of his horse, were effaced forthwith by the whirling sand.

Sywald, on his part, had thought to look back and once more greet his beloved companions, by waving his scarf and brandishing his bright sword; but it was as if a thick curtain had fallen between them. He stood alone in the desert; and, full of a strange emotion, he put his arms round his true steed's slender neck, as the animal drew close to him, almost trembling. But soon he sang with a clear, joyful voice:

> " Stem thou, my steed, yon sandy sea —
>   A knightly hand doth guide thee;
> O snort not thou so fearfully!
>   A hero walks beside thee:
> His powerful aid in utmost need,
>   His safe protection own;
> He will preserve thy life, bold steed,
>   And guard his own renown."

Disturbed by the loud sound, some strange-looking

animals raised themselves from their deep sandy lairs, till they shewed their giant forms, and then, startled, dashed away over the plain.

Sywald thought at first of the phantom-shadow of the wolf Fenris, and imagined it multiplied, to terrify him; but he soon saw they were frightful creatures, with such long fore-legs, that they seemed almost to stand upright; and he knew, from the accounts of the inhabitants of the coasts, that they were called giraffes.

Then he stroked his good horse, and told him that he should not be afraid of these foolish creatures; and the noble beast looked at them with bold flashing eyes, as if only to indulge his curiosity.

Then, also, ostriches sailed by over the sea of sand with their short wings; or hideous camels trotted past, to the great terror of the grey.

But yet the knight and his horse went on and on unopposed.

Sywald knew well that the strongest and fiercest lions inhabited this desert—only traversing the waste of sand when in search of prey, but living, as in castles, in the green spots which were here and there to be found rising in the midst of the frightful waste, with their fruit-bearing trees and fresh herbage. Every lion of a right noble race possessed, said the legend, such an island—or oasis, as it is there called—for his own hereditary kingdom, and kept it with a destructive might.

Yet Sywald wished for nothing so much as the sight of one of these blooming fortresses. He not only hoped there to find a lion strong and fierce enough to satisfy the commands of Alfhilda's father; but his own and his horse's condition made him long for shade and refreshment.

Knight and horse had already travelled for three days through the wilderness without finding a spring: their provisions were exhausted. The good grey often pawed the ground, as if he thought he must discover a cooling stream; he often sought for grass on the sandy plain; and when he could find neither, he looked up at his master, wondering and inquiring.

Oh, what brave knight, well tried in danger, does not feel far more deeply the wants of his faithful horse than his own? For the man knows to Whom he has to look; but the loving creature looks only to his master, and has no trust but in him.

Sywald was sad at heart, and sorrowfully stroked the grey at every step.

On the evening of the third day, there came a refreshing breeze through the scorching atmosphere; but it raised the sand in whirling clouds, and man and horse wandered on in a thick suffocating mist, and could hardly see two steps before them. When suddenly the setting sun shone forth over the plain with slant dazzling rays; the evening breeze fell; and, close to the travellers, the summits of palm-trees became visible above the subsiding sand-cloud.

The thickness soon quite disappeared; and Sywald stood before the most blooming oasis, which, watered by running streams, offered its fresh verdure for a bed, and its dark-green shadows for a cool hall, to the wearied travellers.

The horse joyfully entered the island; he cooled his delicate silvery limbs in the bright water, till it spurted up in showers of pearls like a refreshing fountain; then he drank long thirsty draughts; then again sprang out upon the fresh grass, trotted here and there, neighing; and at last, with eagerness, began to enjoy the sweet pasture.

But Sywald had only quickly cooled his burning face in the water, and poured a few drops over his parched lips, and then stood on his guard with drawn sword and watchful eye; for he bethought himself of the castellan of this fair oasis—the lion. And truly the golden-maned enemy came roaring forth out of the deepest thicket in all his fearful majesty. The horse flew back, startled, behind the powerful shield which the knight had already raised.

The combat began. Soon Sywald was bleeding from many wounds; for the claws of the lion tore asunder the plates of his armour, and several links of his shirt-of-mail were broken by the sharp teeth of the raging beast. But still the weapons of Sywald struck hard. At the first onset his mighty spear pierced the lion's right shoulder, so that a purple stream ran over the yellow hair; and now he drove his two-edged sword with fearful force into the left shoulder, so that the terrible lord of the oasis sank to the ground with a loud roar. The knight could easily have despatched him; but then, what would have become of Alfhilda's commands?

"At worst, we shall have another fight," said he, smiling; "and then I hope you will become wise, and know your master."

At the same time he gathered healing herbs, and filled his helmet with fresh water, with which he cooled and dressed the lion's wounds. The beast roared the louder— not so much because his wounds smarted, but because he burnt with wild rage at having been overcome. Still Sywald went on with his task kindly and patiently; and not till it was completed did he think of his own wounds, and cool and bind them up.

Meanwhile the grey sprang from the grass into the spring, and from the spring to the grass, neighing, and drinking, and sporting about.

Sywald prepared his bed of moss and sweet-smelling herbs under two orange-trees, in the very spot where the lion had sprung from his lair, and reposed there as undisputed conqueror and lord of the island-fortress.

The lion saw this from afar, and roared indignantly at having thus lost his hereditary kingdom. But Sywald slept peacefully, after eating some of the rich fruits which, early ripened under the burning sun of Africa, had fallen from the laden branches upon his golden shield, as a friendly gift.

This night, however, he had a strange dream — it may be more than a dream. There arose from the sand-drifts, near the border of the oasis, wonderful forms, but too well known to Sywald. The shade of the pale moaning Hela wrang her bony hands above her ghastly face, half hid by matted hair; the wolf Fenris, as if performing some mad dance, moved backwards and forwards on his hind-legs; and the serpent Midgard coiled itself into hideous folds, and then encircled the whole island with its giant length, so that its grinning face came directly over the knight, who tried to turn away his eyes, but in vain. Thereupon Fenris the wolf shewed his long, bloody teeth, and Hela said, " Better things are yet to come." Soon all the three turned their attention to the lion : they ventured not, it is true, to come upon the oasis, — it seemed as if they dared not; but Hela muttered many low and powerful words, the while looking fixedly and stedfastly on the lion; and the serpent Midgard shook its head over him, as if shaking in poison; and Fenris howled angrily, till the lion's roar chimed in with the howling, although exhaustion still kept him from roaring out loudly. More and more madly the wolf danced to and fro; more and more diligently Hela muttered; more and more eagerly the serpent shook his head and darted poison. Sywald felt his brain confused, partly from the fever of his wounds, partly from his dream.

Towards dawn of day his steed awoke him, by springing around with frightened movements; and the knight, starting up, saw the lion wonderfully refreshed, and almost healed, drawing near with loud roars to renew the combat.

Again did the knight and lion bleed, and again the lion yielded to the hero after a hard strife, and again did the hero anoint and bind the wounds of his raging enemy. Thus it happened for two days and two nights: by moonlight came the frightful shadows of the three phantoms, by sunrise the renewed combat with the lion, and the tending of the lion by his victor; but each time the victor sank back more exhausted under the shade of the orange-trees. At length it happened, as the phantoms were rising again from the sand of the desert, there stood suddenly behind them a tall, handsome man: he pointed with a threatening gesture towards the stars, and the three fearful shadows vanished at once. The wonderful stranger beckoned the knight to the edge of the oasis; and he, now fully awake and collected, did according to the unknown's desire. But how did he feel when, on approaching, he recognised the dreaded Loki! An adder, which, though so small, was more hideous and hateful than the serpent Midgard, was twined in Loki's hair, and at times darted out venom on the brow of the fallen Asa-god; then he would shake with sorrowful wrath, and his features, at other times almost pleasing, were distorted horribly.

Sywald, shuddering, would have turned away. Then spoke the troubled spirit: "How is this, that thou darest to despise me, thou over-bold young knight? Boast no more of thy victory over me; for even a child could conquer, if directed and led by a wise bard. And what if the Asa-gods have struck me down? Thy valour and thy purity can hardly so be thy defence that thou shouldst not be, like the wretched Loki, driven out of the halls of Walhalla for endless ages! Think, oh think, on the many bad, wild hours of thy life! If they deal with thee better than with me, it is only because they mete to thee the lightest judgment, while to me they have meted the very heaviest."

It was as if the strange form wept. Sywald, deeply moved, was silent.

"And yet I come with a friendly purpose," continued the fallen Asa-god; "I come to deliver thee from all thy dangers, if only thou wilt let me, thou strange, self-willed knight. What good can betide thee with thy ever-renewed combat with the lion? thine enemy each night strengthened and excited to fresh wrath by my evil children, thou each day losing strength and blood through fresh wounds! O, eagle-hero, eagle-hero, all is over with thee, and thou wilt never behold with those eyes the sweet form of Alfhilda. But follow me, and it will yet be well. In a few hours the lion shall be healed and tamed, and shall follow thee like an obedient hound through the desert; and then a prosperous voyage will bring thee, ere autumn begins, to the arms of Alfhilda."

"What is it that thou requirest of me?" asked the youth.

"First thou must solemnly swear that thou wilt never again strike at me with those fearful strokes; and then thou needest only bow down to the lion,—my skill can hold him fast in a harmless sleep,—and breathe a little, little spell in his ear, and the work is done."

Sywald thought for a moment, doubtfully. "What is thy spell?" asked he at last.

A strange convulsive smile passed over the face of the shadow, and all the sweetness of the pale sad features vanished before it. But soon the fallen god looked again with his earnest sorrowful eyes upon the knight, and whispered softly—

"Odin, Freya, all Walhalla,
Oh! how low the fall will bring you!"

"What is this?" exclaimed Sywald. "They are the holiest names of Asgard that thou speakest."

"That may be," answered Loki. "But it is the only spell by which thou canst heal and tame the lion. And how does it harm Freya, and Odin, and all the gods of Walhalla? Dost thou not know that when the day of judgment dawns, they will all be swallowed up by my fearful children? or knowest thou not that solemn prophecy?"

"I know it well," said the knight, thoughtfully. "And then the great Father alone will reign, and the poor sick world will recover its youth; and even the pale dead who, dying without honour, are in the dreary chambers of Hela, will again become free. Then, too, will be freed the young Baldur, whom a murderer's blow struck while at his gay sport."

"Why speakest thou of *him*?" groaned out the shadow, and began to fade away strangely.

"Why speak I of him?" cried Sywald. "He was the son of a god—he was Odin's son; and thy wiles, bad Loki, slew him! It but now all returns to my memory; and surely again I would strike thee with that double blow. But we are standing here to parley; and a northman must warn his enemy before he hews him down. Get thee hence, before I strike thee with my sword."

Then the bad Loki howled, distorted his face horribly, and vanished in the sand-clouds of the desert. At the same time the lion growled, as day broke, and arose from his sleep strong and fiercer than ever. A combat more deadly than any of the former ones began, and soon Sywald, exhausted, sank on his knee, his shield was torn from his arm, and he fought with expiring strength. His faithful steed saw his beloved master's extremity, and sprang forth from the wood with eager longing for the fight: he flew like an arrow between the combatants, and, rearing up, he struck with his hoofs such a powerful blow on the lion's head, that he fell back on the grass, senseless and bleeding. The angry animal would have repeated the blow, but Sywald called to him, quieted him with his grateful caresses, and then hastened first to bind up the lion's wounds, and then his own. He lay in the exhaustion of death under the shadow of the orange-trees, feeling that if the fight began again next morning, he was hopelessly lost. The day passed solemnly and calmly in thoughts of his ancestors, with whom he was soon to quaff mead in the halls of Walhalla, and in sorrowful longing thoughts of Alfhilda: he did not move from his bed of moss. Sometimes his faithful horse came near him, and bent his intelligent, loving face over him. The dusk of evening began to spread over the desert; at the same time the moon, full and golden, arose in the heaven. Then crept far, far over the sandy waste the sorrowful shadow of the fallen god Loki. He sang; and his song sounded solemnly and gravely, even sweetly, in the oasis:—

"O thou so wearily reclined
    Where orange-trees thy bower darken
    The chosen of Alfhilda's heart,
        O, hearken, hearken!

Must I not weep when I behold
    Our earth-born joys how transitory?
When e'en Walhalla vanisheth,
    And all her glory.

Then cherish life while yet it lasts,
    O, pluck her sweetest flowers!
Beyond the grave are howling blasts
    And leafless bowers.

Chill horrors lie beyond the grave,
    O, keep thee from them yet awhile!
Speak but my harmless spell, and win
    Alfhilda's smile!

O, speak it, hero, for her sake!
    A spell can give no mortal wound;
One word, and to Alfhilda's bower
    Thy steed may bound!

O thou so wearily reclined
    Where orange-trees thy bower darken,
    The chosen of Alfhilda's heart,
        O, hearken, hearken!"

With gentle, sorrowfully soothing tones the words of the distant song reached the heart of the wounded knight. He arose, still indeed undecided, but strangely moved to go to the lion, while that unhallowed spell rose to his lips with magic force; but at the right moment he recalled the last greeting of the old minstrel: "Now it behoves thee to keep true, and pure, and strong!" And he angrily threatened the shadowy figure with his sword. It vanished forthwith in the evening breeze; but there arose anew out of the cloud of sand the serpent Midgard, and the queen of death Hela, and Fenris the wolf. The knight collected his thoughts, with a strong effort, to consider whether indeed there was no means of deliverance for him in heaven or earth, and suddenly there flashed upon him as if he had surely found one. He thought deeply on the beautiful Baldur, the son of Odin, who had perished through the treacherous wiles of Loki, and who would rise again from the dark chambers of Hela when the great Father should reign over the new world. Then sang he loud and clear—

"When Loki's hideous shadow-clouds
Darken this world so bright,
When hearts oppress'd the tempter shrouds
In horrors black as night,—
Then shine, thou blessed hero-form!
Grant, Baldur, grant one saving ray;
Thy word can still the raging storm,
And turn our night to day."

Shooting stars darted joyfully through the moonlight, and the spectres howled and vanished. The lion slept peacefully. The wearied knight also sank back to a quiet slumber upon the dewy grass, and bright unearthly dreams passed through his mind. He knew not indeed how to interpret the glorious visions, and gazed almost dazzled on the boundless fields of light which opened before him; but a blessed hope and expectation never afterwards forsook his breast, ennobling and beautifying his whole life. Strengthened also in body he awoke in the glowing light of the following morning.

The lion lay in deep exhaustion on the way to the nearest spring, which he had in vain tried to reach. Sywald filled his helmet with water; and the animal, parched with thirst from the fever of his wounds and from exhaustion, drank eagerly. Then something refreshed, he crawled the short remaining distance to the water, drank, and then again fell asleep. Sywald bethought himself how he could get food for the wounded creature. With two light darts he took his post beneath the tamarind-trees which grew on the island. He did not wait long before three swift giraffes passed close before him; his first dart lamed one of them; his second threw it dead upon the ground.

As the knight took up his prey, the lion awoke; refreshed by sleep and drink, he lifted himself up, roaring fiercely. But he soon sank down again; and when the knight brought him the game with a friendly smile, it was as if the fearful wild beast smiled also. He took the much-needed food, while the grey sprang joyfully and caressingly round his master. This seemed to soften the king of beasts, who looked on attentively.

So passed many weeks one after another. Every night Sywald drove away the bad spirits with songs of the holy Baldur, and every morning fed and tended the sick lion. The hero's own wounds were almost healed: health and strength returned to him by the help of the refreshing fruits, and of the wine which he knew how to draw skilfully from the tall slender stem of the palm-trees. At length this much was gained, that the lion had recovered his full vigour and power, without having ever attempted to injure his victor, or his victor's steed; on the contrary he would sometimes take part in their games. Sywald began to think of the journey home.

It came to pass one evening that the lion lay stretched out quite still and quiet, as if he slept, but his eyes looked out brightly from under his half-shut eyelids. An ostrich sailed past with the swiftness of an arrow, and like lightning the lion rose, and darted after the gigantic bird; they both quickly vanished in the sandy clouds. The grey gazed with surprise on his master, who sighed very deeply, and said: "Is this the thanks I get? I shall never see thee again, lion. Well, then, I must consider how I can tame another of thy kind, truer than thou."

But before the stars had fully risen in the heaven, as the knight sat in the orange-bower, singing the song of Baldur, he heard a rustling on the other side of the island among the tamarind-bushes; he hastened towards them with his drawn sword in his hand. It was none other than the good lion. He was dragging along with difficulty the dead ostrich, which he laid at the knight's feet, and then stretched himself also there, wagging his tail like a loving dog. Sywald gratefully stroked the mane of the noble beast, and pulling out three ostrich-feathers, he placed them as tokens of his joy in his helmet. The grey came up to him neighing, and stretched his beautiful head, as if greeting his new companion, so brave and yet so tame. It was pleasant to see how the gold and silver manes of the two noble creatures mixed and floated together. Now Sywald knew that his great work was done; and he knelt down and sang a holy song to the praise of the Great Father and of the good Baldur.

As, on the following days, he retraced his homeward way through the desert, he met with many mighty lions, for their hunting was now begun; but when they saw how the noblest of their kind followed the knight, as a faithful vassal follows his liege lord, not one of them thought of beginning a combat. They stood reverently still, and ceased from their chase, till the three had passed on.

After a few months Sywald again stood before the gates of Alfhilda's castle. A soft blush rose to the lady's cheeks as she received her victorious knight; and the lion at his signal bowed the knee before her. Then were the races of the lions and the eagles made one in their noblest branches; and never again did the fallen god Loki, or any of his bad children, venture to shew their hideous shadowy forms on the castle-rock of Alfhilda. But the kindly good people often sported there, and the hero-minstrel Wehrmund stood well pleased amongst them, and sang many a kindling song during their dances, while Sywald and Alfhilda smiling gazed down upon them from the windows of the castle.

The Vow.

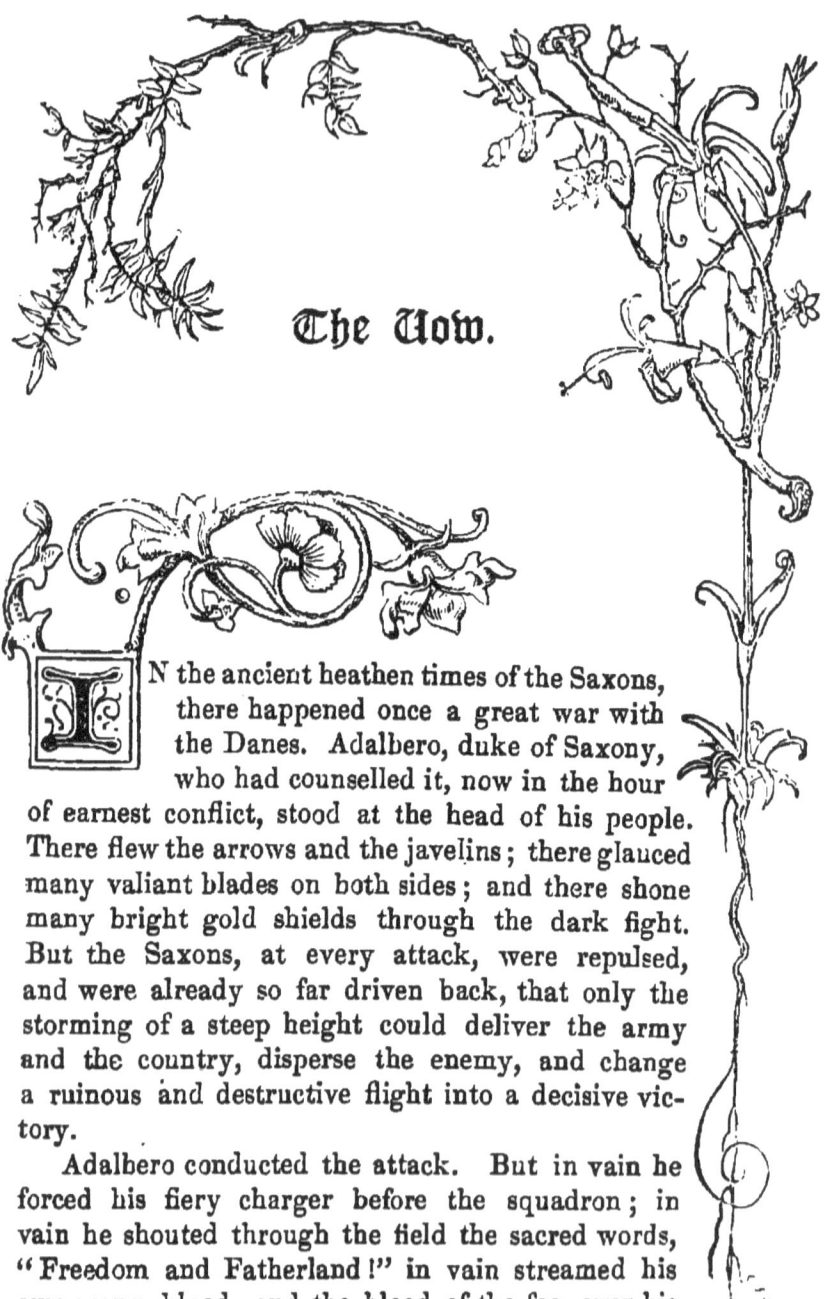

IN the ancient heathen times of the Saxons, there happened once a great war with the Danes. Adalbero, duke of Saxony, who had counselled it, now in the hour of earnest conflict, stood at the head of his people. There flew the arrows and the javelins; there glanced many valiant blades on both sides; and there shone many bright gold shields through the dark fight. But the Saxons, at every attack, were repulsed, and were already so far driven back, that only the storming of a steep height could deliver the army and the country, disperse the enemy, and change a ruinous and destructive flight into a decisive victory.

Adalbero conducted the attack. But in vain he forced his fiery charger before the squadron; in vain he shouted through the field the sacred words, "Freedom and Fatherland!" in vain streamed his own warm blood, and the blood of the foe, over his resplendent armour. The ponderous mass gave way; and the enemy, secure on the height, rejoiced in their decided victory. Again rushed Adalbero on with a few gallant warriors; again the fainthearted fell behind; and again the enemy rejoiced.

"It is yet time," said Adalbero; and again he shouted, "Forward! and if we conquer, I vow to the gods to set fire to the four corners of my castle, and it shall blaze forth one bright funeral pile, in honour of our victory and of our deliverance."

Again was the attack renewed, but again the Saxons fled, and the enemy sent forth shouts of joy.

Then cried Adalbero aloud before the whole army, "If we return victorious from this charge, ye gods, I devote myself to you as a solemn sacrifice!"

Shuddering, the warriors hastened after him,—but fortune was still against him; the boldest fell—the bravest fled. Then Adalbero, in deep affliction, rallied the scattered band: and all that remained of the great and noble collected round him, and spoke thus:—

"Thou art our ruin; for thou hast counselled this war."

Adalbero replied, "My castle and myself I have devoted to the gods for victory, and what can I more?"

The sad multitude, however, called only the louder to him, "Thou art our ruin; for thou hast counselled this war."

Then Adalbero tore open his bosom, and implored the mighty God of Thunder to pierce it with a thunder-bolt, or to give the victory to his army. But there came no bolt from heaven; and the squadron stood timid, and followed not the call.

In boundless despair, Adalbero at last said, "There remains only that which is most dear to me. Wife and child I offer to thee, thou God of Armies, for victory. My beautiful blooming wife,—my only heart-loved child,—they belong to thee, great Ruler in Asgard; with my own hand will I sacrifice them to thee; but I implore thee, give me the victory!"

Scarcely were these words uttered, when fearful thunderings rolled over the field of battle, and clouds gathered around the combatants; and the Saxons, with fearful cries, shouted as with one voice, "The gods are with us!" With invincible courage forward rushed the host;—the height was carried by storm, and Adalbero, with sudden shudder, saw the enemy flying through the field.

The conquerors returned home in triumph; and in all parts of delivered Saxony came wives and children forth, and, with outstretched arms, greeted their husbands and fathers. But Adalbero knew what awaited him; and every smile of an affectionate wife, and every shout of a blooming child, pierced, as with a poisoned dart, his anguished heart. At last they came before his magnificent castle. He was not able to look up, as the beautiful Similde met him at the gate, with her daughter in her hand, while the little one always leaped and cried, "Father, father! beloved father!"

Adalbero looked round on his people, in order to strengthen himself; even there he met quivering eyelids and bitter tears; for among his warriors many had heard his horrible vow. He dismissed them to their families, feeling what happy men he, the most unhappy, was sending to their homes; then rode into the castle, and relieving himself of his domestics, under various pretences, sprung from his horse, closed the gates with thundering sound, secured them carefully, and pressed his beloved wife and child to his heart, shedding over them a torrent of tears.

"What is the matter, husband?" said the astonished Similde.

"Why do you weep, father?" stammered the little one.

"We will first prepare an offering to the gods," replied Adalbero; "and then I shall relate every thing to you. Come to me soon, to the hearth."

"I will kindle the flame, and fetch, in the mean time, the implements for sacrifice," said the sweet Similde; and the little one cried out, clapping her hands, "I also will help; I also will be there;" and skipped away with her mother.

These words, "I also will help; I also will be there," the hero repeated, as, dissolved in grief, he stood by the flaming pile, with his drawn sword in his trembling hand. He lamented aloud over the joyful innocent child, and the graceful obedient wife, who brought the bowl and pitcher, perfuming-pan and taper, used in sacrifices. Then it passed through his mind, that his vow could not be valid; for such sorrow could not find a place in the heart of man. But the answer was given in dreadful peals of thunder down from the heavens.

"I know," said he, sighing heavily, "your thunder has assisted us, and now your thunder calls on your devoted believer for the performance of his vow."

Similde began to tremble as the frightful truth burst upon her; and, with soft tears, she said, "Ah! hast thou made a vow? Ah! husband, I see no victim!—shall human blood ——"

Adalbero covered his eyes with both his hands, and sobbed so terribly that it echoed through the hall; and the little one, terrified, shrunk together.

Similde knew well of such vows in ancient times. She looked entreatingly to her lord, and said, "Remove the child."

"Both, both!—I must!" then murmured Adalbero; and Similde, with a violent effort, forcing back her tears, said to the little one, "Quick, child, and bind this handkerchief on thine eyes: thy father has brought a present for thee, and will now give it thee."

"My father looks not as if he would give me a present," sighed the child.

"Thou shalt see; thou shalt see, presently," said Similde, hurriedly; and as she placed the bandage over the eyes of the child, she could no longer restrain her tears; but they fell so softly, that the little one knew it not.

The affectionate mother now tore the drapery from her snow-white bosom, and, kneeling before the sacrificer, beckoned that she might be the first victim.

"Quick, only quick," whispered she softly to the lingerer; "else will the poor child be so terrified!"

Adalbero raised the dreadful steel — then roared the thunder, and flashed the lightning through the building. Speechless sank the three to the earth.

As the evening breeze rushed through the broken windows, the little one raised her head, from which the bandage had fallen, and said, "Mother, what present has my father brought to me?" The sweet voice awakened both the parents. All lived; and nothing was destroyed but Adalbero's sword, which was melted by the avenging flash of Heaven.

"The gods have spoken!" cried the pardoned father; and, with a gush of unutterable love, the three delivered ones wept in each others' arms.

Far distant, over the southern mountains, roared the tempest, where many years afterwards St. Boniface converted unbelievers to the true faith.

The Unknown Patient.

IN one of the free German towns there happened, about three hundred years ago, the following strange circumstance, which seems well worth relating.

Good old Master Helfrad, the far-famed physician, sat late one autumn evening by the fireside with his wife Gertrude, in edifying conversation. They had let their household go to rest; for supper was over, and the good old couple were unwilling to put restraint on any one. But Master Helfrad had that day received the costly copy of a book of devotion from the monastery of Mariahülf, where he had long before bespoken it; and he could not refrain from reading it aloud the same evening to his faithful companion, for his eyes were yet strong and clear as those of a man of thirty. The heart of husband and wife thrilled with holy joy on reading the wise reflections of the writer, and the beautiful hymns scattered through the book. They spoke with thankful emotion of the whole of their past life, and looked onward with trust at the road which might yet lie before them, and also at the career of their only son, who was now travelling in Italy as a skilful disciple of the painter's art; and they thought with heartfelt content of the bright light which, from their earliest childhood, had shone upon them from above, growing brighter and more full of promise each year, till now it stood before their eyes as a crown of glory awaiting them.

The great clock of the minster-tower had already struck ten, the lights were extinguished in most of the burghers' houses, and Master Helfrad sat yet in his arm-chair, with the silver-clasped parchment volume on his lap, opposite to his wife Gertrude, who let her spinning-wheel stop while she listened with folded hands and sparkling eyes to the speech of her husband, now and then putting in an approving word. The half-hour soon struck, and Master Helfrad looked up in wonder, and said, " Well, well, how far into the night we have talked away! it is not good when men's eyes are open long after the sun has gone down."

" But, father," said Gertrude, " when we are using them to gaze at the everlasting Sun !"—

The old man rose from his seat, and began to take off

the logs which yet burnt on the hearth, repeating the saying,

"If thou wilt prosper in thy station,
Keep e'en in good to moderation."

Then were heard thundering knocks at the house-door from the heavy mallet which hung there suspended by a chain.

"I will come forthwith," said Master Helfrad through the window; and whilst he got ready a light, he said to Gertrude, "Now, indeed, it is well that I am still up; for if this is a dangerous malady, the quarter of an hour which I shall gain may be of much service."

"Were it not better," said Gertrude, anxiously, "to awaken one of the servants, and let him open the door? Who knows what stands without there? Night is no man's friend."

"Therefore will I take *this* with me," said Helfrad, smiling, while he loosened from the wall his honoured old sword. He then put into his pocket a small box of medicines, which he always took with him when he went to his patients, threw over his shoulders a fur cloak, drew on his fur cap, and went, the sword in his right hand, the lantern in his left, out of the room.

The knocking without still continued, growing more furious and impatient. Helfrad said, as he went down the few steps which led from the parlour to the hall-door, "Patience, patience; I am coming!"

Gertrude lighted him out of the room, and whispered, "Ah! husband, there lies a heavy weight on my heart! if you would only awaken one of the men! Do it to please me, and for this once."

"Wife, if it was only my own pleasure I was after, from my heart I would do what you wish," said the old man, as he drew back the bolts; "but in the work of my calling, I must have no misgivings."

The door was now opened; he took up the lantern which he had set down, stepped back, and let the light shine upon the entrance, asking in a friendly voice, "Who is at my door? let him come in, in God's Name, and say how I can serve him."

The autumn wind rushed wildly in at the open door, and out in the dark night was seen a black face, with a strange high head-covering, and a flame-coloured dress, which shone in the light thrown by Master Helfrad's lantern. With a loud cry, Gertrude flew back into the room; even the old man retreated a little, and made the sign of the cross before him with his sword. Then he leant upon his weapon, and spoke with a calm voice, "In the Name of God, say what thou hast to say, and who sends thee."

Perchance the Moor was himself frightened at the appearance of the noble grave old man, with his lantern and his sword, for he trembled violently; but he collected himself soon, and said, "Quick with me to the hostelry of the Three Crowns, master; there lies my lord sick of a fearful fever, which has seized him with such violence, that it will surely destroy him in a few hours, if you aid him not!"

"We will see what may be done," answered the physician: "much may be hoped from God and the healing art." And then he trimmed his light, and went forth, calling back to the trembling Gertrude, "Close the door, and go to bed; but first make up the fire on the hearth, and be not troubled. I have the house-key with me, and I go forth to do God's will. And you, strange messenger," continued he, turning to the Moor, "go before me, and step quickly, that we may soon come to the place."

As they walked hurriedly through the dark and narrow streets, the physician now felt a sort of terror at the bright yellow dress of the Moor, which gave him almost the appearance of an enormous flickering flame. "But," said the old man to himself, "he can hardly be called a 'pillar of light,' I should feel otherwise if he were; and yet who knows? God has put such wonderful power in man, that he can turn all things to his own purpose."

The Moor began to go slower; and as the physician urged him on, he answered, with a not ungentle voice,

"Old sir, I have seen your white hair and your white beard: too great haste might hurt you."

"It is kind in thee to think of that, my son," said Master Helfrad; "but care not for me—I can step as rapidly as the strongest youth."

"Ha!" cried the Moor, and broke forth into a hideous laugh; "then we may run a little race. Off now! who shall get first to the hostelry?"

"Do not speak in that unseemly way," said Master Helfrad. "A thoughtful German burgher knows nothing of such jests and gibes. I will walk as God has given me strength, and as befits me. Any thing unfitting I will not do now or ever, not even for the emperor's sake."

"But we should get there quicker," cried the Moor, and again laughed frightfully, till the sound echoed back from the nearest windows, and was repeated far through the stillness and darkness of the street. Then spoke the old man with the piercing solemn voice of noble indignation, "Be silent!" and the Moor seemed to shrink into himself, and went on rapidly and in silence.

The inn of the Three Crowns was brilliantly lighted up, and the whole house in movement, so that Master Helfrad at first thought some disorderly feast was going on. But as he entered he saw on all faces the paleness of terror, and the household running about in disorder. A little window which opened from the hall into the parlour of the landlord shewed his family kneeling around a crucifix. Master Helfrad asked whether the stranger yet lived?

"If you have the courage to go to him," answered a servant, "go up those stairs and turn to the left; you can make no mistake, for his fearful howlings and imprecations have made the hair of all of us stand on end. We fear that we are lodging the devil or his like."

In truth, hollow cries were heard above all the other noises, coming from a distant part of the building. The physician repressed his secret fear, and went up the stairs; the Moor rushed up in three springs, and was heard running along the passage to the sick man. Master Helfrad followed him slowly through the long narrow passage, which was lighted by a single lamp nearly burnt out. The servant had truly said that no one could mistake the way; for from a room at the further end there came forth a noise which might have been taken for the roaring of a lion, had not the most horrible curses but too clearly shewn that the fearful sounds were proceeding from a being endowed with man's reason. Having reached the dreaded door, the physician once more prayed with his whole heart to God, guarded himself again with the sign of the holy cross, and then passed the threshold with a firm courage.

A dazzling light met his view, for on all sides burnt a quantity of wax tapers; it seemed that all darkness had been diligently banished, as if it had been feared that in every corner where it would have been, there would also have lurked some horror. On a couch opposite the door, a figure, dressed in strange and rich attire, was turning and struggling in the arms of the black man; now a foot in a large purple slipper was darted convulsively forward, now an arm covered with a dark-coloured sleeve slashed with red. It seemed to the physician as if it was no earthly being that he saw; he went forward to look more closely, and a glance at the strange figure had almost made him start back, but that he immediately perceived there was a mask on the patient's face. The latter now kept still, though with an evident effort; it seemed to be the effect of some words which the Moor screamed into his ear in a language which the learned Master Helfrad had never heard.

"Sir," said the physician, "you must take the mask from your face; the face of the patient is an instructive book to the physician."

The sick man shook his head in silence.

"Does not your lord understand me?" asked Master Helfrad of the Moor. "Shall I speak either Latin or Greek to him?"

"He knows all languages," answered he; "you heard him curse in German when you came in. But you will do well to leave the mask in its place."

"Ah! you know nothing about the matter," said the physician; "the mask must be taken off."

"Will you then be driven mad?" cried the patient in a fearful voice, and sprang up convulsively. "He who sees me must go mad; but if you wish evil to yourself, you shall have it. I often threaten my servant with this when he excites my anger too fiercely. You shall have your will; you shall have it!" And he was already loosening the clasps of the mask, but the Moor fell shrieking on his knees, and called now upon his master, now upon the physician, to desist from their intention; warning the former not to drive to madness the physician who should heal him, and assuring the latter that he himself had never looked upon the face of his lord, and yet knew but too well that it was the most fearful sight in the whole world. The sick man let go his hold of the fastenings, and fell back again on his bed; Master Helfrad gave up the point shuddering. Whilst he now felt his patient's pulse, and bent over him to ask him questions and to observe his breathing, it seemed to him as if two such glaring fiery eyes shone out from the mask that he drew back terrified. But the experienced doctor knew well, from the hand, and arm, and whole figure, that he had before him a strong, muscular, but emaciated man of at least sixty.

The good Master Helfrad seized his casket, and began to prepare a salve over the flame of two wax tapers, and whilst it was warming he mixed a costly drink.

"You want implements," said the Moor, and opened a precious chest, in which was an abundance of glasses, vials, retorts, and all possible vessels of the same kind, and all of the best and most beautiful sort. There were also some metal flasks, of such wonderful workmanship that Master Helfrad could not recollect ever in his life to have seen the like, nor could he guess for what purpose they were intended. Then he said, " My son, that chest looks somewhat strange to me; I only make use of those things which I fully understand, and of which I can give a good account to God and man. Close it again, I want nothing more than my own implements."

The black attendant quickly closed the chest, for his fearful master threatened him, saying, " Thou miserable fool! art thou so eager to boast and make much of the very little knowledge thou hast acquired?"

At the same time the malady again seized him with all its strength, and destroyed at once the composure which he had kept with such an effort. The unearthly howlings began afresh; curses in many different languages poured from his lips; the most fearful in that unknown tongue which seemed to be allied to all the horrors of his visage. The Moor held his master in his arms, by turns trembling in all his limbs and stamping wildly on the ground, as he repeated the curses of the sick man.

Meantime Master Helfrad sat diligently at his work, and hummed, with cheerful countenance, a pious song. It was as when, on some winter-night, a fierce storm rolls over the earth, and chases before it the dark and fugitive clouds;—while the moon continues to look down from her height with undisturbed and friendly aspect.

The drink and the salve were soon prepared. The good physician approached his furious patient, saying, " Now control your wild nature; the uncurbed spirit may not hope for help from the Almighty God." And as he gave him the drink, and rubbed his sunken temples and his powerful breast with the salve, he continued to repeat sayings about the ways of God and the wanderings of men, in reference to what he had already spoken. So long as the pain raged in the limbs of the sick man, or began only imperceptibly to decrease, he yielded quietly and gently to all that the physician did or spoke; but hardly had the soothing power of the medicines gained the victory, and life again flowed calmly through his veins, when he said with an angry, displeased manner, "I think, friend, you may cease your tedious sayings and allegories; they are no ways to my taste."

"Not so, I hope," said Master Helfrad kindly, continuing alike his gentle tending and his edifying talk.

"Laugh him dumb with thy jeerings, Nigromart!" said the sick man to his attendant; but Nigromart closed his eyes, and turned away affrighted.

"What hast thou promised? wherefore art thou here?" cried the dreadful figure. "Wilt thou shamefully turn back when half way?"

The Moor now seemed to recollect himself, and broke forth with a torrent of gibes, and jests, and mockeries on the physician; who at first remained quite still, putting in occasionally a holy word, and assuaging more and more the sufferings of his patient; but at length he lifted himself up, looked earnestly at the mysterious mask without shrinking from the fiery eyes, and said, "Man, where wouldst thou be before three hours if I withdrew my hand from thee?"

"Thou needst not think of converting me!" murmured the stranger, turning away scornfully.

"The more, then, must thou care for the little life which may yet be left thee," answered Master Helfrad.

"You would not leave me on account of a few jesting words?" said the stranger; as he muttered to himself, "You would be a good performer of your own words if you did!"

"Listen then," answered the physician, "and I will tell you once for all. If either you or your attendant touch with your impious words those things which are held sacred through all Christendom, then I at once turn my back upon you, and not all the gold of Africa and India shall bring me to you again; but if you choose to jest only on myself, I will be no more angry at it than is natural and excusable, and even that only very seldom, I promise you. Look here at my wrinkled face and white hairs; I think they would be good enough aim for marksmen such as you seem to be."

He looked upon them so kindly and patiently, that neither of them could bring out a word; and now that his sufferings were relieved, the sick man, quite exhausted, sank into repose. The physician gave the black Nigromart instructions what to do to his lord; promised to be there again betimes; and went home in deep thought, after having given rest, by his noble skill, not only to his patient, but to the whole house.

His wife Gertrude lay in a quiet sleep, to which she had composed herself trusting in God, and from which she awoke the next morning at dawn of day, as Master Helfrad was softly leaving the room. "Oh, father! whither are you again going?" she asked. "Will you quite destroy your health?"

"No," said the physician, with a kind smile; "I am thinking much more of restoring that of the man sick near to death, to whom I was called yesterday; and for that purpose I must go forth to gather herbs in the morning dew. Do not detain me, dear Gertrude. I see well you would fain know, after the fashion of women, how the sick man is called, and like particulars; but I have no time; and even if I had, I do not myself know who he is whom I hope to heal." Then he bid a friendly farewell to his wife, and went out singing into the meadows so gaily, that those who had seen him from afar might well have thought it was a youth gathering flowers for his beloved, instead of an old physician collecting healing herbs for an ointment.

The malady of the stranger grew more critical towards mid-day, as Helfrad had expected; but what almost bewildered him was a strange whistling, and piping, and fluttering, which at times sounded through the sick chamber as from the motion of unseen wings. The masked man and the Moor were evidently terrified at it; but the former threatened with his clenched fist, and then for a moment all was still.

"Sir," said Master Helfrad, "I know not what beings you have around you; but I see that you cannot control them, and I must take part against them."

At the same moment there was a more violent whistling, and piping, and flying than ever; and the sick man said quietly, "Master, you will do wisely not to meddle with them in any way."

But the old Helfrad cried out with a loud and powerful voice, "Be quiet, whoever you are, so long as a true and honourable man is here in this chamber: I command you, in the name of my Lord God; and if you do not obey, I must speak yet heavier things to you."

Then, all was so still that the movement of a mouse might have been heard; and Master Helfrad said with an honest smile, "I have now shewn you how one can quiet the like."

"Do you, then, know them?" asked the mask.

"How know them?" answered Helfrad. "I know nothing of such beings; but we need only walk in God's ways, and speak in His name, and all evil things will give way to us."

"Are the means so near, so direct, and so secure?" murmured the stranger. "And could one so simple do more than . . . ." He stopped, and turned discontentedly towards the wall, as if he would sleep; and the physician left the room.

Towards evening Master Helfrad came again; the household seemed in as restless a state as the day before, and the old man listened if the fearful howling was again to be heard; but he soon perceived that the confusion was of quite a different kind. The household was preparing for a riotous feast: in the kitchen there was baking and roasting going on, as for a wedding; attendants with empty flasks were hastening down the stairs, others ran up with full ones. A gay drinking-song reached the physician's ears from the end of the long passage; many reckless words were also heard. As, shaking his head, he now entered the

E

room, he found some young men, the sons of burghers, assembled at a splendid dinner; the Moor was in the midst of them, and he it was who sang the wild but harmonious song, while the rest joined in the burden of each verse. The mask lay on his bed, and laughed often so fearfully that the half-intoxicated youths shuddered and looked round in affright; but the clatter of glasses and the song soon carried them back to their wild carousing. None noticed the presence of the pious doctor except the sick man; but he seemed only to laugh the more violently at Helfrad's distressed and surprised look.

At length the physician went up to the table, saying, "What unholy feasting is this?" and, without waiting for an answer, he took the wine-flasks one after another from the table, and also the dishes, and carried them carefully to the door, saying, " I was well nigh tempted to fling them all out of the window; but God's gifts are not to blame because you have desecrated them."

"Old man, art thou mad?" cried the mask. "Dost thou think that I have touched any of those things? Thinkest thou me such a fool, that, to please my palate for an hour, I would throw away my whole life?"

"One cannot know," answered Master Helfrad, without intermitting his work; "I fear you have been guilty of far worse folly than that. Is not life less when compared to eternity than three hours compared to life? Happily such folly may be repaired as long as a man stands on this side the gulf."

When he had carried all out, he placed himself before the astonished young burghers, and said to them, "You, foolish striplings, go home, and humbly beg your honoured parents to give you a severe chastisement, the smart of which you may feel when you are again invited to such a banquet, and so lose your appetite for the like. Also please to tell those below, that no attendant is to come up here again with such provisions, and that the cook may let his fire go out. March! go!"

With crimson cheeks and downcast eyes the youths left the room; and Master Helfrad murmured kindly, half to himself, " That red colour becomes you, silly boys; it is a livery that shews you yet to be in the service of a good Lord."

The mask meanwhile had taken courage, and once more attempted, with his frightful voice of wrath, to check and terrify the old man; but the curses died away on his lips, as Master Helfrad said, " Peace, speak not against God! a judge for life or for death stands before thee." The sick man, overpowered, threw himself angrily on his bed; and from this evening neither he nor Nigromart sought again to oppose the no less courageous than skilful physician.

Helfrad now devoted his whole time so entirely to save the life of his patient, that he was hardly ever seen but reading, or collecting herbs in the fields, or silently praying to God for light and assistance.

Once Gertrude (who now knew what a terrible guest the Three Crowns harboured in the patient of her husband) asked how, for the sake of such a godless man, he could so waste the precious strength of his old age?

" Wife," said Master Helfrad, " all sick men are alike to be cured. One Higher than the physician must judge whether or not they be worth the curing. But so much can I see, that no one more needs a longer span of life than this poor distracted wretch." Then he took again his cloak and cap, and hastened to the inn of the Three Crowns.

Before the room-door he found Nigromart sitting on a bench, drawing; who made signs to him that his master slept. " Right well," said the physician; and in order to be at hand when he should awake, he seated himself by the Moor, and looked at what he was about. He was pleased to see a fair, bold sketch of St. George, who was sculptured in stone over the door of the neighbouring cathedral, in the act of killing the dragon.

"Say nothing to my master of this figure," whispered Nigromart.

"Wherefore not, young man?" asked Helfrad. "You have done a deed worthy of praise, and that all the world might know of. But one thing I will tell thee honestly does not please me. Why didst thou not put in the strangely beautiful sword which hangs by the side of the saint?"

Nigromart thought it was of no meaning or importance; and when he saw that Master Helfrad was about to return a very serious answer, he hastened to open the book which he had used to support his drawing, and tried to turn the old man's attention to other things, by shewing the beautiful paintings and sketches which it contained. The good doctor looked well pleased at most of these, but put some aside carelessly.

"Why do you not look at those designs?" said Nigromart; "they are taken from the most glorious monuments of Grecian art."

"My friend," answered Helfrad, "I understand none but German paintings, or perhaps Italian, so far as they are related to the German. The other skilful designs I put aside, as an unlearned man does my Latin and Greek books. But a man who would master and practise any art, must learn it thoroughly; therefore I have sent my only son to travel in Italy, that he may lay a firm foundation for the work, which afterwards, by God's help, he shall raise in his native land to the edification of his countrymen by many fair designs. Have you never known him as a fellow-artist—he is called Freymond?"

"Oh! Freymond," said Nigromart,—"yes, Freymond, I know him well." And then he began to relate how highly the young artist was prized by all the Venetian, Florentine, and Roman masters, and how the Italian nobles accounted it an honour to entertain him; with other glorious and joyful tidings.

"May he only not be puffed up!" sighed Helfrad.

"Truly—I may say it behind his back—he went hence with an angel's innocence; and I trust in God *that* has been kept safe by many images of angelic beauty. His mother and I pray for that day and night. See, dear Moor, you have made my heart right joyful with your tale; and so much the more would I that you had not left out the sword of St. George. For, first, a sword is never a mere accessory to a man, as you thought; and then the sword of this figure has its hilt in the form of a cross. I trust my son does not forget that cross-hilted sword in any of his designs. Hearken, my friend; you serve a strange lord, but you have surely never forsworn to paint a cross!"

The sick man moved at that instant; Master Helfrad was obliged to go in to him without awaiting Nigromart's answer; but when he came from the room again, the Moor held out to him the figure of St. George, saying, "Keep this in memory of me. See, I have ventured to trace the sword on it." And as indeed the noble weapon, with its significant cross-shaped hilt, hung down at the side of the saintly knight, the old man pressed very kindly the Moor's hand, and felt a hearty joy in possessing the gift.

At this time, when Master Helfrad went forth of mornings to gather the dewy herbs, there often came to him in the fields a slender maiden, with a lovely though somewhat pale countenance: she helped him modestly and reverently in his work, as a dutiful daughter would help her father. She had soon learnt with quick attention what herbs the physician chiefly needed; she remembered, too, to choose the best and finest of the kind he wanted, since he had given the following answer to her question, "Why he sought herbs for himself with such toil, instead of taking them from the stores of the apothecaries:"—" My fair child, are we satisfied when we see a horse, an ox, or a hound, that it *is* horse, ox, or hound? Do we not ask concerning the strength and good qualities of the particular animal that we need? How, then, can I expect to get good out of dried plants, when we can hardly know at what time of year they were gathered, certainly not what time of day; and therefore know not under what influence they sprang up, nor whether they will be hurtful or serviceable to us?"

One bright morning, as the physician had answered many similar questions of his gentle assistant, and they were both resting, after their work was over, under some shady limes, he said to her, smiling, " It is now time that I should question and thou answer, sweet maiden; it seems to be right wonderful that one of thy sex should find such pleasure in listening. Open now thy fair mouth, and tell me something of thyself; and, first of all, thy name. Truly, if there lay not such a sorrowful paleness on thy cheeks, and if thou didst not speak somewhat broken German, whereby it may be seen that thy home is in a distant land, I might be sure, without asking, that thy name is Angel, thou graceful apparition, so full of all kindliness and humility."

" I know not, dear father, what you mean by that," said the maiden, while a faint blush coloured her pale cheeks, " but truly I am called Angel in your northern tongue, for in Italy I was christened Angela."

" Wert thou born in that beautiful flower-garden, Italy, little Angel?" asked the old man. "What, then, has wafted thee over the high Alps?"

" No hopeful breath of spring," answered the maiden; " but a cold autumnal blast, which stripped all the leaves from my blossoms. Yet I trust to pass here a calm and pious winter; and when the eternal spring comes to me, then shall I wander amongst the flowers of heaven, free from sorrow, and full of peace. See, dear father, I lived with my old, long-widowed mother near the holy city of Rome, in a grove of laurels; and we led a still, quiet life, apart from all the world. We never went into the city; as she lay before us with her old temples and palaces, she appeared to us always as the continuation of the broken columns and walls which still remained in our grove, and under whose shadow I read so happily holy books, or beautiful histories, which my blessed father had bequeathed to us. Now it so happened that a young German painter came into our laurel-grove to sketch the ruins it contained. My mother gave him hospitality for many days; and as he was of angelic beauty and of angelic goodness, he became very dear to me, so that when, after a little while, he wooed me for his wife, with my mother's good will, I willingly plighted my faith to him, and we were betrothed. Then he spoke of carrying us to Germany; and as I had fears of your distant northern land beyond the high mountains, he began to tell me many beautiful things concerning it, and also to teach me your language; and—whether it was that I hung upon him with my whole soul, or that there is an attractive charm in your land for all who learn to know it well—very soon in all my dreams I heard the rustling of your German oaks and limes, with the immeasurable verdure of their extensive forests; and I saw the pure bright mirrors of the mighty streams which roll nobly and peacefully among them. The songs of love and war of your greatest poets were on my lips; and with endless longing I gazed all day on the images which my lover drew of German chiefs, and holy men, and pure women. But the more I now longed to hasten to this beloved land, which drew me to her with a silent welcome, the seldomer did my betrothed speak of our journey. He began with more glowing words to praise the beauty of Italy, and at last declared plainly that he would end his days in that earthly paradise. I yielded to his will, and only prayed him to paint for me many German figures; yet I did ask him whether his parents were dead, of whom he at first had spoken so much, praising their kindness in having given him leave, at parting, to bring home, if God and his own heart so inclined him, a maiden of his choice from foreign lands to be his bride, provided only that she were innocent and gentle. He laughed, and answered, that he believed his parents were in health, but that they led a dull life; and he meant to give me a more joyous one than I had yet known. I felt frightened at this; but I laid all to the state of excitement in which he always returned from Rome, whither he now went almost daily. At this time all German pictures and images of saints vanished from his painting-room; he only designed old statues of heathen times; and he laughed at me when I sorrowfully asked for the figures which in earlier and happier days he sketched for me so readily and so beautifully. 'They were childish trifles,' he said; 'but now he was on the right path of nature and of godlike liberty.' Yet I could trace nothing godlike in his new works; on the contrary, I often saw among them unseemly figures; so that I went no more into his painting-room. My good mother, thank God, did not notice his change, but died in peace and hope, giving us both her solemn blessing. Ah! with what vain, unsatisfying consolations did my lover, once so full of earnest thought, wound my heart! He now wished to take me to Rome · and as I would not hear of it, he went thither himself, in order, as he said, to prepare our future home. Months passed away, and I heard nothing of him; at length I ventured to go into the great capital of the world, and, with tears of anguish in my eyes, my senses bewildered with the tumult that was quite new to me, I went to the part of the town where he lived;—he had often described his house, and once had sketched it for me. Now I stood before the graceful building, which looked to me as fair in reality as it had in his drawing. With like beauty the golden oranges, amid their dark leaves, and surrounded with bright flowers, shone through the garden latticework. And yet this could not, I thought, be the house of my betrothed, for the loud shouts of a riotous company sounded from it, hardly allowing at times a few tones of the melody of many singers to be heard. I was about to turn away for ever, but I loved him as myself; and to

seek the lost was, I thought, a command of God. So I
ascended the marble steps with prayer and confidence, and
entered the door of the banqueting-room. The guests
were startled at my appearance, for I was yet in deep
mourning for my mother; and in the general silence which
now reigned, I went up to my betrothed, who was crowned
with roses and breathing perfumes. I spoke to him of
time and eternity, of the world and of God. At first he
seemed moved and alarmed; but the torrent of his passions soon swept my words from his heart: he spoke much
of the bright inspiring life of an artist; he dared to offer
me to share it with him; he even praised my beauty with
bold, unfitting words. Then I went forth; and I have
never seen him since. I heard, indeed, that he had gone
to Greece as the favourite of a mighty prince. But I
converted my small estate into gold, and have come as a
pilgrim to beloved Germany; for I love it now in place of
my poor bridegroom; and I dare to hope that it can never
be so lost to me as he is lost."

Bright tears fell from the maiden's eyes; and the old
man said, " God will guard our land from being lost to
thee and to all His angels!" But then he spoke with a
low, almost stifled, voice: " Tell me at once, fair child,
was not thy betrothed called Freymond?"

" Alas, yes!" she answered, weeping yet more bitterly. " And since you ask that question, are you not
his father, the far-famed Master Helfrad, who lives in this
city? I have thought so for many days, but never had
courage to ask."

" Truly I am he!" said the old man; " my broken
heart bears witness thereto."

Then Angela knelt weeping on the grass; and the old
man laid both his hands on her dark locks to bless her.

After a while he began again, and said, " Hast thou,
then, no more love for Freymond?"

" Ah, good Heaven!" she answered, " how could I
ever cease to love him?"

"Well then, dear Angela, we will now, and very often, together pray for him." And he knelt beside her on the grass.

They first prayed quite to themselves, then aloud, and louder, stretching wide their hands toward heaven; and instead of disturbing each other, the words of one seemed to kindle those of the other, as we may fancy two seraphs, with wings touching and embracing each other, soar up to heaven.

They were at length interrupted by the loud and uncontrollable sobs of a third person, not far from them. They turned to look, and perceived it was the Moor, who was stooping over a stream close by, and washing his face as eagerly with the water as with his tears. When he lifted himself up, and looked upon the other two, the water and his tears had cleared away the frightful darkness of his face, the high flame-coloured turban fell off, and in its place golden ringlets clustered round his temples. It was Freymond, who in deep sorrowful confusion sank on his knees before his father and his betrothed, repeating through his tears, " O God! O God! they pray for me, and I have broken their hearts!"

" But now you will heal them again," said Angela, bending soothingly over him, and touching his cheek; while the old man took his hand, and with a strong effort raised him, saying, " Will not our heavenly Father receive us when we come again to His house as lost sons? How, then, should a poor earthly father not do the like?"

Then he comforted and kissed him, and thanked God for having hearkened to his prayer; but presently he said, " Now be calm, as beseems a man, and tell us, in a few words, how you came to know that fearful sick man, and how it stands with you now."

" Father," answered Freymond, " I found him in the vaults of an old Roman villa; and when I trembled before him and his mask, he spoke kindly to me, and led me through strange ways to some glorious statues, the like

of which I had never seen above ground. He bound me
fast to him at first by the love of my art, and by his full
knowledge of the joyous life of the old Greeks; and then
he counselled me to follow the same joyous life, pouring
into my hands more gold than I wished for, and more
than I knew how to use. But this fatal knowledge he
soon taught me : I recklessly plunged into all the pleasures
of Rome, and, unsatisfied with what the outward world
could give me, I began to knock at the gates of the unseen
world, not for light, but for might. Thus my terrible
guide had me fully in his power. You have seen, father,
how he is connected with mighty spirits; he promised that
I should become a sharer of all his secrets, and, together
with him, have power over men and over nature, as the
gods of Greece have had."

The father made the sign of the cross upon himself and
his son, and said, " That would truly have been to spring
in your own strength from a pinnacle of the temple."

" But first I was to cast from me," continued Freymond, " all that held me bound to my country, my parents, and our holy faith itself. Till then, he said, I must
remain a servant, have my face disfigured by a hideous
black stain, and bear the hateful name of Nigromart. As
soon, however, as the time of trial should be over, I was
to take the name of one of the glorious gods of Greece,
and assume a marvellous beauty. My master, too, was
again to become youthful ; and, no longer needing a mask,
was to lose his terrific countenance, the result of a former
unhappy spell. In the course of my probation we came
to this good city, to try whether I was so fully possessed
by the evil spirit as to mock my father, and mother, and
home, under my strange disguise ; and then I was to deny
those most holy truths in which the heathen do not believe.
Oh ! praise be to God, who threw that fearful man on a
bed of sickness, and so brought to nothing the ending of
my trial, after which I longed !"

Again he sank down in prayer; and his father and his

bride prayed in silent joy by his side. Then they all three rose.

"Take your betrothed home," said Master Helfrad; "return to your mother, and let her know all."

"Ah!" sighed Freymond, "if only it might be concealed from my pious, sorrowing mother!"

But Helfrad said very solemnly, "Truth is not only a good thing, my son, it is the very best; for without truth there is no love."

Freymond bowed his head in sorrowful acquiescence; and with Angela's soft hand in his, refreshed and strengthened by her loving words of comfort, he went home. Master Helfrad visited the sick man. He approached his bed with a thoughtful face, saying, "I have taken back my son! I should have done it sooner; but I learnt just now for the first time that he was in your service. Reckon him no more as your servant." And then he began to prepare ointments and draughts as before, and to administer them as if nothing had happened.

The masked man trembled violently. At length he brought out these words, "And will you, then, not leave me? will you still heal me?"

"Why ask me such a question?" said Master Helfrad. "I have been called to be a physician by God and by my superiors."

The sick man sighed deeply, and pressed the physician's hand; then he began again: "Has Nigro—"

"That name I forbid!" interrupted the master earnestly.

And the other continued, correcting himself, "Has Freymond confessed to you who I am? A solemn oath binds him yet."

"And he observes it," answered Helfrad; "my son would not begin his repentance by breaking his oath."

"I will trust the secret to you, if you desire it," said the sick man, "and you will marvel. But, ah! I can hardly pronounce it."

"Do not," answered the physician; "I am not curious, and God forbid that I should add to your troubles."

Then he hastened home, and found his son in the arms of his weeping, forgiving mother, and of his happy bride. Soon the wise father took Gertrude aside, and solemnly begged her not to tempt her son to break his oath by her questions: "For," said he, "you like to hear new things, and we know not how firmly rooted the replanted sapling may yet be. In a year's time, I hope, you may question him as much as you please."

Master Helfrad's hope did not deceive him. The true German love and strength soon recovered their former firm power over the heart of Freymond, deepened by the storm of temptations against which he had to struggle. He had to bear a gentler probation in winning Angela again; and the art of his fatherland, on her part, shone brightly on her returning son with heavenly refreshment.

In the mean while the masked man was cured of his sickness; and when Master Helfrad took leave of him, and sent him on his way with many holy words of warning, he listened very patiently, and said at last softly and timidly, "Do you, then, really think that I may yet be saved?"

"Wherefore not?" answered Master Helfrad; "the same God yet lives."

Then the restored man humbly begged the physician to obtain permission for him to do penance in a monastery of the town. He must, indeed, keep on his mask, for his countenance was too hideous to be shewn; even now the fiery eyes shone so strangely through it, that Master Helfrad, against his wont, was forced to look down. He wished also to be allowed to conceal his name, lest it should excite too much terror amongst the brethren, or perhaps awaken an ill-timed curiosity among them, on account of many strange mysteries in his own life and in that of another. Master Helfrad promised to do what he could, and in a short time brought all to pass according to the wishes of the mask.

Received within the holy walls of Mariahülf, the stranger

underwent there such a severe and profound penance that he edified all the inhabitants of the monastery as much as he had at first terrified them. His voice became milder, the light of his eyes less and less frightful, till at last it shone pleasantly. Then, at length, the abbot said to him one day before the assembled brethren: " Penitent, the Spirit has made known to me that thy sins are forgiven, and that thy countenance is again become human, and thou needest no longer conceal it under that dreadful mask. Therefore I command thee to put off that rigid covering."

The penitent bowed humbly, obeying the words of the abbot, and the heavenly smiling countenance of an aged man shone upon the astonished brethren. Then they all together praised God, took the restored penitent into their holy company, and called him Brother Redivivus.

Freymond was now living a holy life at Angela's side, having married her when his time of probation was ended ; and when for the first time he saw Brother Redivivus in a procession of the brethren, and learnt who he was, the last shade vanished from his mind. It then seemed to him as if he first received the full forgiveness of his sin ; and he painted the figure of Redivivus so full of life and love that it was thought the masterpiece of his far-famed pencil. After three years, as Freymond and Angela were carrying home their first-born son after his baptism, their honoured parents with them, they met the bier of Brother Redivivus. He had gently fallen asleep in the Lord. The christening company turned back, and Helfrad and Gertrude, Freymond and Angela, and their sweet smiling infant, accompanied the deceased penitent to his eternal rest.

People who long after saw the portrait of Wagner, the disciple in magic of Dr. Faustus, remarked a great likeness to Freymond's picture of Brother Redivivus; only the one appeared like a descending demon, while the other seemed an ascending angel.

The Victor's Wreath.

LATE one evening an old knight came wearily down from one of the lofty Hartz mountains into the valley beneath. His name was Leuthold; he had once been lord of all the neighbouring lands, but had been driven from the noble castle of his fathers by the might of a rich count; and all that old Leuthold could now do, was every evening to climb the woody heights above his cottage, and to gaze down from hence on the lofty towers of the castle till the sunset. Then would the old man return to the valley, where he was allowed to live undisturbed, as unable to struggle for his rights, his only son having fallen in the defence of his father's hearth.

On his way home, the grey-haired knight always passed by a chapel which he had built in better days, and where now lay entombed the body of his brave son. Then the father would kneel before the door of the lowly building, and offer up a prayer. He did so on this day; and as he rose from his knees, he looked wistfully through the window; but he in vain tried to see his Sigebald's tomb, for it stood in a niche in the wall behind the altar; and Leuthold had no means of getting into the chapel, since, in his overpowering grief after the interment of his son, he had flung the key away into the rapid stream of the Bude. Often had he repented of this, for, poor as he now was, he had not gold enough to have another key made to fit the delicately worked lock; and thus he had shut out himself, his good wife, and his niece Diotwina, Sigebald's betrothed bride, from the sight of all that remained of him who had been their dearest treasure.

But never had his longing been so intense as on this evening: he gazed upon the door with keen sorrow; he had almost intreated it to give way and let him enter, and thought it must grant his prayer; but it remained firm and unmoved, and the rusty lock yielded so little to his repeated efforts, that he became but the more aware of the great strength of the bolts and hinges. At last, after the old man had rattled for a long while at the door of the burial-place of his son, he turned away, and proceeded to his cottage, with tears in his eyes, and mournfully shaking his head at the recollection of his own rash deed.

He found his wife awaiting him for their late evening meal. "Where, then, is Diotwina?" he asked. "Gone to her chamber," answered the old woman: it is to-day the anniversary of her betrothal to Sigebald, and, as thou knowest, she always spends it in fasting and solitude."

The knight sighed deeply, and remained silent for a long space; at length he began again, " How much money have we altogether?" " Nearly two rix-dollars, but not quite," answered the wife. " And the smith asks for a new key—" " Three gold florins." Then the old man sighed again, and looked inquiringly round the room. " Ah!" said his wife, " there is nought here to sell. There might be one thing. . . . The smith thought he could readily give two florins for it." " Dost thou mean *that* up yonder?" said the old man, pointing to his sword. His wife nodded. But he sprang up hastily, saying, " God forbid! I may, indeed, never again use my old weapon in this world, but it shall rest honourably at last on my coffin. My Sigebald in paradise would hardly forgive me if I parted with my noble sword." His wife hid her face in her hands, and began to weep, for she could not but remember how often her dead son, when a beautiful joyous child, had played with this sword, and lisped of his future conquests with it. Then both the old people remained silent, put out the light, and went to bed.

It might have been about midnight when the old man heard wonderful cries and noises sound through the valley; and there shone from the woody heights a light, as of a bright flame, through the shutters of the narrow window of their room. He would have got up to see what it was, but his wife said, " Keep still, husband; I have heard it for some time past, and I am praying to myself. It must be a long procession of the wild huntsman."* " Well," said Leuthold, " I have often heard the wild huntsman hurry past me by night in the forest, but these are very different sounds." " Then it must be some work of the witches," answered the old woman: " who knows what they are doing up yonder on the Brocken? I pray thee keep still, and do not give way to foolish thoughts."

The knight hearkened to his wife: he lay still, and

* See Note, p. 13.

prayed softly. But after a while he began again: "Wife, some one is riding past our window on a grey horse, just as our blessed son used to ride." She trembled, and with a low voice asked him to be silent. But again the old man spoke: "Dost thou hear how some one on the mountain is crying out, 'Strike hard! hew them down?' The night-storm almost carries the sounds away. But just before our Sigebald fell, he would so have called out." "If thou wouldst kill me with horror and fright," said the wife, "or make me go mad, go on with such discourse,—one word more will do it." Then Leuthold was silent; and he drove back into his own bosom the thoughts which were stirring and thronging within him. The wonderful sounds ceased, or were lost in more distant valleys; and towards morning the old couple both fell asleep.

The bright light of day shone again over the mountains. Leuthold's wife sat already at her spinning-wheel, and the knight was going forth to work with hatchet and spade in their little garden; he turned back as he reached the door, and said, "It is very strange. When the wild fancies and mysteries of night have once made their way into a man's brain, he can get no peace from them. I have been dreaming till break of day of our harvest-feast, as we used to keep it in better days in the castle of our fathers." "Strange indeed!" interrupted the wife; "I too have dreamt of it. The peasants were thronging into the castle-hall, with their shining scythes, their wives and daughters with rakes adorned with gay ribbons. The harvest-wreath shone on high against the bright blue summer sky; and, ah! before them all came my own dear child, a lovely boy, with garlands of corn-flowers wound round him; a wreath, as for a marriage, was on his head, and a large red flower in his bosom. I knew that flower well!" Her head sank mournfully; and the knight, to turn her from the thought of her only son's death-wound, said: "The singing was the strangest part of my dream. Even when I awoke I still heard the hymn which the peasants used to sing as they entered, and now I could almost fancy that the same sound is coming over the mountain, and descending the woody hill-side; as I opened the door, it seemed to me that the sound came in stronger." His wife listened likewise, and rose in silent wonder; she took her husband's arm to go out and seek whence came these mysterious sounds. Emboldened now by the cheering morning light, which gilded the stems of the trees, and the dewy grass beneath them; still more emboldened by the solemn strains of the hymn, which drew nearer and nearer, the sounds of flutes and pipes blending with the voices.

As the old couple went forth from their cottage, a multitude of peasants appeared amongst the trees, with green branches in their hats, and glittering scythes in their hands; some of them also carried halberts and spears. " O heavens !" cried the wife of Leuthold, " it is not yet harvest-time. And whither are they going with their songs and music? See only how the morning glow colours their scythes." " They must have been at some very dreadful hay-making," murmured the knight; for he knew the red tinge on their weapons much too well to take it, like his wife, for the glow of morning.

In the mean while the peasants had formed a half-circle round the venerable pair; and while they ended their song with a joyful clashing of their arms, Diotwina stepped forth from among them, approached her astonished parents with a radiant countenance, and spoke thus: " They who go forth early to pray, do not return without a blessing. Here at the entrance of the wood I met these brave men, and they desire that from me you should first hear of their noble deed. They have won back your castle—the country is free—the oppressor dead !"

The old knight gazed around as if yet in his last night's dream. Then drew near to him the oldest of the armed band, grey-haired like his lord; and taking gently from his hand the spade, he put in its stead an old silver staff, inlaid with gold, which the ancestors of Leuthold had possessed from remotest times, and which was now recovered with other sacred heir-looms of the family. Then the men shouted triumphantly the words of Diotwina, " The country is free! the oppressor dead!" and again clashed arms and scythes. " It is indeed so," said the old peasant to the wondering and doubting husband and wife. " Your brother's son Richard is returned from his crusade, my noble lord, and has brought to pass all these wonders since yesterday evening, when he first appeared in the outer court of the castle. He might well guess how in our hearts we longed after our rightful master, for he spoke to us thereof, and bade us take spears and scythes in your cause, as if it was a thing decreed and settled long before, till the most irresolute felt it could not be otherwise. So the alarm-bells rung from the towers, and signal-fires kindled on the hills, and we peasants poured forth in troops, and were quickly marshalled by the young hero, and inspirited by his words. We scoured through the valleys wherever we caught a glimpse of an armed follower of the count. At length we stormed the castle, and the count, in his despair, threw himself on his own sword. The young victor led us on till we came near your abode, and then galloped back to the castle, no doubt that he might have all things prepared for your reception. If it is now your pleasure to let us escort you back, there are here three gentle well-trained horses out of your own stables, ready to bear you and the noble ladies."

With outstretched arms the old lord blessed his brave, true-hearted people; the horses were led forward, the honoured knight and the ladies were placed upon them, and they all took the way to the castle with devoutly joyful hearts.

The old peasant walked beside the knight's horse, and spoke of last night's fight, and of the wonderful deeds of Richard. As Leuthold heard with ever-growing joy and surprise of the magnanimity, and skill, and heroic valour of his nephew in many encounters, his heart swelled within him with thankful pride, till, in the eagerness of his delight, at last he exclaimed, loud enough to be heard by all around him, " Here I pledge my knightly honour and faith, that our brave deliverer shall have for his own that which I hold dearest on earth, my niece Diotwina. She shall be betrothed to him before God and man." He stretched out his right hand towards heaven, as if making a vow. The troop stopped short in amazement, and gazed upon the eager old man; but his wife turned deadly pale with fright, and at last articulated with difficulty, " Husband, husband, what hast thou done? why this unhappy impatience in thy old age? Look around thee where we are. Yonder is the chapel wherein sleeps our only son; and when he died, thou didst receive the vow of Diotwina to live and die the spotless bride of our Sigebald. Which vow shall, then, now be broken, hers or thine?"

The old knight, greatly troubled, let fall his hand, and sighed out, " So it is! Heaven scatters its most precious gifts; and man, in his reckless joy, turns them to his own destruction!" The whole troop looked sorrowful and affrighted on their repentant lord; but Diotwina opened her sweet lips with an angel-smile, and said, " Father and mother, be not troubled. I think our vows are not so very different as you fear." Then turning to the old peasant, she continued, " How know you that your leader last night was Richard?" " What other could it have been, noble lady?" answered the old man; " he wore the colours of our master's house, and its badge on his scarf and shield! Then his words, and gestures, and way of riding, were all quite and entirely after the fashion of our lord. He gave the war-cry of the family with his loud soldier's voice each time that his horse dashed among the enemy. Ay, and oftentimes he repeated to us that we were fighting under a branch of the old tree. Who could it have been but the young lord Richard? It is true no one saw his face, for he wore his vizor always closed."

"Now, then, let me relate what befell me last night," said Diotwina, with a distinct voice and earnest look, "and give good heed to me, for I speak the simple truth, as befits a simple maiden. I stood at my window, and watered, partly with fresh water, partly with my tears, a bright blooming myrtle, which in my happy days was to make my bridal wreath. It was still flourishing and beautiful to behold, but my hopes of earthly bliss were withered for ever. A noise at my door roused me from these and the like thoughts. I could distinctly hear a step on the stairs; it was light and soft, but with a clanging sound, as of armour. My father and mother were long since asleep, and it was midnight; a cold shudder crept over me. Then the door was half opened, and an armed hand was extended, holding the scarf which I had worked for my betrothed, and which had been laid in his coffin. A voice— it was that of Sigebald—spoke from without, 'It is I; can I enter without causing thee to die of terror?' 'Enter, in God's name,' I answered, trembling with fright, and with longing desire to see him. Then a pale, armed figure with open vizor walked slowly and solemnly into the room. I well knew his noble features, and yet I had not the courage to look into his face so as to discern whether his eyes were hollow as those of a corpse, or mildly beaming as of yore. 'Dost thou yet need the myrtle-wreath for thy wedding-day?' he asked gently. I shook my head. 'Never more wilt thou need it?' I again shook my head. 'Ah!' continued he, caressingly and tenderly as when yet alive, 'then weave me a victor's wreath, my own dear bride. For see, it has been granted me to complete the work of vengeance in this pale mortal body; and when it again lies down on its bier, it will take the wreath along with it.' I diligently wove and wove till all the branches were woven into a bright wreath. My betrothed stood at the door silently watching me. When my work was done, he bent a knee before me; I placed the wreath on his helmet; and as he went forth, he looked back and spoke .

'Fear not, sweet love, if the noise of arms reaches you from the valley. God has given the victory into my hands.' Then he greeted me so tenderly that all my awe vanished, and I smiled after him as formerly, when he left me to go forth to a gay tournament. It was not till I saw him on his grey steed passing so lightly and rapidly through the darkness, that dread came upon me again. You now know your deliverer, dear parents, and your true vassals. If you will grant my prayer, and open the chapel and the tomb, I doubt not but that the myrtle-wreath on my bridegroom's helmet will give token of the truth of my words."

They all looked at each other in silence and doubt: there arose, indeed, in many minds the thought that Diotwina's pure spirit had been bewildered by the strange events of the night and a fearful dream; but when they recalled how calmly she had met them on leaving the cottage, this thought could no longer remain. Then they remembered that their leader, after he had assembled them, had disappeared for a while, and returned with a wreath on his helmet. Diotwina's request was granted—the chapel was opened, the fears of his mother lest the beloved remains should be irreverently disturbed being quieted by the promise of the vassals to keep guard over the spot till the fastenings to the door were again carefully closed. But as now the rusty hinges offered a strong resistance, it seemed that a faithless doubt destroyed in all hearts the belief in the apparition. Diotwina's smile alone gave confirmation to her words. The lid of the tomb was at length removed, and there lay the young hero in full armour, a calm smile on his countenance, and on his helmet the myrtle-wreath woven by his bride. Then all fell on their knees, and thanked and praised God. Diotwina joyfully accomplished her own and her uncle's vow—she remained the faithful bride of Sigebald to her death, dwelling near to the chapel in a small house, which Richard, when many years afterwards he really returned home, and had inherited the old knight's possessions, consecrated as a nunnery, under whose shelter the chapel of Sigebald long remained in holy repute, and the object of many a pilgrimage.

NOTE.

"*The wild huntsman.*"

THE tradition here alluded to bears, that formerly a wildgrave, or keeper of a royal forest, named Hackelnberg, was so much addicted to the pleasures of the chase, and at the same time so profligate and cruel, that he not only followed this amusement on Sundays and other holy days, but accompanied it with the most unheard-of oppression upon the poor peasants, who were under his vassalage. After his death, the people conceived they still heard the cry of the wildgrave's hounds; and the well-known cheer of the deceased hunter, the sounds of his horse's feet and of the pack and the sportsmen, as well as the rustling of the branches before the game, are distinctly discriminated; but the phantoms are rarely, if ever, visible. His favourite haunts are in the Hackel, from which he derives his name, and more particularly in the district of Dumburg. He is often heard at midnight, as he drives through storm and rain; or in the dim moonshine, when the heavens are overcast, he chases through the clouds with his swart hounds the shadows of wild animals he once destroyed. Most frequently the chase goes over Dumburg, straight athwart the Hackel, towards the now ruined villages of Ammendorf.

Three travellers had once sat down to refresh themselves not far from Dumburg; the night was gathering fast, the moon shone fitfully through the fleeting clouds, and all was silent as the tomb. Suddenly was heard a rushing like a strong current over their heads. "That," cried one of the travellers, " is the sound of the wild hunter. Hackelnberg is not far off." Let us fly, then," exclaimed the second, in great alarm, "before the monster overtake us." "There is no time," said the other; "and you have nothing to fear, if you will not provoke him. Let us lie down on our faces while he passes over us, and say not a word,—remember the fate of the shepherd." The travellers laid themselves down among the bushes: the loud rushing of the hounds as if trampling down the grass, and high above them in the air the stifled cry of the hard-pressed animal, mingled from time to time with the fierce sound of the hunter's "hu! hu!" Two of the travellers pressed closer to the ground, but the third could not resist his desire of seeing what passed. He glanced sideways through the bushes, and saw the shade of the dark hunter, urging on his dogs as he speeded by. As suddenly again every thing was still. "But what became of the young shepherd of whose fate you spoke?" said one of the travellers. "Listen to his strange adventure," was the reply of the other. "A shepherd once heard the wild hunter drawing near the place where he fed his flock. He could not resist giving the hounds a cheer, and called out, 'Good luck to you, Hackelnberg!' The wild hunter checked his speed, as he shouted with a voice of thunder, 'Hast thou helped me to urge my dogs? so shalt thou have a share in the quarry.' The poor hind shrank trembling away. But Hackelnberg flung after him a half-devoured thighbone of an animal, which smote him as he sat in his cart so severely, that he has never since been able to hold himself upright, or to move backwards or forwards."

This tale, though told with some variations, is universally believed all over Germany. The French had a similar tradition concerning an aërial hunter who frequented the forest of Fontainebleau. He was sometimes visible; when he appeared as a huntsman, surrounded with dogs, a tall, grisly figure. The notion seems to have been very general, as appears from the following poetical description of a similar phantom-chase, as it was heard in the wilds of Ross-shire in Scotland:—

> " E'er since of old, the haughty thanes of Ross—
> So to the simple swain tradition tells—
> Were wont, with clans and ready vassals throng'd,
> To wake the bounding stag, or guilty wolf,
> There oft is heard, at midnight, or at noon,
> Beginning faint, but rising still more loud
> And nearer, voice of hunter, and of hounds,
> And horns, hoarse-winded, blowing far and keen;
> Forthwith the hubbub multiplies; the gale
> Labours with wilder shrieks and riper din
> Of hot pursuit; the broken cry of deer
> Mangled by throttling dogs, the shouts of men,
> And hoofs thick beating on the hollow hill.
> Sudden the grazing heifer in the vale
> Starts at the noise; and both the herdsman's ears
> Tingle with inward dread. Aghast, he eyes
> The mountain's height, and all the ridges round;
> Yet not one trace of living wight discerns;
> Nor knows, o'erawed, and trembling as he stands,
> To what or whom he owes his shuddering fear."

Sir Walter Scott's beautiful ballad of the " Wild Huntsman," alluding to the same tradition, is well known.

Berthold.

THE following remarkable tale is related of Berthold, a young German merchant; and though it can hardly be proved in all its details, it is yet worthy of repetition on many accounts.

Berthold was engaged in speculations of considerable extent, which compelled him to bear about his person a sum of no small amount in gold, jewels, and other valuables; and once, in travelling, he was not a little alarmed on perceiving that he had lost himself in one of the extensive mountain-forests of his native country, and that night was rapidly overtaking him in the middle of a gloomy valley, and in a road to which he was an entire stranger.

It was plain that he had lighted upon a remote and unfrequented district; for the forest-deer no longer evinced any shyness at his presence, and the flight of the owls as they wheeled about him became so daring and undismayed, that he involuntarily drew back his head and shoulders to avoid the noisy flapping of their wings. At length he perceived a man walking on a little way before him, whom, on inquiry, he found to be a charcoal-burner, who resided with his family in the depths of the forest. Berthold's request of a lodging for the night and a conductor in the morning was complied with; and with so much ready frankness that his mind was set at rest, and the two parties made the best of their way to the cottage mutually satisfied with each other's company.

On their arrival the housewife made her appearance at the door with a light; behind her stood a range of youthful chubby children's faces; and the light as it fell upon the person of the man himself shewed one of those open honest countenances, which happily are still to be met with in abundance among our countrymen.

The whole company now entered a small comfortable sitting-room, and seated themselves round a bright, cheerful fire which blazed upon the hearth; and the traveller began to feel as easy about his property as if he had been in the midst of his own family. He had merely removed his travelling-bag from his horse; and having committed the faithful animal to one of the charcoal-burner's sons, he threw his package into a corner of the apartment; and though he retained his sword and his fire-arms, yet this was more from a habit induced by a traveller's life than from any idea that he should have occasion for such things here.

The conversation soon turned upon various subjects. The merchant related stories of the countries he had seen; his host spoke of the forest and his occupation; and the whole family joined in with pertinent questions or modest remarks.

Meanwhile a jug of nut-brown ale was introduced; the cheerful party from conversation soon began to join in other kinds of amusement; and the singing of songs took the place of the stories. The children were in the midst of a lively chorus, when a strange tap was heard at the door. A faint knock was given with the finger; yet, notwithstanding its apparent lightness, the gentle sound was distinctly heard throughout the room, and rose above the clear and mirthful young voices. The singing was instantly stopped; the whole family assumed a grave, serious look; while the master of the house, in a friendly tone, exclaimed, "Come in, father! in God's name, come in!"

The door opened, and a small decent-looking old man stepped quietly in. He saluted the family-circle with a benevolent air, though he stopped with some surprise at the sight of the stranger. In a short time he approached the table, and placed himself in the lowest seat; which, in fact, appeared to have been left purposely for him. Berthold looked with surprise at the old man,—for he was dressed in a costume of the old days; nevertheless the dress exhibited marks of great attention to neatness and decency. His person, as already observed, was very small. At first sight, his countenance might be said to be composed and pleasing; but, on closer observation, there might be seen evident traces of a hidden sorrow. The family seemed to treat him as an old acquaintance, though with manifest signs of compassion. Berthold would willingly have inquired whether the old man were a relation—the charcoal-burner's father perhaps—and whether his pale and sorrowful countenance were the effects of disease or grief. But whenever he was about to open his mouth, the old man looked at him with a half-alarmed, half-angry expression; and that in so strange a manner that he always felt himself checked, though his curiosity was greatly increased.

At length the old man folded his hands as if in prayer, looked over to the host, and said, in a strange hoarse voice, " Come, let us, if you can, begin the evening-prayer."

The charcoal-burner instantly began the fine old hymn,

" The forest now is hush'd in rest," &c.,

in which he was joined by his wife and children; the old

man united his voice to theirs, and sang with a power and clearness which made the very roof of the cottage tremble, and must have excited strong surprise in any one not accustomed to hear it. At first Berthold's astonishment prevented his joining in the chorus. This appeared to make the little old man both angry and uncomfortable; he constantly eyed the traveller with strange dissatisfied looks; and the charcoal-burner also admonished his guest by expressive signs that he ought to follow the example of the others. This Berthold was at length able to do; and every thing was now correct and devotional, until, after a few more prayers and hymns, the old man humbly and quietly took his leave. He had already closed the door, and was about to let the latch fall, when he suddenly dashed it open, cast a wild and furious look upon Berthold, and then slammed it again.

"Ha!" said the charcoal-burner, as he turned with an astonished look to apologise to his guest for this conduct; "this is very different from his usual manner."

Berthold suggested that perhaps the old gentleman was a little disordered in his intellect.

"That," said the charcoal-burner, "is, I believe, very true; but he is quite harmless, and never does any one an injury. At least, for a very long time, we have never had the slightest evidence of such misconduct. I should tell you, however, that the only room which I can offer you has no fastening to it; and it often happens that the old man finds his way there. But do not be alarmed; if he is left undisturbed, he will soon retire of his own accord. Indeed, I fancy you are too much tired with your journey to be roused by his movements; and, as you have doubtless already noticed, he moves about with great gentleness and quietness."

Berthold assented with a smile on his countenance. He felt very differently, however, at heart, though without being able to account exactly for the impression; and, as his host lighted him up to his chamber, he involuntarily grasped his travelling-bag with a firmer hold, and kept a constant eye upon his arms.

The charcoal-burner having suspended the lamp in a place of safety, and commended his guest to the protection of God, speedily withdrew. Berthold, now left alone in his narrow chamber, seemed to feel as if the pious wish would, somehow or other, fail of its effect. He felt more disturbed and troubled in his mind than he had done for a long time before. He retired to bed; and though exhausted with the exertions of the day, sleep was far from him. At one time, he thought his bag too far off; at another, that his arms were out of his reach. Under such excitements he frequently rose; and if for an instant sleep visited his eyes, he started up again at every breeze of wind, with alternate fears and hopes of some great misfortune, or some unexpected and surprising good luck. All his mercantile plans and speculations seemed to form themselves into one great wheel, from which it was impossible to extricate himself, though he was unable to distinguish one single, individual plan, or to separate one spoke from the others. He felt, too, an overwhelming and all-engrossing thirst for gain, excited by the difficulties around him; and surrounded by these perplexities, he fell into a sleep, which might perhaps with more propriety have been called a swoon.

It might be about midnight, or a little after, when Berthold fancied he heard a gentle rustling and stirring in his chamber. But fatigue had so completely subdued him that he lay motionless in his bed; and if at times he raised his unwilling eyelids, and seemed to perceive the little old man passing backwards and forwards near his bed, his drowsy senses assured him that the whole was mere fancy, or that it was only what the charcoal-burner had already forewarned him of. At length, however, these noises became more frequent; a sudden fright thoroughly roused him from his lethargy; he started up, and beheld the little old man quietly seated upon his bag, and looking at him with a sort of scornful pity.

"Villain!" exclaimed Berthold, in a tone of mingled terror and rage, "let alone my property!" The violence of his speech appeared to alarm the old man; he hastened towards the door with a face of mild entreaty, and quickly disappeared. Berthold lost no time in examining his bag to ascertain whether any thing had been taken out. He was not disposed to look upon the little man as a thief; but still the diseased and crazy mind of this singular being might have found amusement in exchanging the contents for rubbish, or destroying some of the important papers which it contained. The locks and straps, however, appeared unopened; and on examination every thing was found as it had been left. Still, however, Berthold's mind was not at ease. Something might have fallen out by the way, something might have suffered by the journey; and under this suspicion he examined every separate package, now rejoicing at the extent of his wealth, and now regretting that it was no greater. In the midst of this occupation he was suddenly disturbed by a puff of wind upon his cheek. At first, he thought it only a current of air penetrating the crazy window, and he wrapped his mantle more closely about him. The puff was now repeated; it became more distinct and perceptible; and as he turned angrily towards the quarter from whence it proceeded, he beheld with terror the little old man's face quite close to his own.

"What do you here?" cried the merchant; "go to your bed, and warm yourself."

"There I am always colder than any where else," croaked the old man, in reply; "and I love to look upon such pretty things as you have got. But I know where there are some much prettier, ay, much prettier."

"What is it you say?" inquired Berthold, who now began to fancy that the extraordinary good fortune which had floated before him while half asleep was to be realised in some way by means of this insane creature.

"If you would but come," sighed the old man, "down below there, deep in the forest, beside the morass."

"Well," said Berthold. "I should not much fear the adventure with you."

The old man now turned towards the door, and said, "I must first get my mantle. I will be with you again in a minute, and then we will set out together."

Berthold had but little time to reflect on his engagement; for the old man had scarcely quitted the room before the latch was raised again, and in stalked a tall and spare man, with a large scarlet mantle thrown across his shoulders, a huge sword in one arm, and a musket in the other. Berthold laid his hand upon his pistols.

"You may as well take those with you," said the red man, "only make haste that we may get into the wood."

"With you!" exclaimed Berthold; "I will not go with you. Where is the little old man?"

"Do but look well at me," rejoined the other, as he removed the mantle from before his face. Berthold now perceived a close resemblance between this fearful apparition and the little old man; only that the one wore a meek and humble air, while the other was wild and ferocious. Berthold felt assured that both he and his treasure were betrayed; and he therefore exclaimed, in a firm voice, "When you choose again to send your half-silly brother for the purpose of seducing people into your net, I think it would be quite as well not to disturb the illusion by so soon making the senseless exhibition of your own person. I am not going with you, and nothing shall make me do so."

"Indeed!" said the man in red, "you wont go?"

"No!"

"Why then I'll make you;" and with this he stretched out his long bony arm towards Berthold, who, in a paroxysm of fear, discharged his pistol. Then there arose a great stir in the house below; the charcoal-burner was heard ascending the staircase with hurried steps, and the man in red, shaking his fist at Berthold, immediately darted out at the door.

"In the name of Heaven!" exclaimed the charcoal-burner, as he burst into the room, " what have you done to our spirit?"

"Spirit?" stammered Berthold, as he looked at his host with astonishment. For his visions of unbounded wealth still floated before his fancy; and finding now that he was not likely to gain any, he began to think it was to be his fate to lose some, and that all the inmates of the house had conspired against him.

The charcoal-burner continued: " I met him on the stairs, looking unusually tall and angry, and wrapt in his red mantle, with his sword and gun in his hands."

Perceiving, however, that Berthold was unable to comprehend what he said, he begged his guest to descend to the room below, where all the household had assembled from alarm at the sound of the pistol, and he would there endeavour to tranquillise both him and his family. Berthold assented; and, taking his bag under his left arm, his remaining loaded pistol in his right hand, and his other weapons in his belt, he proceeded with his host. His chief reason for going below was that he might be nearer the house-door than in his present chamber. As he entered the room, the whole family seemed to regard him with an eye of suspicion; and there was a manifest difference in his present reception from that given him a few hours before. The charcoal-burner now addressed his guest in the following manner:

" When I first took this cottage the spirit was accustomed to wander about in the same térrific form in which you and I have seen him just now. On this account the house had long been abandoned, and no one was venturous enough to live in it, or, in fact, in the neighbouring district of the forest; for the power of these spirits has rather an extensive range. He was one of my predecessors, who was not only very rich, but very avaricious, and his passion for gold induced him to bury his money in the forest; and during his life he was constantly roaming about the spot where his treasures were concealed. On such occasions he usually wrapt himself up in a red mantle, carrying a sword and gun on his shoulders for the purpose of scaring the robbers, as he declared, who would thus be reminded of the city-executioner. At his death he was unable to communicate the spot where his money was deposited: it is possible he may have forgotten it; and it was, perhaps, on this account his mind became so distracted, and that he assumed this frightful attire.

"I, however, said to myself: 'a pious heart, and constant exercise in prayer, is a sufficient protection against even Satan himself, much less against a poor crazy ghost;' and so I came to live here, in God's name, with my wife and children. At first, it must be confessed, our friend of the red mantle caused us a good deal of trouble; for when a man is going about his own concerns, it is startling enough, even to the most courageous, to find some hideous thing jump up before him, and that too of the goblin kind. The children suffered exceedingly from fear; and even my wife too was frequently overpowered with alarm."

"Yes!" sobbed the wife; "and now these awful times will come back again. It was but just now that he looked in at the door, with a wild and angry countenance, taller than ever, and wrapt in his frightful red mantle."

"Do as you did before," said the husband; "be constant in prayer; let all your thoughts be pure and pious, and nothing will then harm you."

Just at this moment the latch of the door was moved up and down with a violent and continued rattling; all pressed close together, and the children cried bitterly. The charcoal-burner alone advanced with a firm, courageous step, and called out, "In the name of the Most High, I charge thee to depart: *we* are beyond thy power."

A noise was heard without like the passing of a whirlwind through the house; and all was quiet, while the charcoal-burner, as he resumed his seat, continued his narrative.

"At that time we considered this a trial; and it may, perhaps, be ordained to be so to us again. We must only pray with greater zeal, and keep a more scrupulous watch over our thoughts and actions. We had succeeded in making him lay aside his red mantle, and he had begun to conduct himself with decency, to attend our evening-devotions, to compose his features into something like complacency, and to reduce his form into a diminutive size, as if his decreasing limbs would eventually disappear from the earth, and the poor creature betake himself to rest until the awful day. My children! you could not help loving him as a meek and quiet household-spirit; it gave you pain that, in his extreme humility, he chose to take the lowest place at our table. You must now cheerfully labour for his repose and your own, by patience, prayer, and purity of heart. I trust in God, we shall soon bring him back to the same condition in which he was before the events of last night."

The whole family stood up, and, putting their hands in his, promised to obey their father's instructions; to maintain the struggle against the spirit of evil with undiminished resolution, in whatever form it might appear.

Berthold alone was still in a most agitated and distracted state. He first conceived himself seized with a fit of delirium, and that all these extraordinary circumstances were the mere fancies of a disordered imagination; he then believed that the whole was a trick devised to make a fool of him; and now thought he had fallen among a band of hypocritical thieves, and that every thing had for its object the possession of his property. With these ideas, he asked for his horse. The charcoal-burner's eldest son instantly ran to the stable to prepare it; but his father remarked, " You had better remain, sir, till it is broad daylight: at this hour of the morning the forest is dangerous, and it is even said to be haunted."

Berthold, however, persisted in his determination; and he soon perceived that the whole family were really glad at heart at the prospect of being relieved of his company, and that they had only pressed him to remain from motives of kindness. He offered the host payment for his repast and lodging; but this was rejected with so much firmness, and even displeasure, that he abstained from pressing it. The horse was now led to the door, and the travelling-bag replaced as before; Berthold sprang into the saddle, and took leave of his strange host with thanks, which were but coldly received, and with a conviction that his departure had occasioned more joy than his arrival. With many anxious misgivings, he pursued the path which had been pointed out to him.

He found it impossible somehow to believe that the inhabitants of the cottage were altogether right, and that the spirit was in the wrong; "for," thought he, "if it be not a spirit, it is clear *they* are deceivers; and if it be, the poor creature does nothing more than what is right in revealing the spot where its secret treasures are deposited, and enabling some mortal to enjoy what is now lying useless." The trees now appeared to assume strange and mystical shapes. The breeze, as it whistled past him, seemed to be charged with notes of golden promise; the mist began to shape itself into a lofty arch over his head, and as he rode beneath it, he thought to himself, "Nature herself favours me; and if this be so, no illusion can intercept my happy career."

"Well done!" he shouted aloud; and had scarcely spoken the words, when he perceived the red man striding along beside him, and nodding assent not only to his words, but even to his thoughts. He felt a little uneasy at this; but the more he reflected on the reasons for suppressing his alarm, the more the red mantle nodded in friendly approbation; and at length began to address him in the following manner:

"To say the truth, friend, I began to be heartily sick of that charcoal-burner's cottage. That eternal singing and praying reduced me to nothing; you saw yourself what a miserable little shrivelling creature I was become; but as soon as you arrived, though I was rather fierce at first, as if something had arrived which did not belong to us, yet we soon understood each other, and then I grew — ay, and I can grow too till my head reaches those stars which are gleaming above us. If you would but entertain the aspiring thoughts you ought, and fancy yourself standing above there quite a different sort of person to other mortals, one endowed by nature with all her riches and gifts, free from trouble and toil, you would then be just what I wish you, and the treasure should be yours. These poor people are far too stupid for such things. Shall we dig?"

Berthold, well pleased, nodded assent; and the man in red pointed to a mound at a little distance strewed with the leaves and cones of the fir-tree. The merchant was wholly unprovided with implements for digging, and was compelled to turn up the earth with his sword; but his labour was not a little checked by fear as he perceived the man in red join in the work; and wherever he dug his hands into the earth, a blue sulphureous vapour rose out of it.

The smoke continued to rise; the earth was stirred; the stones rolled quickly away; and at last two vessels were discovered, which were no sooner exposed to the morning air than they instantly crumbled to ashes. It was in vain that Berthold continued his search; no treasure was to be found. The man in red now evinced considerable uneasiness; he expressed his sorrow by wringing his long bony hands, and at length he pointed to a neighbouring mound.

Berthold applied himself as diligently as before, but with the same result — nothing could be found but earthen-pots, ashes, and rubbish. They proceeded from one place to another, still eager in the pursuit; but all exhibited the same contents. The spirit now became filled with rage; he dashed his long skeleton-fists against the stems of the fir-trees (which at every blow emitted a stream of sulphureous sparks), and at last accused Berthold of having found the treasure, and surreptitiously secreted it. The merchant stood aghast and trembling before the angry apparition, whose person suddenly glowed in one continued flame of red, and rose, as his indignation swelled, far above the tops of the adjoining trees. At this instant the cock crew. With a fearful shriek, the spirit vanished into thin air, and the matin-bell of a neighbouring village sounded sweetly in the breeze, to the great relief and joy of our traveller. Terrified at the danger he had escaped, Berthold now sought his equally frightened steed, which, at the commencement of his treasure-digging, he had bound to a tree; and having thrown himself into the saddle, galloped rapidly forwards toward the nearest habitation.

Years rolled on, during which Berthold, engaged in extensive mercantile pursuits, passed his life in foreign lands and amidst a round of constant and anxious occupations. But varied as were the objects which pressed upon his attention, he never forgot his adventure with the red man, nor the evening spent with the charcoal-burner's family. It constantly reverted to his imagination, sometimes with feelings of dread and curiosity, sometimes of excited, half-satisfied anxiety; and as he was on his return home, and approaching the neighbourhood, he resolved upon retracing his former route; and having discovered the unfrequented path, he arrived at the close of day before the lonely cottage.

His arrival, like the previous one, brought the same cheerful, honest faces pressing to the door; the charcoal-burner's wife appeared with her lamp, carefully sheltering it against the wind, which threatened to extinguish it; and the host himself advanced towards Berthold with friendly expressions of welcome. The stranger was invited in; his horse was committed to one of the sons; but he could see that all, except his host, looked upon his arrival with little satisfaction.

The room looked much as before; the whole party seated themselves at the table; the jug of ale was brought forth and sent round; but, to Berthold's horror, the seat formerly occupied by the spirit was again left vacant, as if his presence were still expected every evening. Little was said; both parties viewed each other with suspicion, and that which had formerly proved the best part of the merchant's entertainment — friendly conversation and the joyous song — were now wholly wanting.

At length the charcoal-burner spoke as follows:

"We know not what passed between you and our household-spirit after you last left us, some years ago; but we have suffered no little difficulty, fear, and anxiety since. You are now about to pass another night under our roof; and I can only wish from my very heart that your mind may be inclined to pure and grateful devotion; that you may disturb neither us nor the spirit. As far as regards him, indeed, it is not very likely that you will now be able to produce any pernicious effects, even if your head and your heart may still be as much devoted to gain and gold. But, silence! children — the hour of prayer is come."

All now folded their hands; the charcoal-burner reverently uncovered his head, and once more began the fine old hymn:

" The forest now is hush'd in rest."

Berthold, with true devotional feeling, joined in the chorus, expecting every moment the spirit's appearance, although in his former quiet garb and figure. But no finger tapped at the door — no one entered; a gentle light alone was seen in the room, and a soft melodious sound was heard, like the notes of musical glasses when touched with the finger slightly wetted.

Prayers were scarcely over before Berthold inquired the cause of the light and the sounds.

"It is our household-spirit," replied the charcoal-burner; "he never shews himself now in any other way.

But to effect this, we have found it necessary to persevere in prayer, and to keep a careful guard over the purity of our hearts."

There was something in Berthold's bosom which told him he was not worthy of passing the night here. He asked for his horse, though in a more friendly tone than formerly; it was soon brought to him by the eldest son in a manner equally friendly; and the family bade him farewell, perceiving that his departure was not occasioned by an evil disposition, and instructed him in his road, which he now pursued with far different sensations than when he travelled it before. He perceived nothing unnatural, except that a beautiful stream of light occasionally rose before him, illuminating with its mild and heavenly radiance the shrubs and plants of the forest.

ROSE.

In the extensive and deep wine-cellars of the senate-house of Bremen, on each side of the narrow walks formed by the high casks containing that gift of God to man which makes him to be of a cheerful countenance, there are small pleasant rooms, where, while day lasts, the light falls cheerfully through the high windows. There friendly burghers often seat themselves with a flask of noble wine; and, made more familiar from being obliged to sit close together, they talk over many weighty affairs of their business or their families; according to the good old German custom, which looked upon wine as more likely to further than to disturb consultations, and gladly saw those things which had been spoken in excitement brought to pass in calmness.

In such wise there once sat two friendly companions together in one of these little chambers. The one was Master Frederick Haubold, a young but renowned armorer; the other, the honourable counsellor and merchant Sigismund Füllrath, even in grey hairs the best support of the commonweal.

"Hearken, Master Frederick," began at length the kind old man: "you have invited me in here to drink wine with you; but, in all my life, I have never sat opposite a more silent companion."

"I would but drink a little courage into myself," answered the youth; "for may be what you will reply to me will take from me all I have in this world."

"Nay, young man," said the counsellor, "who has told you that I am so hard to deal with? I am no tiger or leopard. Only take courage at once for yourself, without seeking it in your wine; and tell me boldly where the shoe pinches. If I can with honour give you any assistance, my hand upon it, it shall be."

They then touched their glasses full of generous wine; and the armorer said cheerfully: "Ay, then indeed shall I be out of all my trouble, if you can honourably help me. For I have no other wish but to gain for my wife your fair and only daughter Rose."

Silently and thoughtfully the counsellor sank his head, and he seemed to be counting again and again the links of the golden chain which hung upon his breast. This, however, did not alarm the youth; for he well knew that it is the custom and manner of Germans not to speak even the most ready assent without due reflection.

At length the old man asked, "Hast thou spoken of this matter to the maiden, my young friend?"

"God forbid!" answered Frederick; "I know well the old saying, The father's blessing builds the children's house."

"Thou hast done what I expected from thee," said Sigismund, "and also this time done very wisely. For,

Master Haubold, however dear you may be to me, once for all, nothing can come of this business."

Poor Frederick was stunned; he became deadly pale, and knew not at first how to behave.

Sigismund looked at him as if a little displeased, and said: " A brave Christian burgher will not lose his self-command even though the Almighty, by the mouth of a fellow-Christian, says nay to that which he most heartily wished for. Be calm, and listen to me attentively. I will tell you how the matter stands. You may have remarked yourself, that by nature I love to aim high, not to gain gold, or goods, or high offices, but all that can bring a renown which will reach beyond the narrow bounds of this life. Truly I strive vigorously to keep under this bold ambition, as beseems and befits a good Christian; but yet I cannot be other than I am; and my daughter Rose has inherited all my disposition. It may well be, indeed, that her bringing up had something to do with it; for her blessed mother died young, and then we read together, the child and I, during long winter nights, all through the chronicles of the Greek and Roman heroes, and the tales of our great German ancestors. And what was not written in books, I taught her from many a beautiful legend, which my grandfather, the brave commander Füllrath, used to relate to me in my boyish days by the fireside. So, though it might perchance happen that Rose, out of esteem and friendship, might give you her hand, yet believe me, Frederick Haubold, my poor Rose would soon wither, to your grief and mine, in the narrow, dull circle of common life, unbrightened by any lofty deeds of renown; and we should have to lay the young, fair corpse in the ground."

With a low but firm voice and burning cheeks the armorer said, "I did not remain behind when lately there was a call to defend the city against the robber-knights; and the blade which I forged for myself with my best skill struck well."

"I know it, I know it, my brave Haubold," said the counsellor, and kindly gave him across the table his honoured hand. "But my Rose blooms high, very high; and she cannot live upon a few occasional sunbeams; she must spring up in the lasting brightness of the firmament.".

The youth bowed his noble head, half proud and half ashamed, and said, " Truly, those things which cannot be changed, an honourable man must learn to bear; and I feel already that I can bear them."

It was now the twilight of evening in the little chamber, and Sigismund said with kindness, " I know you are not wroth with me, dear Master Frederick, and we part good friends. ·Now must I go to the noble knight Everard Waldburg. The senate has decided to accompany him this evening to the wine-vaults, and there to pledge him in their choicest wines."

" He has well deserved that of our good city, the noble knight!" answered Frederick. " Oh! how joyfully he sprang before our squadrons when we broke in upon the robber-bands!"

" And yet much more has he done for us," added Füllrath, " by the commanding skill and wisdom with which he led on our troops, and by the deep earnest spirit which he poured into our hearts. Well may a city be called happy, and more secure than in triple walls and towers, who can rejoice in such a chief. But do you know, Master Frederick, that the wild knight Theobald has collected new bands of robbers, and that in a short time we must again take the field?"

A gleam of the noble joy of war, and perhaps of a yet sweeter hope, shone over the youth's features. He would have said a few words, but they were choked by the fulness of his heart. Besides, as they went out into the street, they saw that already Sir Everard, accompanied by the senators and by some noble matrons and maidens of the first families of the city, came down the steps. Sigismund Füllrath hastened towards him.

It was fair to see the procession pass into the gloomy vault, lighted up by high wax-tapers, carried by the attendants: the grave senators, with their gold chains shining brightly over their dark gowns, and in the midst of them the knightly form of the valiant Everard Waldburg, in the gay dress of a noble, his head shaded by many plumes; and among these manly figures bloomed and twined many delicate maidens, like May-flowers amidst an oak-forest. But the fairest flower that there bloomed was Rose Füllrath, who alone approached the honoured knight, and held in her fair slender fingers the silver goblet, wreathed with fragrant roses, out of which Sir Everard was solemnly to pledge the senators.

Oh, how the heart of the young armorer beat as now the beloved form passed before him, slight and tall as the old masters represent saintly women, gentle and blooming as spring! The young take readily every smile of the present as a promise of a yet more joyful future: so did Frederick; and he joined the procession, cheered and hopeful.

Choice and yet choicer wines had been already offered and tasted, hearts became more open, and tongues more ready to speak. Loud echoed through the vault the "Long may he live!" of the free citizens to the knight. Then spoke out one of the senators: "Would that we could give over to you better fortifications for the defence of the city, my noble lord of Waldburg; but, as you well know, they are indifferent, or something worse."

"And what of that, you brave burghers!" exclaimed Sir Everard with kindling eyes. "Your walls are the valiant hearts of your citizens: what has a free merchant-city to do with other fortifications? If once she were invested and besieged, she would be lost, as concerns at least all that she has of most precious and noble. No, go forth into the field boldly and joyfully, so that none can have to seek you by your own hearths. You who have sailed as far as Novogorod, and you who have conquered on the coasts of Italy,—you may well drive far from your honoured homes a few freebooters and robbers, who again dare hover in your neighbourhood. At least, as long as I am the commander of this noble city, and can wield my good sword, war shall never cease till all evil men are chased far from our walls and our frontiers."

The beautiful eyes of Rose shone brightly upon the knight; she seemed to see in him one of the renowned heroes of the glorious olden times; while, as he gazed on her, he felt that this fair flower would inspire him to noblest deeds of arms.

In the mean while Sigismund had filled again the silver cup; he brought it to the guest, and said, "This wine is the choicest of our city. We give it only to our dearest friends, and on solemn occasions; and we call this pure and costly gift of God, the Rose."

"O pure, O costly gift of God, O Rose!" said the kindling knight, as he bowed before the maiden and drank. But she looked down in sweet maidenly confusion, and coloured deeply. Then poor Frederick knew what would happen, or rather what had already happened; for it was plain that Sir Everard only delayed his suit because the time and place were not fitting for it; and the proud senator Sigismund smiled well pleased upon the far-famed hero.

The youth withdrew, unnoticed, his eyes filled with quiet tears, and rejoicing only in the thought that his good mother would be already asleep, so that for this evening he need not suppress and conceal the deep sorrow of his heart. But the kind old woman was still up; she sat diligently reading in a great book, and was glad when her son came in, because he would now finish reading to her the wonderful story; "For," said she, "my old eyes already hurt me, and yet I should gladly know how it ends."

With a pious strength Master Frederick silenced his bitter grief, sat down opposite to his mother, and read. It was the strange history of two heroes of the North, who possessed a charm which preserved them from the wounds of every earthly weapon, and who were not overcome till their enemies buried them under a thick shower of stones.

"God be good to us!" said the old mother, when Frederick had done. "That must have been a rough, fearful time of the world. And yet, odd enough, next to God's word, there is nothing that I love so much as stories of those days."

But Frederick remained quite silent, and sunk in thought. At first he had only fixed his thoughts on what he read by a great effort, to avoid any outbreak of his grief; but soon—as legends in all their forms had ever a great power over him—the wonderful tale engrossed him completely, till the deeds and the end of those warriors seemed to belong to the present time, and his own sorrows partly to the past, partly to the future. These dreamy sensations accompanied him to his bed, and turned, as they lulled him in his sleep, to a dream of which he remembered what follows when he awoke:—It was as if he saw the armour of a knight, of large size, beautifully worked, and bright with polished steel, leaning against a wall, the helmet above it seemed to have rather sunk down. None could tell him whether this princely armour was empty, or whether it covered a half-fainting warrior. Then there suddenly rattled innumerable stones from the wall upon the armour; and Frederick tried to call out, "That is too much! that is not fair; you reckoned upon two being here, but there is only one!" but his mouth remained as if close sealed; and, in spite of his painful efforts, he could not bring out the least sound. At last one heavy stone struck the joint of the right shoulder. The iron bands flew asunder, blood streamed out, and the whole armour fell clanging to the ground; while a scornful voice cried out, "Oh, ho! oh, ho! how badly has Master Haubold the armorer worked; for this shivered mass came out of his workshop!"

Frederick awoke from his sleep at the first dawn of day, indignant and angry. "I have never forged so brittle an armour!" said he, as he rubbed his eyes. But as he thought over the matter more and more, he remembered that the armour he had seen in his dream was the very same which Sir Everard Waldburg wore most frequently in battle and in tournament.

Now Frederick had not himself made this armour; it was the work of his father, and had been purchased after his death by Sir Everard, on account of the exquisite skill and beauty of the workmanship. A great fear now came upon the dutiful son lest his dream might foretell some mischief to that master-piece of his father, whereby doubt should fall on the skilfulness of the blessed dead, and injury, or perhaps destruction, might come to the honoured commander of the town. He therefore hastened immediately to the dwelling of Sir Everard, and learning there that he had ridden forth to his neighbouring castle, Frederick saddled his swift horse and took the same road.

He soon saw the towers of the knightly building rising above the fruitful fields and meadows; just then there met him some wild-looking, riotous riders, in ill-arranged armour, a sort of herald in the midst of them. The disorder of their accoutrements surprised the skilful armorer; he stopped, and drew his horse somewhat on one side, in order to look more attentively upon the strange figures as they rode past. One of the troop remarked this, and halting, cried out with a laugh: "Do you stare at us, you little burgher? you shall soon have something more to wonder at. See, we belong to Sir Theobald's band, and we have just been challenging your brave defender Sir Everard Waldburg in his own castle; and bidding him give heed to his ears, for in six days we shall come upon him and upon you with fire and sword. Our heralds are already in Bremen. You often say that we lack courtesy in war; at least we give you notice by times and in good form."

"Every beast has his own customs," said the angry

youth, "and you have yours. Who would expect from the like of you courtesy or good manners? But he who dares call me again 'little burgher' shall receive a blow from my sword which will pain him as long as he lives."

The freebooter grasped his sword, but the good weapon of the armorer flashed so, as he brandished it powerfully, that his opponent thought it prudent to call to his companions, who had already passed on. But they only bid him follow them, for it was now no time for such business; he might let the burghers go their way now, they should have them all before long. The man turned his horse, and rode rather quicker than was necessary after the troop. Frederick, on his side, spurred on his horse towards the knight's castle, sorry to have exchanged words with such a set. As he approached nearer, he saw the noble Everard standing in front of the fortress, and examining a part of the wall of doubtful strength; he had bent his head forward to inspect more closely; and though he was quite unarmed, the recollection of his dream of the broken mailed figure rose involuntarily in Frederick's mind. This seemed so full of meaning and of warning, that he hastened to the knight with his utmost speed.

Everard received him kindly, and said, smiling, "Yes, yes, my good youth, now is the time that you and your like must again move diligently your hammers and tongs."

"And our swords likewise, I should suppose," said Frederick, rather proudly: when Everard answered,

"That need hardly be said, brave armorer. We have known each other since our former campaign."

Then Frederick began to speak of armour, till he got to the mention of that which the knight commonly wore. It needed all his caution, lest Sir Everard should take from his words an unfavourable opinion of the work of the deceased armorer. But he was able to say, without hesitation, that after so many years' use, a suit of armour might well want some little repair here and there; and he asked as a favour that he might carefully examine the knight's coat of mail before the approaching severe contest. Everard thanked him for his honest care; adding, that the armour was in the city. Frederick would hardly consent to take the parting cup;—alas, it was offered to him in the silver goblet which Rose gave the day before, crowned with roses, into the knight's hands!—but flew like an arrow back to the town, and to the armory of the noble chief, his mind much more filled with thoughts of the coming strife than with his own sorrow.

On examining the armour, what did he find? the dream had warned but too truly, and it was full time to make repairs. Not only had the joinings of the right shoulder got out of their place, in consequence of the neglect of the squires in not replacing at once a pin which had slipped out, but rust had been suffered to collect around the inner part of the joints and rings, while care had only been taken to keep up the exterior brightness of the beautiful work; and there were now many places which could offer no effectual resistance against either a blow or a thrust. But how could Frederick remedy the evil? Even were he able, through almost superhuman labour, to repair the mischief in the given time, would not every one be aware of this, and shrug his shoulders at the father who needed his more skilful son to hold together his inferior work, while Frederick's declaration of the truth would only be taken for a pious fraud? He stood there sunk in deep thought. At length he collected himself.

"I will do something that will please your lord," said he, confidentially to the esquire of Sir Everard, "and ornament his armour against the combat in a new way lately discovered by me. But say nothing about it to him; only bring the armour quickly into my workshop."

The esquire entered gladly into the plan of the armorer; and soon Frederick was seated and diligently at work, with the armour already taken to pieces all around him. It now stood him in good stead, that, after the manner of all skilful workmen, he had given attention not only to the useful, but to that which is nearly allied to it,—the beautiful. After he had drawn, with a few bold strokes on parchment, the armour as it then was, he began, while new and brilliant ideas poured in upon him, to plan how he could make the necessary repairs on the armour; the Spirit of God was with him,[1] and all ordered itself according to his wishes. Over all the weak places he determined to lay plates of steel inlaid with gold, and to place about the armour brightly gilt devices, representing lions' or dragons' heads (most of these were ready, lying in his workshop), which would serve to conceal the rivets and rings which were necessary to repair the mischief. All was soon arranged, but only in the mind of the artificer. To get it completed in fact within six days required a labour which at first seemed little less than impossible. But Frederick, trusting in God and in his own firm will and experienced skill, set boldly about the arduous work, collecting around him a number of good workmen, who readily obeyed such a renowned master of the craft. By day and by night hammers were heard and sparks seen in the workshop of the noble armorer. Those who saw him out of work-hours believed that he was consumed by a deep heavy sorrow, he looked so pale and exhausted; but it was only anxiety to finish his work in time to vindicate the skill of his father, and to secure the life of the commander of the town. Even Sigismund Füllrath formed a wrong opinion of Frederick, believing that his ill looks were caused by the rejection of his suit, and deeply compassionated the brave youth. But Frederick's mother felt no anxiety for her son, perfectly content with the knowledge that he diligently laboured and diligently prayed.

And by labour and prayer he succeeded so well, that two days before the troops were to march forth, the armour stood before the noble workman strong and beautiful, and free from every blemish; wondered at and praised by his assistants, and by his mother, who had hastened to see the

[1] See Exodus xxxv. 30-33.

work, with the loving joy she felt at all the proofs of her renowned son's skill; but this she praised above all former works. Frederick felt it deserved her praise. He soon fell into the sound sleep of well-earned weariness; and the consciousness of having truly and happily done his duty was to him like the soothing balmy breath of spring.

With the first rays of the morning sun he was awake again, and had the armour, well protected and covered, carried to the house of Sir Everard. When he got there, and had heard from the esquires that their lord was already gone forth to a closer examination of the neighbouring country, he hastened to place the noble armour in the most advantageous light at the upper end of the armory. The wondering pages and retainers helped him joyfully in this work. It was undertaken with zeal and care, yet it lasted till near nine, and was hardly completed when a retainer came in, announcing that Sir Everard was returning from his ride.

"And he returns in joyful mood!" cried a page, who had hastened to the window. "See, then, he must have been to the Counsellor Füllrath's, for he comes back on foot with his betrothed, and with his future father-in-law, while his noble steed is led after him. We must see to their breakfast." And he sprang gaily out of the room. But Frederick turned of a death-like paleness, and leaned back sick and weary against the wall, keeping behind the armour, that he might escape the gaze of all present.

Sir Everard entered, leading by the hand his fair bride, the bright blooming Rose; Sigismund Füllrath followed the noble pair with a deep, earnest joy, and looked up at many foreign weapons and banners on the wall, which had been won in distant lands by the brave hand of his son-in-law.

But Everard remained standing in wonder before the shining armour. "Oh, my sweet, my noble Rose," said he, "can this costly gift come from you?"

But when the maiden denied it, and shewed equal

amazement at the beauty of the work, the delighted page drew forward the pale artist, and said, "The gift comes from this skilful hand."

Then Sir Everard could not speak thanks enough; and Rose, gaining courage from being now a declared bride, gave her hand to the youth, and told him how from her heart she wished him well.

The betrothed lovers overlooked, in their own happiness and joy, the deadly paleness which overspread the brow and cheeks of Frederick; but Sigismund Füllrath gazed upon him with deep compassion and wonder, and this time he did not mistake the youth's feelings. Frederick was almost overcome by sorrow and sadness, as he felt that most beloved form so near, and yet so very far from him. The tears rushed unbidden into his eyes; he could hardly support himself;—then Sir Everard stepped to the wall, and took down a beautiful Moorish sword; its sheath was of purple silk, its rich ornaments and curiously-formed hilt of silver skilfully wrought. He held it out to the youth, and said, " I won it near the robber-nest Tripoli, on the African shores; and I hope it is not unworthy of being accepted by you as a token of my friendship. Besides, you may well use it with advantage in the approaching fight; for though it be somewhat curved and bent inwards, yet it fits the hand so well, that any German warrior may wield it with strength and dexterity. Try but one stroke."

And as Frederick drew the noble weapon from its sheath, and made it flash through the air in his powerful hand, all was again well with him. The approach of the strife for his native land, his mother, and his hearth, and also for Rose, for Rose, for Rose,—so it sounded through his heart like an inspiring echo,—brought back to him a glow of strength and life. He gratefully seized the hand of Sir Everard, bent, as he took leave, over that of Rose; and girding on his sword, he hastened out full of warlike eagerness. But at the door Sigismund Füllrath clasped him in his arms, and pressed him with deep feeling to his heart.

"You are a true Bremener," said he; and his eyes filled with tears while Frederick went forth, strong and fresh, into the bright blue of the spring morning.

He had now to look to the good horse whom he was to mount in the fight, to the sword just given him, which had not yet its full polish, to the light morion which he meant to wear, and which had not been completed while he was working at Sir Everard's armour. Life, with its cares and business, again bore him along with its rapid current, and the keen regrets of love were heard no more. He looked upon his mother with a cheerful, even joyful affection. When the light of duty and necessity falls straight upon a mind so devout and true, there can be no more question of doubt and delay; all then shines clear and beautiful.

But Frederick felt yet more full of courage when, in the morning rays of the next day, with his mother's blessing on his head, he rode forth after the banner of the horse-troops, and halted beneath the Roland's Pillar.[1] The honoured image looked down upon him gravely and kindly; it seemed to him as if he heard his forefathers promise audibly a joyful issue to the coming war.

The bells rang to a solemn service in the cathedral. All the horsemen, and Frederick amongst them, alighted from their horses, and went into the venerable building with an awful joy. As they came out again, service being ended, Frederick heard, close to him, a voice sweet as the nightingale's, saying, "A little while, and we shall sing here, 'We praise Thee, O Lord!'" and looking round, he saw that it was the fair Rose who had spoken this, as she passed near him, leaning on her knight's arm, and greeted him very kindly.

As the troops had now left the city behind them, and even the echo of the farewells had ceased, Frederick sang to a well-known air the following song, which just then rose in his mind:—

[1] This is an ancient stone-figure in armour, to be found in the centre of many of the market-places in German towns.

The Armorer's Song.

Thou fair, thou balmy morning beam,
    So clear and bright,
Thou lurest to the battle-field
    Each warrior knight.

The nightingale she warbles there,
    In leafy grove:
I listen to her song, and hail
    My lady-love!

My lady-love?—another's bride!
    O broken spell!
She hath not given herself to me—
    Alas! farewell!

Farewell, my love! I bear within
    A sickened heart:
Welcome the sword whose edge shall cure
    My bosom's smart!

O German soldier! thou shouldst bear
    A soul more brave:
Bethink thee of thy mother dear,
    So nigh the grave!

Yes! for her sake I'll live; and guard
    Me well this day:
From him who diligently toils
    Grief flees away!

His comrades gaily repeated the last lines of each verse, thinking of it only as a song. Ah! few men guess the secret feelings that give birth to songs; and how deeply ploughed has often been the heart of the minstrel before the rich harvest sprang up! The enemy was nigh at hand; the combat began on the following day. The Bremeners were victorious; and the lawless Theobald, with two hundred of his chosen freebooters, threw himself into a neighbouring castle, which, during the former truce, the burghers had neglected to demolish.

"This comes of want of decision, and of belief in a perpetual peace," said Sir Everard, as, on the evening after the fight, he looked down upon the robbers' nest from a height above it. "Did not Sigismund Füllrath and I urge most strongly that those walls should be broken down? But we were answered, that it was not wise to drive the enemy to despair, that it was unnecessary to exhaust with this labour the burghers already wearied out by the war, —and such-like speeches. But this time the hateful fortress must come down, were I myself to be buried in its ruins."

Night was coming on, and a wet mist was rising thickly from the ground. Everard called the young armorer to his side. "Master Frederick," said he, "the Moorish sword has been wielded well in your true hand to-day; I know that your head is as ready to do service to your fatherland. Let us ride forth together in this veil of darkness towards the robbers' castle, and there spy out how we can best order an assault in the morning dawn. You will easily discover, with your keen practised eye, the weak points of the fortress."

Frederick bowed joyfully, and hastened to bring his horse. Only a few chosen riders followed the two noble companions into the darkness of night. Before long they halted under the walls of the castle.

There seemed to be within a sound of stealthy moving and stirring; Frederick remarked it, and cautioned his chief. But he answered, "Ah! there is something going on there! All bats are wild and active by night, but, for all that, they do not fly at once into the hair of brave men. Any how, two soldiers can guard the door; I know there is no other issue from these walls."

It was done according to his words, and Sir Everard and Master Frederick now separated, to ride in different directions round the castle.

Among the soldiers who went with Frederick was an old experienced retainer of Sir Everard's. He drew near to his young leader, and said softly in his ear, " Master Haubold, you are much wiser than I am, but my senses, practised in many a fight, are very sharp. Be on your guard. There is something wrong going on in that robbers' hole, and they are going to play us some trick. Do you not see something shining through the chinks of those window-shutters? Now all is again dark!—now there is another gleam! Do you hear how the pavement of the court-yard groans under heavy burdens which are being dragged up or down for some particular object?"

" They must be preparing the defences against the morrow," answered Frederick.

" And then that deep, deep silence," added the old man. "If they had their will, not a footstep should be heard, not a light seen. I tell you they have found out that we are before the castle, and they are preparing for a sally, or some other sharp work."

And Frederick, more closely examining and considering, came to be of the opinion of the old man, and rode with his soldiers towards the side of the castle where Sir Everard was, to inform him of what had been perceived; and at the same time to unite the whole of their little troop for resistance.

As he turned round one corner of the building, the chill night-wind drove the clouds asunder, and the light of the stars fell upon a high outwork, on which Sir Everard had mounted, that he might the nearer consider the strength and elevation of the fortifications. He was stooping forward his helmeted head.

" O heavens!" thought Frederick, "it is the very image of my dream!"—and he sprang forward with winged speed to warn the knight of his danger.

At that moment there was heard the rattling of stones; and the whole of the outwork fell crashing over Sir Everard. The horses of the troopers started back; even the

good steed of Frederick reared up; and he had hardly
quieted it, and spurred it on to the place of danger, when
suddenly, with loud scornful laughter, there broke forth
through the ruins the whole band of enemies, on fiery
horses, brandishing above their heads red torches and
flashing swords. The little troop of Frederick could not
resist this unforeseen and overpowering onset; and he
himself was borne back by the wild stream of fugitives
and pursuers. But soon collecting himself, he perceived
that the enemy had imagined that the whole of the Bremen
troops were gathered before the castle, and that this sally
would be a decisive effort. The important point now was,
to give notice promptly to the army. He first thought of
hastening to do this himself; but dreading the slightest
possibility that his going might be taken for a flight, he
gave his orders to one of the troopers who had pressed
close to him in the confusion, and then watched him, as
the stars became brighter and brighter, rushing with the
speed of an arrow up the height where lay encamped the
army. Soon the sound of horns and trumpets was heard;
the horsemen poured forth in close files, and put themselves quickly in order at the loud word of command of
their leaders; the foot-soldiers appeared on the hill, in the
golden light of the rising moon, ready for attack or defence. Then the enemy perceived that they had made a
false step, and turned to hasty flight.

The Bremen troops halted, and received the little band
of Frederick into their ranks. Some of the captains spoke
of a return to their camp, and of storming the castle when
morning dawned. But Frederick broke into the circle,
and cried, with a loud indignant voice, "And is, then,
your hero and your general, the great Everard of Waldburg, to be left to perish under the ruins, or perchance to
be dragged out thence by the enemy, alive, but a prisoner?
And if he is dead already, snall his body remain in the
power of those robbers? Even the blind heathen would
never so forsake the remains of their chiefs. Besides, the

way to the castle has been opened to us by the mad attempt of the enemy. God has given the fugitives into our hands; —up, then, brave Germans! after them!"

All joined in his cry; the cavalry rode hastily against the enemies, who were again collecting. Before they had gained the castle-walls, the wild Theobald had fallen in sudden death beneath the Moorish sword of Frederick, and the freebooters were all either slain or mortally wounded. A loud cry of victory sounded up to the starry heaven. In the mean while, Frederick hastened to the ruins of the outwork, that if possible he might deliver his noble chief. As he passed on, he asked in vain after the old retainer of Sir Everard, he was neither to be seen nor heard of; and Frederick imagined that he must have been struck down from his horse in the confusion of the first flight: but he had cause to think otherwise, after he had sprung off his horse, and climbed the heap of ruins. There shone brightly in the moonlight a sword fast driven between the stones, and broken; near it lay the old soldier bleeding and senseless. It was easy to see that he had been trying to free his beloved master, who lay there buried, till his sword broke, and the blow of some passing foe had stretched him helpless beside his work of faithfulness. Frederick turned immediately to the same honourable task; and as he had more time and more skill, he succeeded far better. He soon perceived Sir Everard's armour shining between the stones; and before long, his noble form lay free, though stiff and still, beneath the noonlight. With a quick glance Frederick remarked that the armour was not broken, and that the knight could not have received a fatal wound; but yet, as he raised the vizor, the fine features were so fixed, that he thought life must have almost departed. Anxiously and in vain he sought for something that might restore consciousness.

Then the old wounded retainer began to move. He slowly raised his shattered head, and murmured with difficulty, "The Rose; that will restore my lord. Oh, do you not understand? I mean the Rose wine. Do not think I am wandering; listen to me; look there, my horse is fastened to that tree; I brought with me of that strengthening wine. Oh, go quickly. The Rose for my knight!" And he sank back again, and breathed out his faithful soul with one deep sigh.

But Frederick hastened to the tree he had pointed out, and found the horse, and, in the knapsack on his back, a silver flask which gave out the perfume of the Rose wine. He quickly rubbed with it the temples of the knight, and, as he seemed to revive, poured carefully into his lips a few drops of the noble wine. Then Sir Everard opened his large sparkling eyes.

"Is the enemy defeated?" he asked.

"Destroyed," was the answer. "Even the wild Theobald is slain."

"All praise and blessing to the Lord God!" said Everard, as he made an effort to rise. He stood up firmly, and tried his strength of hand and foot by rapid and vigorous movements.

"O how skilfully!" he cried out—"how skilfully did Master Haubold the armorer work! I mean, both father and son. Does the noble youth yet live?"

The moon just then shone out upon Frederick's face; and Everard pressed his deliverer gratefully to his breast. On all sides now poured in the victorious troops; and a council of war was held in the first dawn of day, as to what was next to be done. Sir Everard spoke amongst the others.

"My friends and comrades, I am not wounded; thanks be to God and to the brave armorer Haubold. Neither am I dangerously injured by my fall; but I cannot for some days mount my horse, nor ride as becomes the leader of a brave troop. And yet it is necessary to break up the neighbouring robber-holds while we are in the first flush of our victor joy, and they in the first shame of their defeat. This is my advice to you. I will see to the entire destruction of this evil abode; and you, so many of you as are sound and ready for war, must go forth under my lieutenant to new deeds of victory. I give over my command, if you grant me the honour of the choice, to the skilfu. artificer and brave burgher Frederick Haubold."

With a joyful cry the leaders gave their consent, and the victorious march began anew. Before Sir Everard could again appear amongst the soldiers, the fastnesses of the robbers had fallen before the ardent and yet thoughtful courage of the young chief, and the zeal and valour of the Bremeners; and in the first reddening of the autumnal leaves peace beamed softly and securely over the subdued country. The brave soldiers returned to their homes rejoicing and praising the Lord of hosts.

Sir Everard and the senator Füllrath came out to meet the troops as they drew near to their beloved city; the soldiers gathered round their commander with joyous greetings. He made known to them that the senate and citizens had agreed to grant any one request that the brave and good Frederick Haubold should make, as a recompensé for his noble deeds during this glorious summer; and this boon was guaranteed to him by all for each, and each for all.

The colour came into his fair youthful face, as he bent his head thoughtfully. Then he said, with a gentle, grateful voice, " Might I ask to pledge you all in a draught of the Rose wine, and for some flasks of that noble wine as a memorial?"

Everard and the chiefs smiled, well pleased at the lowliness of the request, and attributed it partly to the simplicity of a gay and careless artificer. But Sigismund Füllrath understood him better; and he said, as he reached out his hand to the young hero, " And my daughter shall bring out the wine for your solemn pledge in a cup of silver which is an ancient heirloom in our house, and which shall henceforth belong to you and yours for ever."

Glowing with joy, Frederick thanked him, but added, " I pray that this high honour may not be done to me before the marriage-feast of my noble chief."

And so it came to pass: the fairest Lady Rose Waldburg bore to the youth the generous Rose wine; but this time the cup was not crowned with sweet roses, for they had withered already before the chilling autumn blasts; instead of them a wreath of yellow oak-leaves encircled the rich cup.

Henceforth Master Frederick lived a quiet life, contented and industrious, and many noble weapons went forth from his workshop. He kept up the life and strength of his good mother by the rich wine which had become his, not allowing to himself even the slightest taste of it. She came to a good old age; and the only fault she could ever find in her beloved and only child was, his disinclination to marry. In that alone he could not fulfil his mother's wishes. At her last hour she praised her noble son, and prayed, as her parting blessing, that the Almighty might grant him his heart's desire. And so it was, that soon Master Haubold began to fall ill, and a calm, painless decay brought him near to the grave. The evening of his death, Sir Everard and the Lady Rose visited him as usual; one draught of the Rose wine yet remained; Frederick begged the lovely lady to give it to him out of the silver cup. It was spring-tide, and she had brought with her bright flowers for him, and now wound the sweetest roses around the cup. Hardly had he emptied it out of Rose's hand, when his gentle soul departed in peace and blessedness to God.

p. 28.

Eugenia.

A MILD autumnal evening lay stretched over the rich, fruitful domains of the old Count Frederick of Schlossberg. Before many a house-door of the thriving villages the country-folk had assembled in little groups, talking to each other of the young and beautiful Eugenia, the only child of the count, who, now aged and infirm, had left in her hands the whole government of his earldom. This she administered no less with manly wisdom than feminine mildness; and even now, as was her wont, she had ridden round on her beautiful palfrey, that she might learn from the mouths of the people themselves where any misfortune had pressed, or here any hope had sprung up.

She still lingered in the last village, surrounded by a circle of admiring and talkative peasants; at her side was her equerry, Golding, who, with an anxious and almost angry countenance, hastened her departure. It was, he said, already dark, and it would be impossible for himself and the page, who were her only attendants, to protect her against the prowling bands of the lawless Kuntz. This Count Kuntz was a daring freebooter under the well-known Pappenheim, and for many years the country-people had complained of his exactions and oppressions; for he cared not for the treaty which Count Frederick had made with Pappenheim, but, on the contrary, permitted his troopers from time to time to descend upon the territories of Schlossberg, and to plunder its inhabitants.

" I trust to be able to protect you," said Eugenia to her people, " perhaps even to avenge you : take, meanwhile, as some amends for your losses, what I have now by me."

While she spoke, there poured from her fair hands a shower of gold into the hands and caps of those around; and as with her graceful plume she bent her head hither and thither, greeting and encouraging now one, now another of the bystanders, a mild evening sunbeam played around, lighting up, with golden radiance, the countenance of the giver,[1] reddening her cheeks, and adding splendour to her

---

[1] A similar idea occurs in Retzsch's Illustrations to Bürger's ballad of " The Brave Man," where, in the last scene, a ray of golden light is made to irradiate and glorify, as it were, the face of the generous countryman, who, at the risk of his own life, had just saved a whole family from destruction.

blue kindling eye; while its last lingering glances rested on the happy faces of the rejoicing people. But Golding still persisted in his unfriendly reproofs; till at length Eugenia bade her subjects an affectionate " good night," and rode on, pursuing a meadow path, which, after a few turnings, led her through an alder-wood not far from the foot of her father's castle.

" What, now, was the cause of your ill-humour, Golding?" inquired Eugenia, as they rode on. " You know as well as I that the soldiers of the wild Kuntz will never dare to lay hands upon the daughter and heiress of Count Frederick."

" Perhaps such a thing *might* happen," replied Golding.

" But this was not the chief cause," added Eugenia earnestly. " Am I not right?"

Golding was silent for some time; at last he broke out: " Smile scornfully upon me still, as you have done hitherto, fair lady; I deserve no better: fool that I am, who, though born of a knightly race, and called to nobler prospects, am content to waste the vigour and prime of my manhood in no higher calling than master of the horse to a count!"

" Who obliges you?" asked Eugenia meekly, letting fall a look of mild compassion upon the troubled countenance of her attendant.

" Ah, who else," replied he, more composedly, " but she who is heavenly goodness and benignity itself! But when she averts her glances from me, only to bestow happiness, by her smiles, upon these stupid peasants, jealousy and anger seize me, in my forlorn misery, with their corroding teeth. Pardon me yet, lady; they may gnaw me as they will, but from this day no word of complaint shall escape my lips."

" This surely they need not do," answered Eugenia, ' since you can always reckon upon riding at my side."

Silently they pursued their way through the windings of the alder-wood. While they now entered the most secret and shady spot, Eugenia's palfrey suddenly started back, as if scared by some frightful object. At that moment a savage-looking fellow, on whose shoulders hung a pair of firearms, and a broad blade glittered in his hand, sprung to the bridle; while the bushes around bristled thick with grim bearded faces and forms. Some of these quickly overpowered and tore from his horse the equerry, others seized the trembling groom, and, with guns presented to his breast, kept him silent and motionless. Eugenia, in a firm and collected tone, called out to the assailants, "Freebooters, you are mistaken; I am the daughter of the count."

"Count! what count? what lord?" exclaimed several rough voices. "Money here, quick!"

But as the maiden turned her beautiful eyes upon the circle of fierce countenances around her, the most unmannerly of the bawlers became involuntarily dumb;— without, however, leaving the way free for her to advance.

"I have, indeed, no money with me," said she, calmly; "but take, if you will, this diamond cross, as a ransom for me and my people; and if, as I believe, you serve Count Kuntz, then tell him from me that there is a treaty between my father and his general, Pappenheim, and therefore he may not henceforward oppress the territories of Count Frederick."

The troopers were silent; some of them bowed themselves respectfully, and Eugenia supposed that all danger was now over; when the fellow who held her palfrey by the saddle cried out, "To the wild Kuntz we belong, and we are his fellow-companions. Hurrah! this damsel is my booty! comrades, take you the diamonds; I take the bride!"

Eugenia let fall one of her earnest beaming looks upon the dark-brown visage of the miscreant, but he stared the more boldly in her face, and exclaimed, with a coarse laugh, " I am a Bohemian ! I am the fierce Prymsel, at whose name the very children in their cradles cry out with terror. I will have thee for my bride !"

Upon this he tore from her hand the diamond cross, and threw it to his comrades, at the same time leading the palfrey quickly into the neighbouring thicket. Golding, secured by three guards, panted convulsively with terror; while Eugenia looked up with her bright tearful eyes towards heaven.

The loud galloping of a horse was now heard sounding along the path. " Dog ! Prymsel !" cried the rider, in a voice like a thunder-clap ; and the wild Bohemian sank upon his knees; the others quickly placing themselves in military array.

" What have we here ?" asked the handsome young man, skilfully reining up his snorting steed in the midst of the group, and casting his fiery eyes around from under a strangely formed and richly ornamented casque.

" A prize, Count Kuntz," replied the commander of the troop ; " the lady gives herself out as the daughter of Count Frederick."

Kuntz looked at Eugenia with strange surprise; then, with soldierly mien, bowed himself low before her, down to the very neck of his charger.

" Whither would Prymsel lead her?" inquired he, with kindling aspect. All were silent. He repeated the question in a louder and more menacing tone, turning at the same time towards the Bohemian ; and while the latter trembled in dumb conscious guilt, speedily a bright blade glittered in the right hand of Kuntz; — the Bohemian uttered a loud shriek, and in a moment lay stiff and dead, with cloven skull, under the alders.

" Remember the example of Prymsel," said Kuntz, turning to his people ; and then approaching the shuddering Eugenia, he asked her, " Were you terrified by this cursed dog, beautiful lady? It grieves me much.—Hand me here what you have taken from the countess."

He gave her back the cross, with a few rough apologising words, but with noble warlike mien. Golding meanwhile was courteously assisted to his horse.

" Attention! present arms!" cried Kuntz; and the wild troop stood respectfully, and in military order, before the astonished countess.

Eugenia promptly, and with presence of mind, addressed her deliverer: " In this you had done a piece of knightly duty, valiant captain, if we had stood on other ground; but who gave you leave to bring your wild soldiery here upon the territories of Count Frederick? Do you not know of the treaty with Pappenheim? and do you honour so little the word and writing of your general?"

She paused; but Kuntz yet waited and listened anxiously for her words; at last he said, " If *you* reprove me, fair maiden, I shall indeed listen to you; but know that I would tear in a thousand pieces the treaty of the general. For *that* I care not a rush; but, oh heavens, for *you!*—Soldiers!" cried he, wheeling round his charger, " whoever among you is seen henceforward on these boundaries shall be given up to the vengeance of the people; and whoever takes but a single fowl from one of these peasants shall lie where the wild Prymsel now lies. Shoulder arms! to the right! march!"

While the troop moved off in martial array, Kuntz added, almost sorrowfully, these words: " You drive me, then, thus soon out of your domains, fair lady. Fare thee well!"

" I meant not your own person," replied Eugenia in a mild tone, and with a soft blush, " so much as your warrior-band, Count Kuntz."

" Is it indeed so?" cried the youth joyfully. " God be praised! for then may we meet again soon."

And with these words and a low obeisance, he waved a parting salutation with his glittering blade, and quickly disappeared on his foaming steed into the thick depths of the forest.

In deep musing Eugenia rode homewards. She related at the supper-table to her aged father what had befallen her; and his pale cheeks reddened with indignation at the outrage against his only child, and anon beamed brightly at the mention of the name of Kuntz; till at last, forgetting his feebleness, he sprang erect from his chair, and exclaimed, "The brave Kuntz! With my whole soul I used to love him—the mad fellow—and now he is the deliverer of my daughter!"

"Do you know him, father?" asked Eugenia.

"Who knows him not?—the fiery impetuous youth. I would he were somewhat milder and more pious; but this, I trust, will come in time."

And thereupon he began to lose himself in stories of the knightly deeds of the count—not observing how, as he spoke, the trembling Eugenia looked down with throbbing breast—for the arrow of love had sunk deep and flaming into her stricken heart.

She retired into her chamber, which afforded a solitary view over the woody country, uncircumscribed too by any opposing object; for such was the frowning and almost perpendicular precipice of Castle Schlossberg, that neither wall nor rampart had been thought needful to protect its fastness. All around slept peacefully in the soft moonlight. Eugenia turned herself away from the scene, only the more inwardly troubled by the contrast which its placid stillness afforded to the restless sea of thoughts in her own breast. "O heavens!" whispered she to herself, "can I indeed love him—a freebooter—a ——?" But words and thoughts faltered and were lost, in a silent stream of warm gushing tears.

It was already deep midnight; the lamp began to

flicker unsteadily; and the smiling moon cast her reddened rays through the arched window. Eugenia still walked restlessly backwards and forwards; when she heard the following words sung in a clear voice under her window:—

> " Late through the wood, mid the nightly gloom,
>   Doth the soldier cheerfully speed;
>   Soon the patrol and the field-watch will come,
>   And the freebooter's joyful meed;
>   But dearest of all, the lovely face,
>   And the fair one's arm with its tender embrace."

Surprised and terrified, Eugenia shrunk tremblingly together. "Surely I am distracted," said she to herself. "Here some one sings just under my window, and yet the precipice so near." She looked round her chamber, her eyes seeking the well-known objects, in order to free herself from the strange illusion; and while the song died away, she sighed to herself, "God be thanked! This mad dream had well nigh crazed me. Now it is gone, and I will to rest. I have been awake too long, and have wearied my senses."

But again the song began:

> " Ah, lovely fair! ah, smiling grace!
>   Thine own is all the spoil;
>   Fear not the dusky bearded face,
>   Nor the bloody armour's soil;
>   On the warrior's arm who safely sleeps
>   Is watched by his love, and his courage keeps.
>
>   This song, when after ardent fight,
>   Did once my thoughts beguile;
>   Full oft it served me, day and night,
>   To many a kiss and smile:
>   But now a maiden flies from me,
>   And all my love is mockery."

Eugenia was transfixed with amazement; and looking through the casement, she beheld a tall powerful figure striding backwards and forwards quickly and impatiently on the very edge of the precipice. Ah! but too well she knew that form; and trembling with anxiety, in haste she opened the window, and called out into the night, "For heaven's sake, Count Kuntz, why do you venture here?"

In his first surprise he bent his knee, but immediately raising himself to his full height, he replied, in a half-laughing tone, " Did you speak of *venturing*, fair vision? Then surely I must be the most cowardly warrior on earth, if such an enterprise as this is any thing wonderful to me, and especially now, when such an object draws me forth."

Eugenia, suddenly shrinking back in womanly mood, said, with earnest voice, "And what object, then, leads you up this steep precipice, Sir Count?"

"Ah! you well know it," replied he. "I would see you, — hear you, — and draw light from those soft beams that play around your fair form. O, you are so wondrously beautiful, so stately, so divine! Heavens! I have already been for hours as if enchanted; and it must be so, I well see, all my life through."

"It appears, however, from the last verse of your fine song, that there are many in the question," replied Eugenia, proudly. " But if, as you say, *many* salutes have fallen to your share, you may probably find, nevertheless, that you have overreckoned in the matter. *Here* you have, most certainly. I wish you a good night, Count Kuntz!"

" O mercy!" cried he, sorrowfully, "do not disappoint a poor warrior, by thus retreating so speedily. It was certainly very stupid of me to sing that silly song at this time. It sprung involuntarily from me, because, at the moment, I could think of nothing better. The *last* lines, however, do nevertheless, from my inmost soul, apply to you:

" But now a maiden flies from me,
And all my love is mockery."

"But you have yourself composed the whole song, have you not?" asked Eugenia.

"Oh yes," said he, as if half ashamed; "I composed it, as the words themselves tell plainly enough, when, after we had chased some dogs of enemies, we came to a halt on the banks of a wild mountain-stream, and a female captive of wondrous beauty fell to my share;—nay, go not away from the window; beshrew me, if I tell you not all truly and properly;—well, the fair captive told me she had a bridegroom; and then, to be sure, my fine rejoicing was speedily at an end. I caused the odious fellow to be searched for; and when he was found among the wounded, there was nothing for it but to procure a good wagon, and to send him home, with his beautiful bride at his side: but to me it was a cursed vexatious disappointment."

"And she, then, was the *one* you spoke of?" asked Eugenia.

"No," answered Kuntz, confidently. "The last lines ran differently once. I cannot sing them to you now. I have forgotten them, in fact, since I saw you; and these new ones came strangely and loftily upon me in a wondrous dream. They displease you at me so very much, fair maid, that I begin to think some accursed dog of a magician has been playing his hellish game with me; for, truly, from my inmost heart they flowed forth."

Eugenia remained thoughtfully silent. There was much that attracted her—much, too, that repelled her, in the wonderful man that stood before her. At last, recollecting herself, she said, with strange half-smiling lips, "I know not how it has happened that I have been so indulgent in standing here so long."

"Indulgent!" interrupted Kuntz. "And I, all the while, incur a very death-agony for such an indulgence! I know not how the affair will end, and whether, at last, I had not better throw myself headlong down the precipice, as the least dreadful alternative. O you lovely, you beloved lady—"

His warlike voice sank down in the last words to an unexpected softness, and it seemed as if, blinded by the tears which pressed from his eyes, he staggered heedlessly towards the edge of the precipice.

"Stop! Count Kuntz," cried Eugenia, anxiously, "and listen to me for a moment. It is not that I would altogether drive you away. Only be reasonable, and hear quietly what I have to say."

The warrior stood in an earnest, peaceful, and almost submissive posture; while she proceeded: "What wild scheme is this, that you should climb up here by this dangerous path? You come more in the fashion of an enemy than of a friend; and by such conduct you shew, in the most repulsive manner, your own rude and ill-regulated mind. We are at peace with your general. My father, I can assure you, is well disposed towards you, and will rejoice to learn your deeds out of your own mouth. What hinders, therefore, that you should seek companionship in this castle in a proper and becoming manner?"

She would have proceeded; but the strange movements of Kuntz, who, at the last words, had suddenly thrown himself from the humble posture in which he stood, into an attitude of proud defiance, and had begun to stamp with his feet, and impatiently to pull his beard, caused her to stop in astonishment.

Then Kuntz broke out into a half-angry, half-laughing exclamation: "The devil! People little know how it is with others. As to this about the field-general, I will say nothing of it; for how little I care for that wild stormer is well enough known to every one in our band. But then the worthy old count! Heavens! this is truly a joke. Am I to seat myself quietly and orderly beside him in the large chair, and talk him off to sleep with my warlike adventures? And then, perhaps, scarcely have the joy of seeing you once pass through the chamber—ah! I see already how it would be—you, my charmer, my"—

"In discourse of this kind," interrupted Eugenia, "I

think that it becomes not me to listen to you either here or elsewhere."

He stood once more as if petrified, and then moved slowly along towards the declivity, in order sorrowfully to descend, when the last moonbeams fell upon Eugenia's countenance, and made visible therein a whole heaven of pity and concealed love. Kuntz hardly knew how to interpret what he saw; but,—his whole soul filled with anxious anticipation,—he sank upon his knee, and said, in a gentle tone, and with upraised hands, "O! you are not, after all, so hard upon me. I have been very foolish, very daring; but it shall be so no more."

Eugenia could not forbear a smile when she heard how a rough oath had melted away in the end into the soft whisper of a love-request; and she felt herself so inwardly touched and attracted by the rude yet blossoming wilderness in the spirit of this valiant, loving man, that before she was aware, she had nodded a friendly assent to his parting question, "May I venture to return to-morrow?"

Kuntz waited not for farther answer, but, transported with joy, wheeled down the rocky descent; while a magic slumber, in which were mingled dreams, half of love, half of fear, soon sealed the eyes of Eugenia.

Many a night after, Kuntz was found standing on the same spot, seldom without having first obtained permission: the intimacy became ever more dear, and, at the same time, the rude manners of the warrior grew more mild and gentle, so that there was scarce an evening in which Eugenia did not permit him to draw joy from her life-giving glance and her sweet instructing words, even as from a pure fountain of ever-flowing wisdom and virtue.

Golding had discovered something of these nightly conversations; for no lover, or at least no despairing lover, is deprived of the frightful faculty of reading his melancholy fate in all things, and even tracing it out in manifold ways. He intended one day to reprove Eugenia in an angry jeering manner; but she turned loftily away from him, saying,

"I wish, Mr. Equerry, that you would look better after my white palfrey. It seems to me that he is ill."

And on the following evening Kuntz sung the following words from his rocky seat:

> "Where the eagle flies,
> No screeching owl may dare;
> Where the lion hies,
> The wolf's brood in their lair
> Must lie down with fear.
> Hence, away! thou beast of prey,
> Lion and eagle both here stay."

Golding no longer ventured to approach Eugenia, whether with word or look; only as a dark frowning mist-cloud he seemed to hover near the bright path of the hero and favourite of the noble count.

Kuntz stood once in a moonlight but tempestuous night over against the beloved lattice, and as the tender speech of Eugenia fell upon his ear, his courage rose at last to the utterance of a long-cherished request—" Ah, lady," sighed he, " it is so far from hence to the window, and this thick ugly wall stands up so stiffly between us; how charming would it be to wander through the deep night, the fair beloved one on my arm! And if this would be too much for her to grant, yet to walk humbly by her side; yes, how charming this would be! O thou fair image!"

"Wild, senseless youth," replied she, "what is it you ask of a young and tender maiden?"

" Oh, lady, I am already become more mild and peaceful; I have even almost left off the rash oaths I was wont to use towards my warriors: only come down to me! Hearest thou not the hollow voice of the storm whistling around the battlements? Seest thou not the dark flitting clouds as they sail over the face of the pale moon? Within—in the castle-garden—all is sheltered and still; there is the screen of the high walls, and of the green waving beech-trees—and only in the hardy tops of the old lindens the low earnest rustling is heard. I can easily pass over the wall, if you will promise to come down the steps and meet me. Come, dear lady, I entreat you, come!"

Touched by his kindly manner, Eugenia nodded a friendly *yes*, and vanished from the window. Kuntz flew swift as an arrow over the wall, filled with the most transporting joy. While he now stood in the dark leafy grove, and waited in earnest, longing expectation, and still Eugenia came not, neither was there any light seen descending the winding turret-stair, his former wild impatience began to seize him; it burst asunder the soft bands which had lately begun to twine themselves around him; and just as Eugenia stepped into the garden, the LION was pacing about chafed and fiery as before. Kuntz hastened towards her so impetuously that at the first look she started back terrified, taking him,—now so strangely altered,—for another person.

"What dost thou fear?" said Kuntz, with a loud confident voice; " it is I, sweet love; follow me, be not afraid. Hearest thou how the free woods rustle yonder below? Hearest thou the night-song of the stream? O leave this little cage, and follow me forth, my sweet bird, into the dark green shade of the forest, and be as a queen upon the vanquished, submissive earth! Hearest thou not? Dost thou not come?"

" Alas! how you have betrayed me!" sighed the maiden sorrowfully.

" Let the devil betray, for that is his art," cried the incensed warrior: " it is not the way of the bold Kuntz; he takes with his valiant arm what belongs to him,—and he takes *thee* too!"

" O go, go from me, unheard-of deceiver!" exclaimed Eugenia.

He uttered a wild laugh, and approached to embrace her; but the maiden stepped back with graceful agility, and in a moment a large yew-tree divided them from each other; then she raised her shining white arm menacingly towards the night-sky, and cried, "Hence with thee! hence to the alder-wood, where the bloody Prymsel lies mouldering in the earth! dig up his miserable skull, and place thy head under one cap with his;—for wherein art thou better than he?"

Struck with amazement, the warrior stood rooted to the spot, while Eugenia vanished into the castle, calling out to him, as the door closed behind her, "Never more!" In wild despair Kuntz fled over the wall and back towards the window; but, alas, this opened not to him again, how sorrowfully soever he begged and repentingly complained. Night after night he came and watched, even to the appearing of the morning-ray, but no form approached the lattice; quiet and motionless burnt the lamp in Eugenia's bower. But within, the damsel wept many a burning tear. And ofttimes when he would beseech her earnestly and hopefully, and when, perhaps deceived by some illuding fancy, he would exclaim, "Oh, heavens, she comes! she comes!" and would joyfully clap his hands;—then she seemed to pine away for sorrow at the sound, and to be dissolved in the flood of grief which oppressed her tender heart. She would lie for nights immovably before a picture of the Saviour; and sometimes when she would change her apartment and remove to the innermost part of the castle, where she could no longer hear the complaints of her lover, she would say to herself, "No, no, I must bear this burden as well as he; for was not my weak and foolish compliance the cause of his undoing?" And truly he was very near his final undoing; for the thought once came into his mind to throw himself headlong in despair from the top of the precipice; but he saw as it were the white menacing arm of Eugenia in the clouds above, and drew back from the horrid purpose.

The mournful cry of the poor wild Kuntz had sounded for the last time. In vain did Eugenia sit by her window at night-fall tremblingly expecting his plaintive voice; and when sometimes she would arise from her couch and exclaim, "He comes! he comes!" alas, it was but the cold spring wind with its shivering sound, or the doleful cry of some wandering night-bird. She now learned, moreover, from her servants, that the soldiers of the wild Kuntz had dispersed themselves, and withdrawn from the country; it was said also that their master had somewhere perished, for they had sought him long and anxiously in vain.

And now there descended as it were a dark mourning veil over all the days of Eugenia's life. In deep grief she passed away her time; the reins of government slipped from her feeble hands, and the old Count Frederick was obliged himself to resume them, albeit the unaccountable withering away of his darling child pressed him every day more sorrowfully to the earth. No cheerful discourse availed to cure her grief—no gift—no pleasure. The teardrops stood ever moist and bright in the eyes of the poor maiden; and when these precious grief-pearls were about to fall, she would hurry, with buried face, into her own chamber.

One day Golding stepped unannounced into her apartment. She was about to reprove him angrily, but, ere she could speak, he addressed her thus:—"Countess, I come with honourable purpose, and therefore your displeasure terrifies me not. It is as if I made my last testament. Listen to me. I can no longer bear to witness your suffering. I go out, therefore, to seek him for you in the wide world—you know well whom. If I find him and bring him back to you, well and good for you both, and I need not then be ashamed to appear at your weddingfeast. If he is dead, or if he is no longer worthy of you, —and was he ever this?—then, lady, we have many examples that true love and manly wise discretion can at length achieve a triumph, and attain their lofty aim. But say nothing to me on this. It is my last life-spark, and you may well leave me to cherish it." Without waiting reply he quitted the chamber, and left Eugenia in a strange sea of perplexity and hope.

She heard her father tell next day that Golding had gone forth, no man knew whither; only he had left behind him a letter, to the effect that he should return again,—that they must wait for him with patience,—and that during his absence such and such persons of the household should act as his representatives. Eugenia was somewhat grieved that the poor man, out of attachment to her, should attempt so hazardous an enterprise in the uncertain world, while yet she felt herself elated by the flattering hope which it seemed to promise;—before, too, she had been oppressed by the presence of the anxious, jealous Golding; and it seemed now as if one at least of the weights which drew her towards the joyless grave had fallen off.

Her mind now recovered itself so far as to make her long again for a sight of the outward sky; and one bright winter-day she felt her spirits so enlivened as to induce her to try a pleasure-ride. Her palfrey stood saddled in the court-yard, ready at her beck, and a tall portly man, with a thick white beard and hair, held the stirrup. She gazed wonderingly on the old man, and was amazed to find that not only had the government of the people become strange to her, but even the household itself, since there stood here before her, as her equerry, one whose face she did not so much as know. He was called Pertinax, they said, in answer to her inquiry; he had served for some months, humbly and quietly, in the stables, and Golding at his setting out had appointed him to the duties of his office. While she still stood musing, the old man said, in broken German, with a hollow voice, " I am Pertinax, the trusty Pertinax; I am an outlandish man—a Bohemian—but true-hearted."

Eugenia remembered the Bohemian Prymsel, and involuntarily started back. The old man looked, much troubled, towards the ground; while she, repenting that she had vexed him, stepped quietly into the stirrup, which he presented to her in his hand. He lifted her up cheerfully, and with much adroitness, into her seat, and then

K

rode respectfully and heedfully by her side. She tried on the way, by kindly words and looks, to make amends for the pain she had given the old man, and he seemed, by his gestures, to be sensible of her favours; but with his imperfect German he could reply but little to her discourse; he even appeared to be unwilling to speak much, and seemed to wish rather to ride on silently, with his head bent down before him; which, with his extreme kindliness and attention, made a strange and awkward contrast. Perhaps it was owing to this very strangeness—but so it happened—that Eugenia conceived a liking for the old man, and often after this rode out in his company; perhaps, also, because his love of silence allowed her to nourish uninterruptedly both her griefs and her uncertain hopes;—of which last she herself hardly knew whereon they rested.

One day she happened, from a window which overlooked the court-yard, to see her old favourite dragging an enormous load of wood towards the kitchen. She threw up the window indignantly, and called to him, "Pertinax, let go that burden!" In a moment the wood lay at the feet of the obedient old man. "Who desired you to carry it?" continued she.

"Pertinax himself—the old Bohemian himself," was the reply. "I am a servant; I am acting as a servant, and I am satisfied to do so. Pray let me carry it, lady!"

"If it be thus in your country," answered Eugenia, "it is otherwise in our free land. Here you are no servant, but my equerry. There are services which it does not beseem you to perform, and this is one of them."

But he only repeated, holding up his hands imploringly, "Oh, lady, give me leave, I pray thee, to carry it!"

She at last consented to his strange fancy; whereupon, with joyful alacrity, he swung the burden again over his shoulders; and afterwards, laden a second time in the same manner, he moved quietly across the court. Eugenia, on inquiring of her household, learned that Pertinax, at such times as his duty permitted him leisure, took upon himself the heaviest and most fatiguing of the servile occupations of the castle, and that he lived with his fellow-servants in constant unvarying friendliness; of whom some looked on him as one half-crazed; others, again, as a kind of saint. When Eugenia once, during their ride, remonstrated with him on the subject, he replied in some half-intelligible words, by which he seemed to wish to intimate that a vow or penance obliged him for the present to such a life. Thus it went on; and at last Eugenia, who ever regarded him with a kind and gracious eye, left him, without further remark, to his own unaccountable ways.

The spring had again come round; on every tree and bush hopeful buds and blossoms sparkled in the cheerful sun. But, alas! the hopes of Eugenia revived not. Count Kuntz remained, as before, a lost, unknown knight; and Golding had sent no intelligence as to the issue of his search.

Once when, in a melancholy hour, Eugenia was musing upon these things, a servant stepped hastily into her chamber, and called her to her father. She supposed that a sudden indisposition of the old man was the cause; but what was her amazement when she found him clad in full armour, which two esquires were hastily adjusting; while a strange warrior, with wild, insolent looks, stood before the door. The venerable old hero smiled from under his yet unclosed visor, and said, "Eugenia, you see me engaged here in shewing an ambassador how an adversary's challenge ought to be replied to, even though his opponent be an aged man, who has neither son nor son-in-law to espouse his cause. The troop of the wild Kuntz is again in motion, and more eagerly than before. But the letter, I see, is addressed to you: there it lies."

Eugenia, pale and trembling, took up the paper, and read as follows:—

"Countess Eugenia! I promised to return to you; and I am here again on the borders of your domain. I am Golding, not Kuntz. Kuntz is dead and gone; no one of his followers can hear any tidings of him. But the remains of the troop gathered themselves round me as their leader; others poured in from all sides; and I am now as powerful as ever Count Kuntz himself was. Recollect, I am sprung of a knightly race. I have served you peacefully for many years in faithful, devoted service. Accept me now! Your father will possess a brave, powerful son-in-law; you, a husband who adores you. If you will not consent, then shall my soldiers carry fire and sword into your villages, and at last into your castle. Ask me not further how all this has come to pass so strangely; suffice it, that I rode forth with quiet, peaceful intentions, and the troop chose me for their captain; I also choose you heartily for my bride. And so things are as they are. Make your choice, then, countess; make your choice, old count. Early on the morrow you see a wealthy and powerful lover before your gates, or else an incensed and deadly enemy."

Eugenia tore in pieces the detested scroll, and turned her back upon the astonished ambassador. "Right so!" cried Count Frederick. "You have now your answer, messenger!" And the latter left the apartment with a scornful grin.

"What horse may it please you to ride?" asked an esquire of the count, casting the while a mournful look on the pale, but gigantic, figure of the armed knight.

"Bring my good grey," said the count; "he is quiet, and knows me well; and he surely will not refuse to carry me to my last battle."

"Ah! Sir Count, the good grey has been dead these two years."

"Then bring me out the little Moorshead, which I have so often ridden in the chase. He is no battle-horse, it is true; but then he will not throw off a weak old man."

"You rode Moorshead somewhat nard for five years in hunting; since then he has been laid aside, and he is now dead too."

"Ah! my poor good horse. Now indeed I suffer the punishment of my errors. Then there remains only in the stable the wild, snorting young steed?—for I may not lead my daughter's gentle palfrey into the fight."

The squires sorrowfully answered in the affirmative, and were speechless.

"Well, I know what to do," said the old man, with a serene look. "When I was a boy, they used to fix me on the saddle of my pony with a leathern band. This I have preserved in remembrance of my youth, and I will now at last use it in good earnest. My hands and arms are yet firm and strong; and if once I am well secured, I can tame the maddest steed. See, here it is!" cried he, bringing forth from a cupboard the red and beautifully ornamented band; while Eugenia hastened, secretly weeping, to her chamber.

Her resolution was taken. Was it indeed so, that Kuntz was dead; or, at least, so despairingly sunk in the rude whirlpool of life, that even her soft love might not avail to draw him thence? Why, then, should she force her aged and infirm father into an unequal contest, and involve her peaceful subjects in all the miseries of a bloody war? She determined, therefore, to take refuge at once in a neighbouring convent, which was well guarded by the protection of a powerful prince, and from thence to make known to her father, as well as to the odious Golding, that she wished henceforth to live as a nun, and as a nun to die.

At her desire, Pertinax repaired to her chamber. "Old man," said she to him, "wilt thou, for the love of me, accompany me on a far-distant journey, and without any one in the castle knowing of it? I go to the convent of Mariaschein."

Pertinax bent himself reverently, with his hands crossed upon his breast.

"It would take too long, and would hardly be intelligible in your un-German ears, if I were to tell you all that has happened. But art thou willing, my faithful servant, —if I should never return, and if thou must also avoid the castle because of this,—art thou willing to go forth with me?"

Pertinax repeated his obeisance more reverently and joyfully than before.

"Gold shall not be wanting," added Eugenia; "I will take enough with me. Only, in half an hour, let horses await us at the garden-gate which looks towards Mariaschein."

"Oh, no gold! no gold! perish the gold!" exclaimed Pertinax, in a rough displeased tone. "But let us ride, fair lady—let us ride whither thou wilt. Repair quickly to the postern. In a minute the horses shall be there."

He vanished. Eugenia now hastened through the castle-garden with a casket of gold and jewels on her arm, leaving behind her the long and much-loved home of her fathers. As she stepped along through the garden-walks, it seemed as if the bushes, which waved to and fro in the humid breeze, were laying hold of her to arrest her flight, while the lofty lindens shook mournfully their aged heads at her departure. But she bade them all a kindly though stedfast adieu, and soon arrived at the gate, where Pertinax already awaited her with the horses.

"Once more, Pertinax," said she, as she mounted into the saddle, "remember that you speak not a word to me during this journey, unless in answer to my questions; see too that you make no remark or objection to what I am doing. Do you hear?"

The old man bent himself again before her with folded hands; and the pair rode forth on their way in melancholy silence.

They had already reached the confines of the count's territories, when the evening began to set in, not with its usual peacefulness, but with sharp gushing torrents of rain, and with ever-darkening and howling storms. In the narrow copse through which they rode, the solitary fir-trees would push out their tall heads into the dark grey heavens, and waving to and fro with their pointed leaves, whistle mournfully in the growing tempest. Eugenia perceived this with increasing anxiety; and the thought that she was now, as a sad exile, travelling away from her ancestral home, and leaving the whole kindly world behind her; and that she must soon, too, bid an eternal farewell to her last remaining friend, the faithful Pertinax, pressed like a stony weight upon her heart.

Pertinax, who had hitherto kept respectfully behind her, now rode quickly up to her side, and gently pulling her cloak, pointed with his hand towards a rising ground on the left, from which Eugenia perceived a number of mounted warriors advancing. "How shall we give place to these troopers, Pertinax?" inquired she anxiously.

"I think—I hope they will pass to the right," said the old man; "but quick trot!"

Scarcely, however, had they put spurs to their steeds, when fresh riders shewed themselves right before them in their path. While they began now to think of retreat, they perceived with dismay that the thicket behind them was fast filling with armed troopers; and quickly from all sides a crowd of horsemen rushed forward, so that in a moment they found themselves surrounded by a circle of bearded riders and wildly snorting steeds. Pertinax appeared not to meditate resistance,—which, indeed, would have been a frantic attempt against so overwhelming a force,—but he measured the whole band with his keen eye; while the troopers paid so little heed to the presence of the old man, that it had not even occurred to them to deprive him of the sword which hung by his side.

The leader of the band now rode up to Eugenia's side, and said to her, "I know not, fair maiden, whether you recognise in me the ambassador on whom a short while ago you turned your slender back so proudly and scornfully. The game is changed, and the contest seems to be at an end; for you are now in the power of the valiant Captain Golding, before whom we intend to place you as speedily as possible. Come, then, with us without resistance." So saying, he gave the signal; and the warriors put themselves in motion with shouts and songs, and marched on, having Eugenia and Pertinax in the centre of the troop.

The old man rode close beside his mistress, and looked inquiringly into her face.

"Know you any way of deliverance for me, Pertinax?" whispered she, tremblingly.

"Well I know it," replied the old man, "if only I am allowed the use of my speech, and liberty to act according to my desire."

"O, all that you wish," was the answer; "no risk appears to me now too great."

"And you will not drive me from you? you will suffer me to remain near you?"

"Why should I not, my brave deliverer? here is my hand upon it."

The soldiers who rode nearest began now to listen to their conversation. Upon this Pertinax raised himself in a moment to his full height with a noble and joyous mien; his cap, his white hair, and his long white beard, suddenly flew off, and dark locks waved wildly around his gleaming eyes.

"What, in heaven's name," roared he, in a voice which shook the very ground, "what are you doing here? Halt! Stand!"

They stood as if struck by a thunderbolt, while he sprung — his glittering sword in his right hand — upon the leader of the band. "Wolf," cried he, "know you not your commander? know you not Count Kuntz? What insolent dog has ordered you here, and upon this errand?"

Wolf looked tremblingly to the earth, while the sharp blade of the warrior glanced fearfully over his head.

"I ought to hew thee in pieces on the spot," said the Count at last; "but all shall be forgiven, if you bring your Captain Golding, as he calls himself, within three hours, disarmed and bound, to the castle of Count Frederick."

"It shall be done," answered Wolf, putting himself in military posture. "Have you any other commands, Sir Count?"

"The whole troop must accompany you," said Kuntz, "drawn up, and equipped in the best manner. And remember, speedy justice shall be done upon that man who shall touch a hair of any inhabitant of this earldom. Now wheel about—march!"

Wolf, hastily saluting the count, sprung quickly with his troopers up the declivity, and in a few moments all were out of sight.

Kuntz stood in anxious thought beside the fair rescued one, who, in sweet confusion, looked silently towards the ground. At last he said, "And do you then hold to your word? and may I venture to dwell at your side, when I have conducted you back to the fortress, and have placed you in safety from the wild troop?"

She was silent for a while; and the dismayed warrior sighingly exclaimed, "Oh, heavens! Then must I go again into the wild world, for I am shorn of my sweet hopes! I should truly have become gentle, peaceful, and courteous; no more imprecations should have passed my lips. As Pertinax, you have never heard from me other than pious and becoming speech. And I should have been called again by that dear name which my blessed mother was accustomed to use, ere she died, and left me to wander forth into the rude world. She called me *Conrad;* and the friendly, peaceful Conrad I should again have become. You will have it otherwise. Let us, therefore, hasten to the castle, and all shall then be at an end."

But while he rode by her palfrey, Eugenia stretched

out to him her white, tender hand. "Gracious heaven!" cried he, "what does this betoken?"

"Dear Conrad, dear bridegroom!" whispered Eugenia: and, with souls full of blissful emotion, the reconciled pair rode on their way. The storm was now over. The night-sky was still and clear, and the moon shone peacefully upon their path.

Many were the dear discourses and explanations that passed between them, as they pursued their journey;—of the griefs and sorrows of Eugenia, and of the repentance and penances of the youth under the disguise of Pertinax. At length they approached, at midnight, the castle of Count Frederick, and descried its towers by the watch-fires which shone from its heights. The troop of Count Kuntz stood in fair military array before its walls; while the aged Frederick himself, astonished and incredulous, spoke down from the battlements to one and another of the strange host, and sent servant after servant round the castle to seek for his lost child.

When the latter rode up at Conrad's side, and arrived in front of the troop, a rejoicing "VIVAT" resounded loudly through its ranks. Guns were fired off as a soldierly salute; and many a waving blade glittered high in the clear moonshine. They approached the main gate of the castle; and Conrad said, "Let us both enter together, fair bride. It is fit that we should set your father's mind at ease as soon as possible, and give him an account of all that has happened. As to all others, it is time enough by and by."

The great hinges of the door turned quickly at the call of Eugenia; and she and Conrad rode together into the fortress, which was again closed behind them. But when Frederick, the aged warrior, had heard from the mouth of his daughter the tale of her love, her distresses, and her deliverance, and of the lowly penance and stedfast faithfulness of the valiant Kuntz, then every gate of the castle rushed open at the rejoicing words and gestures of the old man. The gallant band poured like a stream into the moon-lit and torch-illuminated castle-yard, and there rejoicingly drank the health of the betrothed pair.

Golding, disarmed and bound, was placed before them. "Have you any thing to say in your defence?" asked Conrad.

"Not much,—or rather nothing," replied the prisoner. "If you cause me to be cut to pieces, or to be hung up before you, I cannot call it injustice. But if you allow me to go, then will I, knowing that I have been guilty, not only of folly, but of wickedness too, remove myself as far as possible from your sight. In the northern coasts of Germany is my home; there I would live as a quiet householder, and strive, by a wise old age, to make amends for my past follies. Decide according to your pleasure."

Conrad looked inquiringly at Eugenia. She made a signal to her esquires, and they unbound the prisoner.

Golding, supplied by Eugenia with money and provision for his journey, rode forth, humbled and ashamed, from the castle, and was seen no more.

Count Frederick had, in the mean time, put off his ancient, stately armour. He then caused the bridegroom to put it on; and as he presented to him the bright polished saddle-band, he said, "This shall be for thy first-horn son, dear Conrad!"

The Privy-Councillor.

 CALM, still Saturday evening, with its setting sun shining brightly on the woody heights of Schleswig, found the worthy woodman Klaus returning from the distant woods, where he had worked diligently and alone all the week, that he might spend the last hours of Saturday with his family in their small but pretty cottage, accompany his wife and children to church on

Sunday, and then on Monday return to his laborious weekly work in the woods. It was a very happy time that Klaus thus spent. The joys of home seemed rooted yet deeper by their regular interruption, sanctified by the Sundays passed so holily, and enlivened by the merry jests of the good father, who would often relate the adventures of his woodman's life with a humour peculiar to himself.

Old father Klaus's heart always beat high with joy when, from the top of a hill, he saw below him the little village, and the soft grey smoke rising from his own hearth, announcing to him that his careful wife, dame Elsie, was preparing a favourite mess for his supper. But then, at times, he would think very anxiously—"Ah! during the week that I have been away, there may have happened many serious, perhaps sorrowful, things in my little household. Who knows whether my old wife Elsie may not have fallen ill, as has often happened of late? and then it is only the maid who stands before the fire and prepares, along with my supper, some broth for the patient. And my good daughter Agnes sits near her sick mother's bed, and will try to smile at me as I go in, and will not be able, because she has been crying with anxiety for her mother; and she will rather look down, that I may not see her distress. And then my little fatherless and motherless grandson Hans will creep up to me, instead of jumping and shouting as usual, and will stand on tiptoes and whisper to me, 'Grandfather, you must not cry or look sorry; for the wise woman in the village says that would make grandmother a great, great deal worse.' And my heart will be broken, and I must not shew it. Perhaps my dear Elsie will ask with a sigh, 'Ah, husband, have you no tidings of our dear son Gotthilf, since he went forth to seek his fortune as a farrier?' And I can only answer with a sigh, 'Alas, no!' and my patient sufferer will weep secretly and gently."

Once or twice before, all this had indeed happened to father Klaus: and often since, a foreboding spirit had made him feel sure his fears would come true. This evening especially the dread quite stopped the joyful beating of his heart at the sight of his dwelling. But he knew there was one cure for it—an earnest childlike prayer and a cheerful hymn. He clasped his hands as he walked on, and prayed inwardly,—no sound came from his lips, and the words were hardly formed in his heart. This still breathing up to God was especially dear to him; "for," he would often think to himself, "our heavenly Father knows better what I would say than I do myself." But now, with the joyful certainty that the sighing of his heart was heard in the right place, there broke from his lips the following words, in so clear and strong a voice that the echo could not but repeat them :—

"God hears the spirit's groaning;
Our prayer, through blood atoning,
He grants—our gracious God:
This is my heart's confession.
O joy beyond expression!
All bountiful is God!

Though now my courage fail me,
Though fearful thoughts assail me,
Yet trust I all to God!
Through joy or sorrow, never
My heart from Him shall sever—
Its watchword still for ever,
'On, on, thou man of God!'"

And as he now walked on, rejoicing in heart and in words, his little grandson Hans came flying towards him with outstretched arms. It was easy to see that he brought important tidings; but whether they were very good or very bad, could not yet be known: even the quick, eagle eye of father Klaus could not at that distance discover the expression of his childish features.

Klaus ceased his song, in order not to lose a word of the

child as he drew nearer; but there still echoed strong and clear in his heart the words,

"Its watchword still for ever—
'On, on, thou man of God!'"

At length the voice of the child could be distinguished: "Shout, shout for joy, grandfather! shout for joy! There are come news of uncle Gotthilf—good glorious news!— and a letter from him! And it is an old trooper, in a shining cuirass and shining helmet, who has brought us the good news, and sits within by the fire between grandmother and aunt Agnes, and repeats so many stories about the war that it is a pleasure to hear him. Only let us walk fast, grandfather, that we may not lose much of his beautiful stories. And now you must shout and be merry!"

Woodman Klaus remained quite silent. But as he held his hands firmly crossed and pressed against his breast, and as his eyes, sparkling with joy, were turned towards heaven, whilst he walked briskly on, his little grandson understood that he was shouting and rejoicing in his own way; and the boy thought to himself, "Though I cannot hear what he says, the angels in heaven can." And he trotted on joyfully by his grandfather's side, taking five or six steps to each stride of the strong old man, but keeping up with him, and talking all the while of the strange trooper, and still more of his long bright sword, which hung behind him on the wall, and seemed to give light to the whole room; and then of the tall, tall black horse in the stable, which kept prancing and stamping till he could be heard in the house, but would not the least hurt the cows, for the brave trooper had expressly answered for him, and had said, "You may take my word for it."

Klaus, in his thankful joy, only heard the chatter of the child as if it had been the noise of a bubbling streamlet along his path; but a word here and there fell upon his ear. So that when he entered his cottage, the soldier, who sat between the mother and daughter, and was refreshing himself with meat and drink, did not appear to him like a stranger, but as a dear friend, to whom he stretched out his hand, saying, "It is very kind of you to have brought us news of our dear son,—oh, how we have longed after him! Welcome a thousand times to our house, dear guest!"

The trooper received the greeting as heartily as it was given, and seemed to feel himself quite at home; only he drew somewhat aside, in order to leave more room for the easy-chair of the master: and this he would surely have done as reverently had he been in his own far-distant home; for it was easy to see that he was no upstart adventurer, but the son of decent and honourable people.

Mother and daughter in the mean while welcomed the father with joyful caresses; and when he was seated at his supper, with a tankard of foaming ale beside him, they begged the soldier to repeat his good news.

"Ah! one could never hear too often such happy tidings, if they were to be repeated again and again through a blessed eternity!" exclaimed the mother, her eyes shining with joy through her tears. And then she sat down at her spinning-wheel, anxious to make up by her diligence now for the time she had lost during the first hour of that absorbing joy. Agnes followed her example, and turned her wheel rapidly and dexterously; little Hans placed himself familiarly near the soldier, looking up at him admiringly, as if he would catch the words as they fell from his lips.

"Yes, truly," began the stranger, "fortune has been kind to your brave son. After he had thoroughly learnt his honourable calling in many distant and strange lands, it happened that before he returned home to you, the ship, in which he was, cast anchor on the coast of Zealand. Near the place of landing there had met, just at that time, a great hunting-party, assembled by your and my gracious master, Christian IV., king of Denmark." The trooper touched his helmet as if to salute; reverently the wood-

L

man raised his cap and bowed his head; then the guest continued: " The merry sounds of the hunting-horns, and the barking of the dogs, and the cries of the huntsmen, attracted your son, and drew him on farther and farther into the depths of the woods. It fell out that the hunted stag passed suddenly by him, and disappeared again amongst the trees. Then followed a hunter of very noble presence on a tall white horse, and surrounded with eager dogs. In order to shorten the way, the hunter spurred his steed to leap over a high hedge; but it was too high, the horse caught his fore feet in it, and fell with such violence on the greensward, that his rider was flung from the saddle full ten paces off; and both horse and man lay motionless, and as if dead. Your son ran up, and shook the hunter violently in his strong arms until he came again to his senses, and asked, with flashing eyes and imperious voice, what that meant. ' It means, sir, so much as this,' answered your son,—' that you would have been suffocated by the blood that had rushed to your head, if a less strong arm than mine had shaken you.' Then he helped to raise the horse on his legs again, to put in order the saddle and bridle, and finally held the stirrup for the stranger to remount. After which he walked off, displeased and silent, without heeding any of the questions which the hunter now asked kindly and thankfully."

" There I know my strange Gotthilf," said the old man, shaking his head, but with a pleased look. " As ready as an angel to give help, but as restive as an overdriven horse if he is treated unfairly. Well, what came next?"

" Your son," continued the trooper, " heard, some days after, as he walked through the fair city Copenhagen, how a reward was offered by the king to whoever could cure his favourite horse of a bad lameness. Your son desired some one to shew him to the royal stables; and as he was taken, according to his desire, to the sick horse, he saw, with some astonishment, that it was the same creature which he had seen fall in the wood. But, as was his wont, he had only eyes for the work he had just undertaken."

The old man nodded approvingly. The trooper continued:

" He put aside other thoughts, as needless for the present, and began to examine thoroughly the noble horse, which, contrary to custom, seemed well pleased with his surgeon, as if he would have said, ' Now this is a good, clever fellow, to whom I may trust myself safely.' At last your son discovered that the wound was not, as was supposed, high up in the shoulder, but only in the hoof, which had been injured by the fall; and he engaged to cure this by skilful shoeing; so that the king should ride again his beautiful steed in a fortnight, as well as if he had never been hurt. The wiseacres—as usual in all places and on all occasions—raised a senseless cry against this promise of the strange, unknown farrier. But, as not one of them could give better advice, they agreed at last that it was wisest to let the stranger make the attempt, and ruin himself; and so they gave up the horse to his care. Such a proceeding is more common than is generally thought, even when other and more important objects than horses are concerned. But it also often happens as then with the king's horse. In twelve days he was perfectly cured. As he was then taken before King Christian, and your son stood near, the king knew him immediately to be the same who had been so ready to help him in the wood, and then so displeased ; and said, with a good-humoured smile, ' If thou art not the angry smith Wolundur of the legend, but a living Christian man, I would fain keep thee near me.' Your son answered, bowing respectfully, ' I am a Christian man, sire, and of the faith for which you have fought so zealously in Germany with your true sword.' ' Had I but had better fortune with it!' said the king, sighing deeply. ' Well,' said your son, ' you fought gloriously, because honourably and bravely ;

and God and all good men rejoice at that, whether the event be victory or defeat. Now we have an honourable peace, and all the land is again yours.' 'You are the man I want,' said King Christian, and stretched out his hand to your son, who shook it heartily but reverently. I stood by; and we all rejoiced, both high and low; and again we rejoiced when your son accompanied the king every where as a skilful farrier, and as a brave squire and huntsman to boot. Yet he will not remain with the king, but means to return home to you, and carry on his trade here, feeding his forge with your wood."

"That is well," said father Klaus; "we had agreed to that before we parted. 'Go up and down the world,' said I, 'as long as you take pleasure in it, and have strength for it, and can learn something new and good. But only forget not to come back. One's own hearth is worth its weight in gold.'"

"And when will my best-beloved son return to his own hearth?" asked mother Elsie; and Agnes moved her lips as if she too would inquire after her brother's return, though the words were not audible.

"That you will find in the note," said the trooper; and he pointed to the well-sealed letter lying on the table.

"Have not you yet opened it, mother?" said Klaus.

"The direction was to you, not to me, dear husband," answered Elsie.

Klaus nodded, well pleased; but he said kindly, "Man and wife are one, especially when their children are concerned." He opened the letter, and read it through attentively, while the soldier said to the women, "I only know so much as this, that your son will follow the king in but one more campaign before he returns to your happy household; and that will soon be over. The campaign is against the Ditmarsen,* that strange people who have often revolted against the kings of Denmark in former times, and now again are rising with new complaints of the infringe-

* They inhabited a small province to the west of Scnleswig.

ment of their rights. But our army will soon silence them; and then, my kind hostesses, you will again have your son and brother with you, to be yours once more, and for always."

" God forbid!" said father Klaus, solemnly, as he slowly folded up the letter, and put it thoughtfully into his pocket. The others looked at him with astonishment.

" Your words did not apply to my words?" asked the trooper.

" Yes, and no, as a man may take it," answered Klaus; " and yet I am no friend to yes and no in the same breath."

" That can be seen as plainly in you as in your son," said the guest.

" But sometimes," continued Klaus, " it must be so when human things are concerned. My words, however, related to the ending of the letter."

" There is nothing bad in it?" asked Elsie, with an anxious look.

" Nothing bad for our son," answered the father; " for he is not answerable for what is going to be done; and that only can be called bad for a man of honour, which leads him to do an injustice in the sight of God. But there are other people very near to my heart—one more especially." He looked up as if he saw a steep ascent just before him. Then he looked around with a smile, and drew a long breath, like one who has a heavy weight taken off his breast, and said, " Well, now, it is no business of mine to give counsel. Things must come to pass as they may." And therewith he began to talk of other matters in his usual earnest, and free, and cheering manner. But again it seemed as if that weight returned, and he often fell into deep thought. His wife and daughter inquired no further. They knew well that when father Klaus could and might disclose to them any thing which moved him deeply, he was quick enough to do so. But if it was otherwise, he was as a casket, the key of whose curiously wrought lock was lost. The wife and daughter trusted so entirely to the strong and wise firmness of the father, that they never felt tempted to remonstrate with him when once they knew that he held the rudder in his powerful hand.

The evening passed cheerfully and hospitably. In the morning the trooper rode away. He took leave thanking his hosts for the hospitality they had shewn him, and receiving their thanks for the good news he had brought them of the brave Gotthilf. The family then went forth to church, Klaus himself, more than usual, grave and silent. The preacher spoke of the woe pronounced on those who, having put their hand to the plough, turn back and leave their day's work unfinished. And then he spoke of the blessedness of those who complete their work.

The face of the good Klaus was sad at the first part of the discourse, but looked cheerful again at the end. When it was over he fell on his knees, and prayed so earnestly and so long that his wife and daughter had to wait for him, and at last to touch him, as they were about to shut up the church. Klaus looked well pleased as they walked home, but he did not speak.

When he had dined he began to make up his bundle, and desired his wife to give him a provision of meat and drink; which made her ask him,—" Must you, then, go forth to the wood again this Sunday evening? Why can you not stay with us till Monday morning?"

" I am not going forth to the wood now," answered the woodman, with earnest kindness; " I am going a much longer journey. Whatever you wish me to say to your son, mother Elsie,—and you, Agnes and Hans, whatever messages you have for your brother and uncle,—think of them quickly, and let me know them in the next hour; for as soon as it is passed, I shall be on my way to the capital, Copenhagen."

" On Sunday evening?" asked his wife. " Is not that like profaning the Lord's day?"

" It is the Lord who bids me go," answered Klaus, " and my own conscience. I have no time to lose. But be not troubled and sad, my dear ones. I have a sure hope: the Lord who sends me will also bring me home again to you, and perhaps in great joy. If all goes as I expect, I shall return, and our Gotthilf with me; if it goes otherwise,—well, then, let us leave it all to Him whose love and power has counted the very hairs of our head."

The little family were at first well-nigh stunned by this sudden departure; but a firm trust in God helped them, and, next to that, trust in the understanding and strength of the father of the family. With moist eyes, but firm step, Klaus an hour afterwards left his home. With weeping eyes, but hopeful hearts, his family gazed after him.

———————

Some time after there stood before the royal castle of Copenhagen a crowd of respectable people, who waited to see their king, Christian the Fourth, ride out. His beautiful white horse stood already at the gate, held by the brave squire and farrier, Gotthilf; who since he had cured the noble animal would give up the care of him to no one. The king rode almost every day at this hour, about ten in the morning; but he was so much beloved, that it seldom failed that many persons were assembled, who gladly saw their knightly monarch spring on his horse, and with a kind greeting to his subjects ride gaily forth to the fresh bracing sea-coast, or to hunt in the dark forests of the valleys.

And now King Christian passed from the castle-door in a simple but rich dress, and laid his hand on the saddle-bow in right knightly fashion. Just then he looked on the face of the brave farrier, and said, " What ails thee to-day, my good Gotthilf? thou seemest to me to be much moved?"

Gotthilf answered:—" Nought but good has happened to me, my royal master; I have just seen my old father, the woodman Klaus, standing there in the crowd, and I looked not to see him here. What brings him from his

Schleswig woods I do not yet know; but as he is ever in a good path, it can be only good that has brought him here."

"Call him hither," said the king; and, at a sign of his son, Klaus drew near.

Gotthilf hastened to tell his father not to greet him before he had done reverence to the king. But there was no need for his caution. It seemed as if in this moment Klaus saw in the whole world but one man, King Christian the Fourth of Denmark. With uncovered head he approached the king very reverently, but with a look and gesture full of trust and confidence. "God is with me!" he said. "As I have been so quickly brought to my king, it will be granted me to speak to him those words which lie nearest my heart. It is very important that which I have to say, my gracious king."

"Does it concern your brave son?" asked the prince.

"One higher than he, sire."

"You, his father?"

"Higher yet, sire?"

"Then it must be me, your ruler."

"Truly it does concern you. But yet I must still say, One higher still, sire."

"Oh!" said the king, smiling. "But you must know, woodman Klaus, that even if your message concern either the German Emperor or the Pope, I acknowledge neither of them to be above me."

"And I too acknowledge neither to be above me," answered Klaus; "for I am the subject of none other but your majesty. I am a free peasant; and you hold your kingdom from our Lord God alone. What have we to do with pope or emperor?"

The king looked well pleased into the woodman's large blue eyes, and asked, "Are you in haste to deliver your message?"

"It may be that on every moment hangs something important for time and for eternity," answered Klaus very earnestly.

Then said King Christian to the farrier,—" Now, brave Gotthilf, take back your grey; truly, without your good aid he would not now be mine; take him back to the grooms. I shall not ride him to-day; your father must be attended to first."

He again saluted the crowd kindly, and then went back into the castle with the woodman at his side; whereat many wondering speeches passed between the attendants.

In his innermost apartment the king took his seat on a gilt arm-chair, whose cushions were covered with purple silk. Klaus stood before him reverently.

" How is this?" said the king. " You need rest far more than I do. I was about to ride out for my pleasure and wholesome exercise; but you have hardly ended a toilsome journey. Draw a seat near here, and sit down."

" Sire," said the woodman, " do not so lead your subject into temptation. It is true I have been brought up in villages and woods, but yet I know so much as this, that it would ill befit me to sit down near my lord and master, as equal with equal, comrade with comrade. And had I not known it before, I should have learned it from your kingly presence. You are God's anointed, sire; endowed with a marvellous and heavily pressing power."

" Heavily pressing power!" repeated King Christian, as if to himself. " Yes, yes, goodman Klaus, often have I felt that in my heart. You use words very full of thought, as is often the case with people who have grown up in healthful solitude. But you will not refuse, I trust, a cup of noble wine? I will have one brought to me likewise." He touched the little bell that lay beside him, and commanded the page who entered to bring two goblets of Rhenish wine for him and for his guest.

" Sire," said the woodman, as the page left the room, " although, truly, my richest drink at home is only of good strong ale, yet I believe a cup of noble Rhenish wine will bring me a blessing; especially when I think of the great honour granted me of drinking it in the presence of my sovereign lord. But if it seems good to you, let me first speak out my errand, and then we may enjoy the rich drink together. When work is over, it is good to feast."

At this moment the page returned, bearing the richly gilt cup on a silver salver; he offered it to the king on bended knee. " Place it on the table by the window, my child," said King Christian, " and leave us."

As they were both alone again, there arose between them the following solemn discourse:—

" Now, good Klaus, what is thine errand with me?"

" Sire, they say in town and village that you mean to carry war into the country of the brave Ditmarsen, and that you have made your preparations already. My son, too, has written me a letter wherein he states that thus it is."

" People have spoken truly, and your son has written truly, friend Klaus. Have the Ditmarsen sent you to me?"

" No, sire; I do not know a man amongst them. But I know the Lord my God, and He has sent me with a message to you."

" By means of a vision?"

" By means of my own conscience; *that* said, Klaus, thy king must not go forth against the Ditmarsen."

" What has it to do with thy conscience, old man, whether I go against the Ditmarsen or not?"

" My conscience would have had much to do with it, had I let you go forth without warning you. Henceforth my conscience has nothing to do with it, since I have warned you, even should you now go against them."

" I see very well the cause of all this, woodman Klaus."

" I think you in no ways see it, sire."

" Hearken, if I have not rightly guessed. You would

gladly have your son at home again; and you look upon this expedition against the Ditmarsen with an evil eye, because the brave young man has promised me beforehand to follow me in the campaign. But we will make good terms together. Let me go out against the Ditmarsen without disquieting yourself about it, and I will let your son return with you at once to your home well rewarded and high in my favour. Why do you shake your head? What is there which is not yet right?"

" Nothing is yet right, my honoured king. That may indeed be called making terms together, but not *good* terms; and on that *good* just depends every thing for time and for eternity."

" Well, then, propose some other articles of capitulation between us, friend Klaus; and a better one, if you can."

" To say truth, sire, I do not well know what is meant by articles of capitulation. But what I mean in my conscience is this:—It is now almost sixty years ago that many high and precious rights, which had been before granted to them, were by force of arms torn from the Ditmarsen by your royal predecessor. They defended themselves manfully as a free nation, for only on certain conditions had they in former times placed themselves under the protection of Denmark; and many drops of good blood were shed in the contest. And now is it to come to pass again that the few remaining rights yet left them are to be violently torn from the Ditmarsen. May this be far from your thoughts, sire!"

" It is very near them, very near indeed, friend Klaus. But do not misunderstand me. I am only about to inflict suffering on the Ditmarsen in order to do them the more good afterwards."

" Sire, that might beseem a man who was like the God of heaven. But you, though the anointed of the Lord, and appointed to great things, are yet only a man on earth; and the greater your anointing and your power, the greater is your responsibility."

"Friend Klaus, why should the Ditmarsen have greater privileges than the inhabitants of Schleswig and my other subjects?"

"Because they are another people, sire."

"A better people?"

"Another. Every man has his own coat."

"But would it not be better, Klaus, if all coats were after the same pattern? then in time of need men could help each other, and there would be far less of envyings and idle scruples."

"No, sire, with your permission, it would not be better, but worse; for then all men would look as like one another as so many eggs; and, besides the dulness of this, what confusion we should all be in, if Peter was to be taken for John, and John for Peter! And although it is true that one man could help another to a coat, yet altogether there would not be more help to give than now, when the tall man can gather fruit from a tree for a short one, the swift can run for the slow, the strong support the weak, and so on with all the numberless good offices which may be exchanged between men. The capital of good offices is a very beautiful capital,—and, God be praised! a very large one also, sire. It is therefore that I have prayed and warned at the same time, in the name of the King of kings. Let the Ditmarsen keep their own coat, and do not cut it without being called to do so. Act so by all of us your subjects, then will things flourish and stand fast in your whole kingdom."

"I want no prophet," said the king in an angry tone.

"And yet," answered Klaus, composedly, "the prophets under the old covenant were often unlearned men, with no other merit than that of simple obedience to Him who sent them. It is true that I am not gifted, like them, with wonder-working powers. But yet, sire, a good conscience is a precious gift of God ; and my conscience is very sad, my beloved king, on account of this expedition against the Ditmarsen."

"You have done your part, woodman Klaus; and your conscience is clear of my deeds."

"Not quite thoroughly, my lord and master. That great, beautiful, polished sword, which shines yonder on the wall with your other arms,— is it the same which you wielded in Germany for the defence and protection of the faith?"

"The same, friend Klaus."

"Now, sire, I think that you would do very well if this time you left that noble comrade behind, and chose another good sword out of your armory to use in this war against the Ditmarsen. For see, now, such a seemingly dead instrument has often as it were a sort of life in it when a man has won with it something good and beautiful for his fellow-men, as you did with this sword; or even has had good luck with it, as when I, some years ago, killed with my axe a wolf that was close pursuing my little daughter Agnes, as she was bringing me my dinner in the wood. I have never since used that axe but for some particular and good purpose, such as when I wanted to make some changes in my little house which would add to the comfort of me and mine, or when I made a cradle for my little grandson Hans, and such-like joyful works. Leave your good sword at home, sire, for this time."

"You are a very wonderful man. But since it is not kingly to say often in one breath, ' No,' to a suppliant, yes, I will leave that sword behind when I go against the Ditmarsen. And your son, too, shall stay behind; and although I shall greatly miss him, you may take him home with you. You have not yet asked me this, so the more willingly I prevent your request with my royal yes."

"Let it not displease you, sire, if I interpose an humble earnest no. And this 'no' you cannot hinder, sire."

"Woodman, I a king, and cannot hinder? Wherefore not?"

"Because you *will* not, sire. *There* lies a strong bar for all God-intrusted power on earth. My son is your squire; but were he only your farrier, he could not so leave you at the beginning of a campaign. When danger draws near, no true man will turn aside, or the fairest fame would be tarnished."

"But, friend Klaus, if I let your son depart richly gifted and in my high favour, who will dare say a word against him?"

"Perhaps no one, sire. But perhaps also evil tongues may wag against him in secret. And that may eat into his fame, as decay eats by degrees into a tree once sound. Alas, alas! not with fire, nor with iron, can that tree be made again sound. And it gives the solemn warning, Beware in time, O man! guard the tree of thy honour against the first speck of decay. And even should no man from without say an evil word, something within would say to my son, and to all like him in the same case, 'Farrier, hadst thou not left thy master when he went to that war, perchance he would have escaped such or such an overthrow of his horse, if thou hadst had the shoeing of the animal. Squire, hadst thou, according to thy duty, remained close at thy master's side when he dashed against the enemy, thou mightest have turned from him that cut of a sword, or that thrust of a lance, which now thou wilt sorrowfully hear of far away from him.' And he will seem to himself as a cowardly traitor, and nothing in this world will again bring him joy, and hardly will he be able to think with a true joyful faith on the blessed heaven of God. No, no, sire; you never would decree that your and my Gotthilf should come to this sorrowful pass—it would be poor thanks for his faithful services. And therefore you will not dismiss him till the expedition against the Ditmarsen is over. If Gotthilf then lives, send him back to me honourably, sire. If not, there is in blessed heaven, for all true men, a joyful, endless reunion. Is it not true, sire, you will take my Gotthilf to the war with you?"

"And you can ask that so joyfully, Klaus, and yet blame my war as unjust? It is very strange, very strange!"

"Not at all strange, sire! Each one must give up his own reckoning when, at length, before the throne of the King of kings, the word will be, either 'Depart from me!' or, 'Come!' My Gotthilf, if he falls honourably in your service, will, I confidently hope, hear the 'Come!' And I, too, afterwards. For now I have done my part here, sire, and I go forth from your presence with a quiet conscience."

He bowed with deep reverence, and went towards the door.

The king called to him: "Stop, woodman Klaus! You must first empty that cup of wine in my presence."

Klaus stopped.

"If you command me, sire, truly I must obey. But, if I might ask, do not bid me drink it. Good wine only tastes well after a good work is completed. And we have not so happily finished the business between us."

"Yes, Klaus, we have!" said the king, rising, and stepping quickly and firmly to the table where the two goblets had been placed; and taking one up, he brought it to the woodman. "There," said the king, "take it and quaff it down. Peace, and joy, and safety to the brave Ditmarsen, so long as King Christian IV. lives; and yet afterwards, so long as his will has influence with his successors!"

A violent emotion shook the strong frame of the woodman. "My king," he said,—" my noble king, my good king,—I feel as if I must kneel down to you!"

"Now, shame upon you, honoured messenger of God! Do you not know the saying, 'Thou shalt kneel to God, and not to man?'"

Then woodman Klaus knelt down, folded his hands together, and said: "Well, then, I kneel to God,—that may be done at all times, even in kings' presence,—and I thank Thee, O my God, that Thou hast given to our king such princely thoughts, and such a fatherly heart! I thank Thee that he listens to Thy word in the mouth even of the meanest of his people! And for that, may he one day hear that most joyful of all words from Thy mouth, the blessed 'Enter!' But first leave him with us for a long course of happy years, for we need him much, and love him dearly." He rose, and took joyfully the cup out of the king's hand, saying, "You have given me a good toast, sire; and I will give a good toast to you, and I have full assurance that it will be granted: 'Long live our king, Christian the Fourth of Denmark!'"

The king and the woodman both emptied their glasses slowly and solemnly, looking the while steadily in one another's face; and each saw that the bright eye of the other was moistened.

"You must take the cup with you, woodman," said the king; "and let it go down to son and son's son."

"That will I right readily, sire," answered Klaus; "and should I drink nothing but beer out of it, it will seem to me to taste like your fragrant Rhenish wine."

"But why not stay with me, friend Klaus, and always have Rhenish wine to drink out of your cup? I would not let it fail you; and I would see to having your whole family carefully brought to you."

"And in what capacity should I stay with you, sire?"

"You should be . . . . yes; you should be one of my privy-councillors."

"Not so, sire. You have already a multitude of such lords; and they are a very different sort of men from me. I saw some of them once when I went to the city of Schleswig, and, if I am not mistaken, here, too, in your royal city. They are very wise grave lords and masters,—some pale and thin from many night-watchings,—some round and broad from long sitting at the table—the table where they write, I mean,—they talk little, and are long silent, and they write heaps of acts. Besides, they are richly drest; and they are obliged to take great care of their costly clothes: no, no, sire,"—and the woodman laughed heartily, —"old Klaus would never do for a privy-councillor."

The king laughed too. But then he said very earnestly, "And yet, friend Klaus, you have been my privy-councillor. With whom have I ever held such secret council as with you? Whose council ever seemed so mysterious to me at first, and yet unravelled and made clear so many deep secrets, as thine?"

"Sire," answered Klaus, "all that I can readily believe. For what I had to say to you, and the manner in which I ought to say it—all seemed to me dark and mysterious, like a shaft sunk deep in the mountain. I only knew thus much: The conscience of thy king is in danger, and the salvation of thy king likewise is in danger. Then I could find no rest by day or by night. Afterwards I heard in church some texts of God's word, full of warning,—the preacher truly spoke them with a very different purpose; but they laid hold on my heart, as telling me one particular thing and nothing else, and pricked my conscience, and drove me here, over mountain, and valley, and sea-coast. And here I am now, and have spoken,—spoken in a way which seemed, and still seems, very mysterious to me,—and the council of a poor woodman has reached to your heart, my beloved king. It was the work of God, not of man."

"Klaus, thou who hast been the chosen messenger of God to me, wilt thou henceforth deprive me of so precious an adviser?"

"Sire; a thing done once is not to be done always. And, 'shoemaker, keep to your last.' Your last, sire, is the sceptre together with the sword. My last is the woodman's axe, which will do for a battle-axe when any wild beasts cross my path. Still the last remains a last; and each of us has a very different one. But that privy-council,—we held it both in common, sire; and it would not be at all according to rule that I should turn privy-councillor to you, or you to me. The real privy-councillor sits with you there, beneath your gold-embroidered purple mantle; and with me, beneath my dark woodman's jacket: he is called

Conscience by name; and he is a true and faithful friend, that is, when he is often bathed in those waters of eternal life, which flow freely for us all, rich and poor, high and low, out of the Holy Scriptures."

"Farewell, faithful woodman!" said the king. "You have left me indeed a true councillor in your stead."

———

Some days afterwards, king and woodman parted with great affection. The woodman took his dear son Gotthilf with him; and there was great joy in the household when they reached home. The king and the woodman lived many years afterwards,—the king, alternately in honourable peace and in just wars; the woodman, in the quiet happiness of his home. But neither of them ever forgot that solemn and happy council. On the days of family rejoicing in the woodman's household (and these, by God's blessing, were not few) he was wont to say, "Now reach me down the king's goblet from the shelf. This day deserves to be ended by a draught out of it." And when purifying trials came upon the king—as they failed not to do, by God's grace—he would, after he had held council with men of worth, shut himself up with none but himself and his Bible, saying, "Now let no one disturb me; now I am going to hold the true council."

The Lantern in the Castle-yard.

IN a very wild and remote region of the Scottish Highlands there stood on a rocky height an old fortress. One stormy evening in harvest its lord looked from his window into the darkness, and over the well-guarded court of the castle towards the opposite hills, where the tops of the trees, still visible, rustled and waved in the dark-blue heavens. The rivulet in the valley sent forth a wild and strange sound, and the creaking weather-cocks clattered and brawled as if chiding the storm.

The scene and the hour were congenial to the mind of the lord of the castle. He was no longer the mild and indulgent master. His only daughter had fled from the fortress with a handsome youth, far inferior to her in birth, but a sweeter singer and harp-player than any inhabitant of the wide Highlands; and soon after their flight, the lover was found dashed to pieces in the bottom of a rocky valley, into which, in the darkness of the night, he had fallen. Thereupon the daughter, by an unknown pilgrim, sent a letter to her father, saying that, night having robbed her of her lover, her eyes were opened to her fault—that she had retired to a convent to do the most severe penance, and that her father would never see her more. After this event, the lord of the castle had become almost as obdurate as the surrounding rocks, and unfeeling as the stony pavement of his old fortress.

As he now looked from the window, he saw in the castle-yard a lantern, moved backwards and forwards as if in the hand of some one, who, with tottering steps, stole across the area.

Angrily he called out, " Who goes there?" for his domestics had strict orders to admit no one within the walls; and since the flight of the young lady, these commands were so rigidly obeyed, that it seemed as if lifeless statues alone dwelt within.

To the lord of the castle there came a soft voice. " An old, old woman," it said, " begs some food, noble knight." But the humble demand was impetuously refused.

"Spy! vagrant! witch!" were the appellations showered upon the beggar; and because she did not immediately retire, but reiterated her petition with a fervent though weak voice, the knight, in the wildness of his wrath, called on his bloodhounds to hunt the beggar-woman away. Wildly did the ferocious dogs rush forth; but scarcely had they approached the old woman, when she touched the strongest and fiercest with a slender wand. The domestics, who had come out, expected that the raging dog would tear her in pieces; but, howling, he returned, and the others laid themselves down whining before the beggar. Again the lord of the castle urged them on; but they only howled, and moaned, and lay still. A strange shuddering seized him, which redoubled when the old woman raised her lantern on high, and her long white hair appeared waving in the storm, while, with a sad and threatening voice, she exclaimed, " Thou in the heavens, who seest and hearest!"

Trembling the knight retired from the window, and ordered his people to give her what she demanded. The domestics, frightened at the apparition, placed some food without in a basket, and then secured the doors, all the while repeating prayers, until they heard the strange old woman carry away the food ; and as she stepped out of the castle-gates, the hounds moaned mysteriously after her.

From this time regularly every third evening the lantern was seen in the castle-yard ; and no sooner did its strange twinkling begin to be visible through the darkness, and the light steps heard to totter softly over the pavement, than the lord of the castle hastened back from the window, the domestics put out the basket of food, and the hounds moaned sorrowfully till the apparition vanished.

One day — it was now the beginning of winter—the knight followed the chase in the wildest part of the mountains. Suddenly his hounds darted up a steep height, and expecting a good capture, at the risk of imminent danger he forced his shuddering horse over the slippery, stony ground. Before a cavern in the middle of the ascent the hounds stood still; but how felt the knight when the figure of a woman stepped to the mouth of the abyss, and with a stick drove back the dogs! From the long silvery locks of the woman, as well as from the restless and low moanings of the hounds and his own internal feelings, he soon perceived that in this drear spot the lantern-bearer stood before him.

Half frantic, he turned his horse's head, buried his spurs in its sides, and galloped down the steep, accompanied by the yelling hounds, towards the castle.

Soon after this strange occurrence, the lantern was no longer seen in the court of the castle. They waited one day—several days—a whole week passed over, but the apparition did not come. If its first appearance had alarmed the lord of the castle and his domestics, its disappearance occasioned still more consternation. They believed that the former prognosticated some dreadful event which the latter betokened to be near. On the knight this anticipation had a terrible effect; he became pale and haggard, and his countenance assumed such a disturbed appearance, that the inmates of the castle were of opinion the apparition gave warning of his death. It was not so.

One day, as was his custom, the knight rode to the chase, and in his present distraction of mind he approached unawares that part of the country where the old woman with the white hair had appeared to him, and which he from that time had carefully avoided.

Again the dogs sprung up the height, howling and looking fearfully into the cavern. The affrighted baron in vain called them back. They stood as if fascinated on the dreadful spot; but on this occasion no one appeared to drive them away. They then crept into the cavern, and from its dark bosom the knight still heard their moanings and cries. At last, summoning resolution, he sprung from his horse, and with determined courage clambered up the steep height.

Advancing into the cavern, he beheld the hounds crouched round a wretched mossy couch, on which the dead body of a woman lay stretched out. On drawing near her, he recognised the white hair of the formidable lantern-bearer. The little horn lantern stood near her on the ground, and the features were those of his only child! More slowly than the faithful hounds, who from the beginning had known their young mistress, did the unhappy knight become aware whom he saw before him; but to dissipate every doubt, there lay on the breast of the dead body a billet, on which with her own blood her hand had traced the following words:—

"In three nights the wanderer's hair became white through grief for the death of her lover. She saw it in the brook. Her hair he had often called a net in which his life was entangled. Net and life were both by one stroke destroyed. She then thought of those holy ones of the church, who in humility had lived unknown and despised beneath the paternal roof; and as a penance, she brought alms from her father's castle, and lived among the rocks from which her lover fell. But her penance draws near its end, the crimson stream fails. Ah! fath—"

She would have written "father," but the stream was exhausted, which, with unspeakable sorrow, the knight perceived had issued from a deep wound in her left arm.

He was found by his servants near the corpse in silent prayer, his hounds moaning beside him.

He buried his daughter in the cavern, from which he never afterwards came out. The unhappy hermit forced every one from him—his faithful dogs alone he could not drive away, and mournfully they watched together by the grave of their young mistress, and beside their sorrowing lord; and when he also died, their sad howlings first made it known to the surrounding country.

The Prince's Sword

NOT far from the free imperial city of Nuremberg, so renowned in story, two young companions, both born within its walls, met on a delicious summer morning. The one was called Leutwald, and sat under the fresh dewy boughs composing lays, as was his wont; when the other, named Adelard, rode up to the spot, mounted on a beautiful fiery steed.

As soon as the two youths beheld and recognised each other, they were glad at heart; the horseman sprang from his horse, the singer to his feet, and they clasped and embraced each other right lovingly. They had much to tell, for they had been a long while parted; Leutwald at home in the fair city, under the teaching of the most accomplished minstrels; Adelard with the renowned Count Albert of Bayreuth, who for his beauty and his knightly prowess was surnamed Albert Achilles. With him had the warlike youth lived after his heart's desire; and he too had become dear to the German Achilles for his skill in arms, and for many proofs of dauntless contempt of death displayed in hard-fought battles.

"So, then, it was a grief to you to leave him?" asked Leutwald of his friend.

"Indeed it was," answered Adelard; "but what could be done? As soon as the count mustered his troops against our beloved mother, the holy free city of Nuremberg, I made myself ready, fastened my horse to the gate, and then, resolved in mind, and with girded sword, I mounted the stairs to my beloved lord, saying, 'You have been a gracious prince to me; but as things are at present, I must use against yourself the skill I learned from you.' I thought the valiant Achilles would have broken forth in anger, as is sometimes his way, but he smiled quietly to himself. 'Thou art a brave fellow;' then again a little time he was silent, jingling the large knightly sword, inlaid with gold, which never leaves his side, and spoke: 'This sword might one day have made thee a knight. Now, however, it may strike thee after another fashion. See only that thou comest honourably under its stroke; so will it be for thy good, whether it touch thee with the flat edge or with the sharp—for life or for death.' Then he dismissed me after his gracious manner; and as I rode forth, a solemn stillness came on my soul; but since I reached our own borders, and still more since I have met with you, I have become light-hearted as before. But are you ready here? It is full time."

"That we know well," answered Leutwald. "Only come you to-day to the aged Councillor Scharf. There will be a cheerful meal; you will learn what is about to happen; and be of good heart."

Then the two youths embraced joyfully; and leading the horse after them, approached the city, singing battle-songs with all their heart and voice, through the flowery country.

At the house of the venerable councillor Adam Scharf there was an assemblage of the brave citizens of every sort. Some whose hoary heads, bowed down with age, seemed to look forward to their last deed of arms, and close beyond it to an honourable grave; others who, in the midday of life, moved on with lofty resolve; others, and many more, with fresh colours on their cheeks and bright hopes in their hearts.

Here the two youths, Adelard and Leutwald, were right welcome; and as every one gladly beheld the latter on account of his graceful songs, so they took no less pleasure in the knightly-trained pupil of their valiant foe, the German Achilles.

All took their places at the table; the beakers passed swiftly round, and no word was spoken but of the welcome dangers of the approaching war. Adelard had much to tell; and all listened eagerly to him, who knew so much of their renowned adversary. And as the great Achilles had always seemed to Adelard to resemble the splendid consecrated sword of a prince, his discourse ever returned to the gold-inlaid sword of the Achilles; so that not only in his own, but in the hearts of all who were present, he stirred up a vehement desire after that far-famed knightly weapon — " Either to win it, or to fall beneath it." There was many a young citizen who made that vow in his secret heart; and only the authority of the aged men hindered the pronouncing a general vow for the willing and the unwilling.

At last, the aged Adam Scharf inquired of Leutwald

concerning the song of the banner; and when the latter answered that it was ready, they all entreated earnestly that he would sing it. On which he began in the following manner :—

> By maiden fingers woven,
> Upheld by warriors bold,
> For holy cause uplifted,
> By counsel of the old.
> Such, Nuremberg, thy banner waves on high,
> Bright, strong, and gorgeous with emblazonry;
> And under it we conquer, or we die!

The last three lines were repeated in chorus by the guests; and now arose such an impatience for the banner, that every one desired to see it first, and then in the presence of the sacred ensign to sing the following verses of the lay.

"I think the maidens must have finished their weaving and embroidery," said Adam Scharf, and invited his guests to follow him; at the same time explaining to Adelard that his daughter and other honourable maidens had made ready a new city-banner for this enterprise, and were at that very time completing it in the apartment occupied by the females of his family.

It was pleasant to behold when they entered the spacious and neat apartment, where round the large white folds of silk sat the delicate maidens diligently employed upon their labours, some busied on the golden fringe, others embroidering the border; for the banner itself was already finished, and the solemn imperial eagle was to be seen with a golden glory round each head, with the sword and ball in his claw, rising dark and gigantic from the silken surface. Directing the whole work, and diligently forwarding it with her own slender fingers, sat at the upper end Elisabeth Scharf, the only child of the councillor; one of these forms which the pencil of our beloved old painters so willingly portrayed, and which foreigners of every land would so deeply envy us, were they capable of feeling their surpassing excellence. When the men entered with old Adam Scharf at their head, the maidens rose from their work, drew back a few steps, and made room for the banner to be seen by those who were to defend it, and perhaps to dye it purple with their blood. The men stood around it in thoughtful silence, pondering on things to come, and wondering in themselves whether that Achilles who was now threatening them, might not play such a game with their fair city as he of old with Troy. Each one was resolved at least not to outlive such an event; and therewith they clasped each other's hands, both young and old, to form a chain which carried the electric spark circling round the sacred banner. The maidens stood behind them, each with her slender white hands modestly folded in the same form; so that between two glowing manly faces, with kindling eyes, there appeared the gentle supplicating countenance of a maiden with drooping eyelashes. Between Adelard and Leutwald, who here least of all thought of separating, stood Elizabeth Scharf; and the two youths sometimes looked back from the inspiring tissue to the inspiring countenance.

Then the aged councillor made a sign to the minstrel who stood opposite to him, saying, " Now for the rest of the song, dear youth; this is the right time for it." And Leutwald raised his voice, and sang,

> An Eagle was encradled
> Within a rosy nest;
> But now, for waving blossoms,
> The billows he must breast.
> Such, Nuremberg, thy banner waves on high,
> Bright, strong, and gorgeous with emblazonry;
> And under it we conquer, or we die!

And again all echoed the last three lines with sparkling eyes. Leutwald continued the song:

> The Eagle soon, my comrades,
> Will witness fearful sights;

> The blood of burghers flowing,
> Shed freely for their rights.
> Such, Nuremberg, thy banner waves on high,
> Bright, strong, and gorgeous with emblazonry;
> And under it we conquer, or we die!

And once more the men echoed the last lines. They then embraced each other with overflowing eyes, and departed in silence to their homes. But the maidens seated themselves again to their work, wept softly, and sang a simple hymn, imploring the divine protection for their beloved native city. Thus, at length, was the work completed; and the maidens parted, with many a gentle wish and many a heartfelt prayer upon their quivering lips, to prepare themselves against the morrow for the ceremony of the consecration of the banner.

The dawn of the following day beheld men and women of every condition assembled in the cathedral. Their hearts were raised to God, and the noble banner was given forth by the consecrating hands of the priest as a hallowed thing.

Then were chosen nine youths of the chiefest families of the city, and each himself of acknowledged worth, who should advance to the altar, that the priest might decide by lot to which of them the honoured ensign of the army should be entrusted. Adelard and Leutwald were of the number. High beat those young hearts, ever thirsting after honour and virtue, with the desire to bear that sacred ensign.

The calmest to behold was the minstrel Leutwald, and he was so in truth; for that blessed spirit of poetry is wont, where she has once taken possession, to nurture humility and gentleness in a soul devoted to God, as the fairest flowers which can bloom in the hearts of her children.

Most ardent and impatient of all swelled the spirit of Adelard; and, in truth, he had learnt other lessons in the school of the German Achilles, than had his friend at the feet of the poet. Moreover, he glowed with the warmest love for the fair and skilful one who had woven the banner, Elisabeth Scharf; and he thought that only in the foremost place could he rightly win and deserve the foremost beauty of the city. But the lot was given forth, and the banner sank from the hold of the priest into the right hand of the blushing minstrel.

Adelard had almost felt angry; but he took shame to himself for his own bitter feelings, when he saw how calmly, and sweetly, and devoutly his friend moved under the wings of the floating eagle, so that the beholders were at times tempted to think of the Lamb with the sacred banner, as it may be seen in some mystical paintings, or on some ancient coin full of deep meaning. The solemnity of the festival relaxed towards evening into a stately assembly of the chief families in the saloon of the Town-hall. Thither came the maidens of the city, all in their gayest and richest attire, the youths in the like array, and moved together in graceful measures through the hall, to the inspiring music of various instruments. At first they were led by the honoured elders and matrons; but when these had taken their places round the hall as spectators, the young were indulged with livelier dances. As long as they moved through the spacious hall in pairs, Leutwald had been the partner of the fair Elisabeth Scharf; an honour yielded to him by all, as having been that day appointed within holy walls the bearer of the standard. Adelard withdrew sorrowful and lonely into a recess. But no sooner did the livelier measure begin, than Leutwald bent modestly to his fair companion, and said, " It would be unjust in me to encumber your graceful movements by my unskilfulness. May I bring to you a noble friend, better practised in the dance? I will betake myself to my more fitting place among the musicians; there I may hope to embellish what here I should only mar."

And when they stood before Adelard, he placed the hand of the fair one in that of his friend with a manner as kindly as it was graceful, and hastened to join the musicians. When with them he inspired the dance by touching so sweetly now one, now the other instrument, and looked down with such gentle smiles from the balcony, especially when Adelard and Elisabeth glided past, that one might have taken him for an angelic musician.

His friend and the fair maiden, meantime, fell into low and earnest conversation; or rather Adelard spoke, and Elisabeth only listened, but with eyes so sweetly cast down and tenderly glowing cheeks, and sometimes with such gracious smiles on her delicate lips, that Adelard forgot the banner in far sweeter hopes. So passed away the evening; and one parting look of Elisabeth wove a whole wreath of blooming roses round the heart of the youth. But the fair maiden had a wise and tender mother, and her true eyes could not fail to discover that which was passing in the pure bosom of the damsel.

And now, when every one in the dwelling of the councillor had retired to rest, the matron rose again, threw on her mantle and hood, and stepped softly to the little chamber where slept her blooming daughter; though well she knew there was no slumber there. She nodded kindly to her darling child, set down her lamp, and seated herself at the foot of the bed. Then began in low tones a confiding earnest conversation. The gentle Elisabeth, more by blushes than by words, yet truly and openly confessed, that the young Adelard was not indifferent to her; and as truly and openly did her mother make known to her that she was already a bride affianced by her father's will and word, and that to her first partner of the evening before, the noble minstrel Leutwald, the beloved and honoured friend of her family.

"My father's word is sacred as my honour," said Elisabeth; and though her cheeks became as pale as before they had been blushing red, there beamed a heavenly serenity in her large blue eyes. She kissed in token of gratitude her mother's caressing hand; and when the good matron had left the chamber, two warm tears indeed stole down the maiden's cheeks, but a silent heartfelt prayer was her help, her spotless heart again beat evenly, the pious child sunk into a calm and almost happy slumber, and the angels pursued their blessed course through her dreams.

But this night passed quite otherwise with the daring Adelard. He scarcely slept; or if any thing like sleep or dreams came near him, then did Elisabeth's lovely form ever rise from their mysterious waves; he started up as though to seize her; and in such waking and such slumbers he dreamed away the time, till morning was far advanced.

The trumpets sounded through the streets, the hautboys blew their subdued notes of farewell, the troops mustered in the plain beneath the walls, and, as they were to march on the morrow, the city gave on this day a public feast, at which the noblest maidens were to present the farewell cup to the young warriors and drink to their success. Never before had Adelard so joyfully helped to marshal the troops, never before had he wielded his arms so joyfully; since he alone can truly understand and love the joy of arms and warlike music, who bears in his mind the image of a beloved and loving one, or at least the remembrance of having possessed such a blessing.

How proudly beat the heart of the youth, as they sat at the table, when Elisabeth Scharf, with evident design, advanced first to him and filled his cup. The German Achilles was at that moment too weak for him, and the golden sword too slight, for he thought that by no victory could he deserve the honour he now enjoyed.

But, now, Elisabeth bent towards him with a grave demeanour, saying, " Fair sir, you receive this draught from an affianced bride." In her countenance he immediately perceived the immeasurable change since the evening before; and the manner in which she turned from him and passed on, took from him all power to approach her with a single word; the joy in which he had lived for a while was extinguished in bitter and secret grief.

When all the splendour of the feast had passed unfelt by Adelard, and every one had sought his own home, the unhappy youth would yet make one last attempt. He went to the venerable Adam Scharf, and addressed the following words to him: "My honoured sir, you have, as I learn, betrothed your fair daughter to a husband."

"That have I indeed," answered Adam Scharf; "and who dares to say aught against it?"

"He who would willingly have gained her for his own," said Adelard. "I suppose a man might make such efforts as would win his love even from an enchanted dragon."

"From an enchanted dragon, truly," said Adam Scharf; "but from a father who has once betrothed his child to a deserving husband, not the German Achilles could win her. In this there can be no change."

"And if a man should bring home the mighty sword of the German Achilles himself?"

"That must the city recompense, and doubtless would; but the father's child remains still the property of her betrothed; and so, young sir, good night. Do not force me to think less highly of you, by idle talk of things which cannot be changed. For the present I say to you, with great esteem and friendship, farewell, against the morrow's march." And with these words the old man courteously opened the door for his guest, and Adelard departed, half impatient, half submissive, and altogether despairing.

Far other than he had hoped the day before did he ride forth the following morning with the horsemen to the field. Truly, he now wished for nothing more than battle; partly because it was his life, and, according to the saying, the wounded fish takes to the water as readily as the whole one; partly because, for the first time in his young life, death appeared to him in an inviting form.

When they were so far from the city that the sound of farewells and good wishes seemed to die away in the distance, Adelard rode forwards to join his friend Leutwald; wishing, under the folds of that banner which Elisabeth had woven, to lament to him his loss of her, and his desire of death.

But he could not, beneath those beaming happy eyes of the young minstrel, find words befitting his woe; and presently Leutwald said to him, in his childlike singleness of heart, "There rides not in this troop a happier being than I, beloved Adelard; for she who wove this banner is my bride. Her father has betrothed her to me; and I trust that warlike deeds and gifts of song may win the favour of my inspiring Elisabeth. Shall I not fight and sing for a glorious prize? When we return from battle it will be made known to her; and then shall I, God willing, have done somewhat which may give me courage to tell her how inexpressibly dear she is to my heart."

Now first did Adelard comprehend the whole of his misery, for now even the right of wishing was taken from him. He only said, "So, then, Elisabeth is thy bride! My bride shall be the knightly sword of the Margrave Albert." And he rode forward to meet the foe, in gloomy silence.

But the war took no such rapid decisive course as Adelard had desired. The knightly sword of the great Achilles did not glitter before him for victory or death; but lightning in the distance it described magical circles, rather threatening than striking, so that for a long time it could not be decided what precise purpose the terrible warrior bore in his iron soul. In all this time there was but little fighting, and that of small consequence to the mind of a bridegroom seeking honour, or of an unsuccessful lover seeking a glorious death.

At length it happened, after long marching to and fro, that news came suddenly from the city of Nuremberg how the Achilles had appeared before their very gates, which he had reached by rapid marches, and how the troops must hasten home to protect their native hearths. Without rest or stay they hastened to the deliverance of their dear native city; and though it seemed incredible that the Margrave should have gained such an advance upon them, the prize was far too precious to allow of relaxing the speed with which they ran their course,—more willing to make the greatest needless exertion than to risk falling short in the least.

It was evening, and already dark, when they entered the walls of the free imperial city. Weariness both of horse and man summoned all to immediate and profound repose; and as these brave warriors felt a consciousness of strength and courage to guard their homes, a deep feeling of security lulled them sweetly to sleep in the bosom of the mother whom they came to protect.

But hardly had the morning dawned in the east, when messengers came from the advanced posts with a whole troop in flight behind them. "The foe!" they cried; "the foe!" And horns were blown from the walls, and trumpets in the streets, and the red banners displayed their colours from watch-towers and battlements through the uncertain dawn. The Achilles was not far from the city; and he who till then thought least of Troy and of destruction, now in this fearful morning, startled by sounds of terror from his sleep, felt such thoughts whirling through his bewildered mind. All, too, was distraction and confusion in the city. Women were weeping, children screaming, commanders giving orders, foot-soldiers and horsemen were hurrying, no troop was in array, and no one passed through the gates.

Leutwald meanwhile, calm and bright as ever, held the city's banner in the market-place, not far from the dwelling of Adam Scharf, and let the imperial eagle float joyfully over his head in the cool breeze of morning. Then sprang Adam Scharf from his threshold towards him, "Forth with the banner, my son-in-law!" he cried. "The foe is not yet so near as the people suppose; and he must be met upon the plain, or he will press too near our walls. If once the banner is gone forth, I will soon send numbers to follow you. Forth with Leutwald, whoever has youth and heart among you! Here we must depart from accustomed rules."

And Leutwald urged his swift steed thundering over the pavement. He raised a joyful cry, " For the banner! For Nuremberg!"

The youths nearest at hand hastened after him, Adelard amongst them; and so they passed at their utmost speed to the gates, and over the bridge, through cornfields and meadows, to the appointed plain. Here they halted, and beheld the enemy advancing from afar; but the young warriors had perhaps ridden forward too rashly, for only sixteen, Adelard being one, had kept pace with the standard-bearer. And right before them, although yet distant and hardly ranged in order, but numerous and every movement more prepared for fight, moved on the squadrons of knights and squires, and a forest of spears rose threatening from a cloud of dust. Those who were to come to their support were yet only advancing from the gates of the city, and scarcely discernible. Leutwald said to his companions, who were measuring with doubtful eye the space before and behind them, " Till our friends come up to us, we may well make a stand here. If we have ridden forward too rashly, some among us may, indeed, bleed for it; but should the banner of the city turn to flight, it would strike dead at one blow the courage of all who may follow us."

They saw that it was so, and remained stedfast at their post, whilst Adelard rode to a height to watch lest they should be cut off on the other side. He halted at the top, and saw nothing of the enemy's troops but one single horseman, who advanced slowly, mounted on a lofty and richly-caparisoned steed, himself lofty and majestic, in his complete suit of armour glittering with gold, a mighty plume streaming from his helmet; and like a proud eagle he turned here and there his slender neck, shielded and adorned with glittering scales, to survey with his keen glance the bearing of the field, and again rode slowly forward,—quite alone, quite careless of his safety, intent only on the order of his troops,—giving such tokens of a Prince of Hohenzoller, that Adelard could no longer doubt he beheld before him the German Achilles, his great and terrible master.

"Now welcome, thou fair morning, to the most glorious death or the most unheard-of victory!" Thus spoke to himself the impetuous youth, fixed his steel-cap more firmly on his head, seized his sword with convulsive strength; and though the natural feelings of youth mourned his approaching death and shrunk from the full-armed gigantic knight, yet thirst of fame and disappointed love exulted within him. He sat firmly on his steed and self-possessed, and in right horsemanlike guise rushed upon the Hohenzoller. But he, as if rejoicing mightily, spurred his snow-white steed, and on a sudden shot like lightning forward; not upon the daring youth, as Adelard in joyful tremor had expected, but, without observing him, straight to the floating banner amidst the fifteen who surrounded it. Adelard stood stupified for a moment, like one who witnesses a desperate leap over a precipice. There sat the Hohenzoller already in the midst of the troop; many a weapon whirled and rattled upon his harness and helm, but his mighty sword flew like lightning round. Here fell a horseman, there hung another stunned from his saddle; there staggered a horse without a rider, there rushed another wounded and maddened towards the city. The Margrave's troops shouted from afar after their lord, and hastened to follow the solitary hero. Adelard flew to the standard; and just as he reached the troop, the Achilles with his powerful charger had borne down Leutwald's steed to the ground.

Such of the fifteen as were not bleeding or prostrate stood motionless as if enchanted. But Leutwald held fast the staff of the banner with desperate strength; Adelard rushed forward from the left, struck the left arm of the Margrave which had grasped the staff, and shouted with wild energy, " Now for death or thy sword, thou Achilles!" At the same moment the blade of the prince thundered over Adelard's head; but the thick plumes of his steel-cap intercepted the blow; only the fastening was loosened, and Adelard remained unhurt.

But then shouted the prostrate Leutwald, " He is rending the banner from me. Give help, whoever can!"

" Elisabeth's banner!" cried Adelard; and reckless of every other danger, seized fast the staff of the banner.

The Margrave thundered forth his war-cry. " Ye rash boys, let loose. You have your fee." And twice the fierce blade glittered on high; and while both youths fell bleeding to the ground, the arm of the victor waved the two-headed eagle high above his helmet. The Margrave's troops had reached him, and exultingly followed their Achilles to attack the advancing Nurembergers. The tumult had long passed by, when the two youths raised their languid heads.

" Hast thou the banner?" asked each youth at once of the other, and then again sank back exhausted on the dewy sod. After a while, Leutwald again raised himself and spoke.

" Hast thou already fallen asleep, Adelard? I mean to thy last sleep?"

" No," said Adelard; " but the time may not be far off. The wound in my head pains me sorely."

" Not so mine," answered Leutwald; " but weary am I, as after a night spent in the dance—a sweet weariness. What thinkest thou?—we die a noble death. It seems to me as if this were almost the spot where we met together on thy return from the Achilles, and now that Achilles sends us both to our home."

" If we had but saved the banner," sighed Adelard; " Elisabeth's banner!"

" We held it fast so long as we were able," said Leutwald. " Our merciful God will give to each of us in paradise a fairer banner, woven of the ruddy dawn and the deep midnight blue, and sunshine and moonlight, embroidered with stars for flowers—Oh, lovely flowers!" Then the youth was still.

Adelard raised himself up, and saw by the quivering smile of his mouth that even now the loving childlike soul had parted from its pure tabernacle. In grief for his departed friend and for the lost banner, and overcome by the fever of his wound, Adelard sunk back insensible upon his bloody couch.

The encounter was in the mean time ended. Margrave Albert, seeing that the city was far too strong and well-garrisoned for a sudden storm, contented himself with driving his adversaries back to their gates ; and then went forth, with the captive banner, and the glory of a victorious day, to other deeds of arms.

Then came forth both citizens and peasants to search for the wounded and the dead ; and they bore the two friends, one in the paleness of death, and the other approaching to it, back into the city.

So often as Adelard awoke partially from the stupifying delirium caused by his wound, it ever seemed to him as if he lay in that spacious chamber where he first beheld Elisabeth and the banner ; often, indeed, as if Elisabeth herself sat by his couch, smoothed his pillow with her own delicate hand, or brought him medicines, or bound up his smarting head. He smiled then gratefully, thanking God that he vouchsafed to the fever of his illness such lovely visions. "What am I better than other wounded men," said he sometimes aloud to himself, " that some should see fiends by their bedside, and that to me an angel should appear?"

But the stupefaction of fever departed from him more and more, and more and more distinct appeared the spacious room to Adelard's eyes, and at length clear and undoubted the sweetly-blushing countenance of the beloved maiden.

Happy as the reviving youth felt himself, yet the hou-our of a warrior claimed its rights; he inquired of his beloved one after the banner. More deeply blushed the noble maid of Nuremberg, and a low-breathed "Lost" escaped unwillingly from her sadly-quivering lips.

"For Leutwald I dare not ask," sighed Adelard; and the sick man and his nurse shed the tears of a friendship which reached beyond the grave. In the abandonment of his grief, the youth took the hand of the maiden, hid his glowing face upon it, and when his tears flowed more gently, he felt with astonishment that Elisabeth yielded her hand to him without resistance. Amazed, he gazed upwards into the angel-face; it seemed as if he might hope every thing, and yet he durst not utter a word. But the question hovered so beseechingly in his eyes and on his lips, that Elisabeth at length, with eyes cast down, half turning away, spoke: "Could a maiden attend thus on a youth, Adelard, were she not his bride? My father has made this vow for your recovery."

Then seemed it to the heart of the restored youth as if a dream of childhood were fulfilled. Now first he held that fair left hand clasped fervently, and covered it with kisses; and with her soft right hand, Elisabeth half timidly, half tenderly, stroked his cheek, which was suffused with the returning hue of health. Then was heard the sound of spurs and of men's footsteps on the stairs; the door opened, and Albert Achilles entered, led by the aged Adam Scharf.

"Oh, I have then been dreaming!" sighed Adelard; and sought to hide his head in the pillows.

"Why talk of dreaming?" asked the Margrave. "I have made peace with thy native city, my good youth, and I am here for the solemnity of thy betrothal. I will return for thy wedding when thou art entirely healed of the wound of my sword." Whilst he spoke, the golden-hilted knightly sword re-sounded by the hero's side, and Elisabeth shrunk timidly back. But Adelard raised himself up joyfully at the well-known sound.

Then said Albert Achilles, "Give me your hands, fair youth and maiden. I will place on them the ring of betrothal."

But Elisabeth moved another step backwards, and said softly in the ear of her honoured mother, who now stood beside them, "Must I be betrothed by the hand which robbed our free imperial city of its banner?"

The Achilles heard her words, and answered: "To take it, gentle maiden, was the deed of a brave warrior; to give it back is the deed of a generous prince. Because your bridegroom defended it so bravely, I will restore it to-morrow to your cathedral."

Adam Scharf fervently embraced his son-in-law, and dropped some manly tears over his wound. Elisabeth, bowing meekly and gratefully, gave her hand to the Margrave; and as he exchanged between them the rings of betrothal, he said:—

"Young warrior, I well know that you had fixed your eye upon my sword, and another had done so with you. This time that sword has made a friendly return to those who strove to possess it. It has helped the one to heaven, the other to his bride. But for the future have a care in such matters. The gifts of princes' swords are solemn, and weigh heavily."

The Siege of Algiers.

Chapter First.

IN the last third of the month of October of the year 1541, the fleet of the Emperor Charles the Fifth, which had for several days been separated by a sea-storm, collected on the coast of Africa, not far from Algiers, then so noted for pirates, in order to disembark the bold land-troops chosen carefully out of three great nations for the seizure of the Mohammedan castle.

Still many of the four hundred transports which formed the fleet were missing, though confidently expected; and the landing, after a council of war had been held, was deferred till the dawn of the next day; while the bright and innumerable stars began to sparkle on the clear southern night-heaven.

The late contrary wind had not been the first which the Christian emperor's squadron had had to encounter since the sailing of the thirty-six imperial galleys from the harbour of Genoa; for it was not without almost constant combats against wind and waves, that after fourteen tedious days he had at last reached the island of Majorca. In this harbour he found many German and

Italian ships, but was obliged to wait a stated time for the Spanish fleet, under the command of Admiral Madoza, two hundred sail strong; for this bold seaman had attempted a long time, but in vain, to guide it through the rough autumnal sea to the appointed place of rendezvous.

He had succeeded at last, and they were now close to Africa.

Silent, gloomy, void of habitations,—for the threatened Algiers was not in sight,—Cape Matifo, the destined place of landing, frowned on the Europeans.

Upon the noble galley of the young bold Genoese Gianettino Doria, nephew of the doge, sat the old, but still powerful steersman, Ruperto Sansogno, at his post; his left hand supporting his head, which was sunk in thought, his faithful right hand leaning upon the helm that had been entrusted to him, while his long white hair flowed down over his brow to his long white beard. You might almost fancy he was one of those old river-gods sculptured upon the monuments of Romish antiquity, with dripping locks, leaning upon his oar.

Walprecht, a young German trooper in Gianettino Doria's chosen body-guard, let his silver-tipped swordsheath, as if by chance, slip down from his arm upon the deck, and burst into a fit of unrestrained and hearty laughter, as the thoughtful old man started up a little frightened at the alarm.

"Foolish jester!" said Ruperto, angrily, sinking back again into his former position. "Thou mightest have spared thy silly grins for the time when that moon-like German mask of thine shall have dropped from the empty skull beneath. That, under the existing circumstances, may very soon happen, and then you may grin on as long as you like."

"Yours are not very flowery similes," returned Walprecht, in unrepressed merriment; and yet it seemed to him as if an icy hand was laid upon his shoulder; but shaking off the gloomy feeling without any perceptible emotion, he added, laughing:—" And, nevertheless, you Italians are proud of being born the children of the south, whose little hands, even in the cradle, grasp two bright bunches of flowers and fruit of a never-fading kind. It was indeed a beautiful picture, a child with bright swelling bunches of flowers," he said, after some consideration, kindly, and with a softer voice; but then again adding, with a laugh,—" only it is unfortunate, old Ruperto Sansogno, that your observations about skulls are appropriate to nothing in the world less than to an Italian flower-garden, like those which, to my great delight, I have often strolled through at Genoa."

"Every thing has its season," said the old steersman. "When God chooses to send a warning death-worm—they call it also a death-watch—to me, to you, and to others, what have you to say against it? and what can I do for or against it, if I am only once commanded in this manner by the great Admiral on high? Have you never seen a butterfly of a sad-coloured kind, which is called the ' mourning cloak,' rise up out of the bright chalice of a flower? But hark! close by lies the galley of the young noble Spaniard, who has the command of ten vessels, Don Felix Carrero, who dreams of nothing but victory and renown; and with him is his beautiful beloved Donna Lisandra, more angel-like even in the beauty of her song and the notes of her guitar than in the perfect gracefulness of her form. Listen, and disturb not the lurking spirits of the air, for she sings."

And as the notes of nightingales pass over beds of flowers, a sweet woman's voice breathed forth the following song in the language of Castile:—

>" Slumbering on a couch I lay,
> And a dream passed through the air,
> As the soft, soft breezes stray
> Over beds of blossoms fair:
> Bright the glorious future spread
> Rainbow-like around my head;

As a princess I was crowned,
And in the triumphal train
Proudly o'er the flower-strewn ground
Don Carrero led me on.
Don Carrero, noble knight,
Listen, and thy love shall tell
How the vision clear and bright
On her sleeping eyelids fell.
We had landed in my dream,
And thy purple banner hung
A flag of victory in the gleam
Of the glorious setting sun;
And thy sword-blade through the air
Sounded like the last faint groans
Of the dying, here and there
O'er the field of battle borne.
Round thee on the field of blood
Towered a bulwark of the slain,
While I in bridal vesture stood
On a hill above the plain,
Breathing hopes of love and joy
Through the tumult of the fight.
But amid the trumpet-call,
Sounding through the gathering night,
Fainter, lower grew my song,
Dying like a lute unstrung.
Then a conquered Moor drew near—
Conquered, else he had not dared,
Spirit of evil, near to me,
Glowing star of victory!
' Beautiful lady,' then he said,
' The purple flag thy hero waves
In token that his foes are dead,
Or numbered with his conquered slaves.
To thee, who in thy lofty mind
Viewest the issue of the fight,
Belongs a purple star, to bind
As on the glorious brow of night.
Bow down, lady! Man must bow
When he honour would receive.'

But the bowing pleased me not.
' Moorish slave, I'd have thee know,
I no little flower am,
Bent about by every breeze.'
But the thought unto me came
Of the noble crown of state
Soon upon my head to stand,
And I bowed before the man :
But upon my head he set
No wreath, or gem, or coronet.
No! upon my breast there bloomed
Suddenly a purple rose.
Hero of the conquering flag,
Noble knight, Don Carrero,
Thy bride, thy love, in purple shone,
To ornament thy victory!"

The song ceased, or it was overpowered by a joyous burst of trumpets, that suddenly broke loose upon the deck of Don Carrero's galley. The proud Castilian did honour to the dream of victory of his beautiful lady and bride with a warlike greeting.

Called upon deck by the joyous sound, the beautiful blooming youth, Gianettino Doria, appeared on the deck of his vessel, and at his side a grave, somewhat aged man, of a noble countenance, with fiery, almost burning eyes, his arms folded over his breast, and veiled in the white black-crossed mantle of the German order of knights.

Upon the deck of the neighbouring Spanish galley still strolled her captain, Don Felix Carrero, tenderly leading his tall graceful bride—a wondrously beautiful Castilian, somewhat pale, but her features of the most perfect symmetry, and with silent large dark star-like eyes, and jet black hair parted over her proud alabaster brow. The rising moon shone upon her figure, now wholly veiled in its white drapery, surrounding her as it were with a glorious light. The two ships greeted each other solemnly and respectfully.

"Yonder knight, Don Felix Carrero, would be an enviable man, if one dealt in such unworthy feelings as envy!" said the young glowing Genoese, Gianettino, to his companion. "But away with such thoughts! This tall knightly Castilian deserves to be an angel's bridegroom, and with noble right bears his name, 'Felix, the happy.' Think you not so, Baron of Marbach?"

"I!" answered the German lord with kindled, almost angrily sparkling eyes; "I and that Don Felix Carrero! It is always against my will that any appeal is made to me concerning him. The man displeases me from first to last. In my whole life I never saw any one with such lofty, overflown, and unbearably proud ideas and manners. You laugh, Signor Gianettino. Might I ask you why?"

"Bold knight," returned the young Doria with engaging sweetness, "permit me to speak to you to-night a little more freely and more boldly than it else might beseem my youth to address your ripe age of manhood, already crowned with honour. But hearken: days of fierce battle are close at hand; then shall we all seem of the same age, at least as regards this particular object that we have in view. Age and youth can contend equally with the undisciplined troops rising up before us on these Moorish coasts."

"I love you always, Signor Gianettino Doria," answered the German knight with heartfelt, and to him rare but most pleasing cordiality; "but most of all when danger draws near, or is already in existence. Then are you the most dear to me. Therefore say what you will; you have laughed at me just a little—and why?"

"Does it seem so right to you," said the young Genoese, "whom thousands call the bold, the proud, the brave Baron Marbach, to blame so hastily the ideas and manners of this Don Felix Carrero as something altogether wicked and unheard-of? Have you then no looking-glass in your cabin? or has the sea-wave, when it is still, never reflected back your own noble self?"

"To-night is a vigil, I suppose," said the German knight, with difficulty disguising his rising passion under a kind of raillery. "Indeed, young gentleman, though it may be necessary for me to repent, yet I cannot but say that the boldness of your speech exceeds the wisdom of it."

"I did not wish to offend you," returned Gianettino Doria, gently but firmly.

"Enough!" said Baron Marbach somewhat sharply. Yet soon recovering himself, he fondly took both the hands of the princely youth in his, and looking kindly at him, said—"Gianettino, I have a mind to give account to you of my pride, in comparison with the pride of this Castilian; but mark me—only to you. Therefore know, a lofty mind searches throughout the swarming stars in order to find the polar star, and having found it, to measure the form and order of the whole. Pride will climb to heaven in order to prepare itself a throne therein; that is a giant's dream and foolery. Have you understood me?"

"Yes, sir knight," answered Gianettino, "as far as your definition goes I understand you. But as to why your aspirations should be all of the noble and excellent kind, and the aspirations of the Don Felix Carrero all as certainly of an ignoble and evil kind—excuse me, this I am by no means able to comprehend."

"Young man," said the Baron of Marbach in a strangely moved voice, while two big tears sparkled in his ..aming eyes—"young man, my striving is after a divine idea of a new world, and a new era of time; the aim of this poor Carrero is confined to his temporal knighthood and his childish love. God grant that you may perceive the difference; and I hope it of you." Then, with a tone and manner strongly contrasted with his former energy, he added: "And now, to set the crowning point to his vanity, he leads about his ostentatious bride, as if she were a bird in a bower on purpose to be looked at; he even takes her into the very midst of the tumult of battle, as if to point her out as a prize of victory for the Mohammedans."

Gianettino Doria, with a proud look, and some haughtiness in his tone, returned: "Baron Marbach, whatever we may bring with us to these barbarous coasts, under the protection of the invincible Emperor Charles the Fifth— and permit me at the same time to add, the admiral, my uncle, Andrea Doria, the Doge of Genoa, who ranks next to our emperor as a naval commander—whatever we bring with us at this time can never be intended as a booty for the barbarians, but only serve to render our victorious trophies more brilliant and more complete. Donna Lisandra de Sarmontada y Balcosta, the richest and most beautiful heiress in Spain, cannot possibly be more secure in one of her strongest castles than in this victoriously-winged armada, under the protection of her beloved Don Felix Carrero, flower of the Castilian knighthood."

"Gianettino!" said the German lord, suddenly breaking forth into an unwonted laugh; "Gianettino Doria! are you still a merry thoughtless Italian, or have you suddenly changed into a solemn Spanish Hidalgo? for, in truth, I scarcely recognise your own words under such a solemn garb."

Gianettino laughed without restraint, and then added: "Indeed, as our Italian language has in its sound so great a similarity to the Spanish, the two nations must, one would think, have more in common with each other, and be more closely united, than we generally suppose. If we Italians by any chance rise into the heroic style, we are certain to fall down into the Spanish grandezza, scarcely knowing how. However, thus much I must say, to pursue the subject of my Castilian brother in arms—that by thus bringing the dearest and most beautiful treasure of his life to these barbarous coasts, as to a triumphal procession, he gives surety that he possesses at any rate one great quality of a soldier, namely, the certainty of victory."

The German lord angrily shook his head. After some

silence, he said, with scarcely repressed passion : — " Take it not ill, young prince, if I say that this boasted quality of a soldier is shared in the highest degree also by the common mercenary. Nor is it of much real value: for if in the midst of his certainty of victory, a lost battle, or some other great misfortune befalls him, he suddenly forgets his short-lived confidence, and wonders that he ever had such a certainty. The commander-in-chief, on the contrary, or the thoughtful warrior, must consider upon and weigh every chance beforehand, and keep himself prepared for whatever may happen. Then, if an unexpected piece of fortune — but in prosperity every man knows how to act."

"I would unwillingly," said the princely youth, "most unwillingly, contradict so famed and experienced a warrior as you are, but just as unwillingly would I enter into your views. Ah! it would banish all the joy from my soldier's life. No, Baron Marbach. For this same noble confidence of success, I would praise our emperor, and this young noble eagle of Castile, ever hoping for victory, and so for that reason victorious."

"And I think with your uncle, the great doge and admiral, Andrea Doria," answered Marbach quickly, "with regard at least to this seemingly unprosperous expedition of ours. Has he not"——

"Pardon me for interrupting you," said Gianettino; "but your voice is loud, and your words in no way suited for the ears of the sailors on watch, not even for my old brave steersman, who turns on us from his post every now and then such sullen piercing glances."

"You are right, and I am a fool," said the knight, full of noble resentment against himself. "They have a mocking proverb in Germany, that we Swabians never become prudent till the fortieth year of our life. If it is the prudence of the world of which the proverb speaks — the rules of which our rash Swabian blood often breaks — a dozen years may be added to the proverb for my sake;

for though arrived at such an age, I must, notwithstanding, allow myself to be tutored by your young Genoese prudence, and unfortunately with perfect justice. Nevertheless my own heart is too full, and yours too dear to me, for me at once to break off our conversation. Step with me to the forepart of the ship; there we shall be undisturbed, and I will speak softly."

They stood on the beak of the galley, and after looking with a serious glance for a few moments over the gloomy coast of Africa, the German baron whispered to his young friend: — " Have you forgotten how your wise uncle warned the emperor not to undertake this expedition at a time when the sea-storms are at their height? at that time of the year when an experienced sailor leaves the mischief-bringing salt wave, and seeks a secure harbour ?"

" I have not forgotten it," said the young Doria; "but neither have I forgotten how the Emperor Charles the Fifth answered my uncle and other prudent counsellors: ' Permit me once to act as an emperor, that I may satisfy myself.' It was a noble saying."

" It was the saying of an emperor certainly," answered the German knight gloomily ; " but whether it was a humane and wise saying — that, indeed, the issue will soon teach us."

The youth, burning with noble rage, returned hastily: "Teach!—the issue! My baron, the issue may indeed teach many things; among others, prudence for future times, in so far as the same example can assist and be of value where the object is extended, and always different in some way from any former occasion. Still is there something over which the issue has no influence; and that is, the real intrinsic wisdom and right of every human resolve. You must, I am quite confident, after a beautiful and varied life, still bear in your nobly beating heart the remembrance of many a heroic and courageous resolve of your soul, which afterwards bore bitter fruit both for yourself and others, and whose influence would last for time and for eternity. It is not the skill or seeming wisdom with which an enterprise is planned that at all times gives it value. You know how this deserter from our holy faith to the standard of the crescent, Hassan Aga, who now reigns in Algiers, shamefully throws back upon Christian men and Christian countries, as evil, what good he has before learnt in our Christian army! How this reckless Sardinian renegade has not spared his own native island from his pirate squadron; how, with the most savage, and bloody, and, pardon me for the expression, brutish violence, he has pillaged the beautiful coasts of Sicily and Naples, so that they stand desolated, and mourn not only on account of the misery they have suffered through him, but also of the disgrace suffered from him! He is indeed the Corsair of the Corsairs."

"And well skilled in war by land as well as sea," added the knight Marbach; "and in the art of fortifications. It was not without a hard-fought contest that our imperial master returned in former years from the victory of Tunis, and no Hassan Aga commanded there."

"Well, and so much the better that he commands here!" exclaimed Gianettino Doria. "If we would kill the one powerful head of the hydra, we must do it by one decisive attack, and as it were by one stroke of the sword."

"May it be so!" said the other; adding in a low voice: "and you now, noble Gianettino, speak in somewhat a louder voice than is necessary, if you would keep the tenor of your words from the ship's watch, and from the steersman. Yet I grant that they will do no harm, for they carry with them the trumpet-sound of victory. And so, good night; God forbid that I should disturb any of your knightly dreams of joy."

He was about to leave him; but Gianettino seized the right hand of the German lord with both of his, and said, with the perfectly irresistible sincerity of youth:—" Bold baron, think not my heart is so childishly sure of the issue of our enterprise that I cannot endure the thought that it may perhaps prove unsuccessful. All rests in the hand of God; but I feel, however the event may be, an unextinguishable joy in my heart, assuring me that the remembrance of my name shall not be lost in the future waves of time, because I dared to conquer or die in a great undertaking. Though stranded or broken to pieces on a neighbouring cliff, every noble ship leaves the track which follows her keel behind her course upon the mirror of the waves."

"Trust not the mirror of the waves, and still less the foam that rises for a moment on their surface," said the baron, shaking his head. "Many a beautiful image has vanished unnoticed, as a fool with cap and bells disappears after a banquet."

"Well," returned Gianettino, somewhat downcast, but with a firm and manly tone, "if after-ages may hear nothing good of me, they shall at any rate hear nothing that is bad. This at least is in the power of every man."

"Indeed!" said Baron Marbach gloomily to himself, and he drew his knight's mantle close around him, as if he were shivering in a winter's frost. "Well, think as you will; but for my part, it seems to me that you still persevere in your hopes of victory."

"Troy fell, and Hector remained great!" exclaimed Gianettino joyfully.

"But," Marbach answered, "then Hector had good luck; and yet not altogether good luck, for to this day every schoolboy relates how Hector ran three times round the walls of Troy as a deserter, before he could make up his mind to fight with Achilles, who was pursuing him. You must know, young knight, *that* I consider to be as untrue, as I should consider it if it were told of you or of me. Yet schoolboys explain it thus, and their honoured tutors cry 'bravo!' to it; and old Homer was, in the main, a great poet, and moreover a worthy man, who was well acquainted with war, as may be seen from many parts of his works. Now if a poet, after two or three hundred years,—though there were scarcely so many years between

Hector and Homer,—happens to judge unjustly of you, can you hinder it?"

"I cannot, and neither do I wish to," said the young Doria, proudly, while he leaned upon his long beautifully-shaped rapier. "The African Moorish poets I do not fear, with regard to my fame in after-ages; and the Italian poets shall not be able to think otherwise of me than I would desire they should think."

"As if there were only Moorish and Italian poets in this widely peopled world!" exclaimed the German lord, with a scornful laugh. "Only think, after some two hundred years, a young poet may spring from the race of Marbach, who shall be inspired by the Muse to write an historical tragedy, or epic poem, or some such thing, concerning these our times; and it may occur to him, in a wild fit of humour, to bring in Gianettino Doria (it may be because it will give weight to the plan of the poem) as a careless spendthrift, as a silly blockhead, as a weak, perfectly uneducated child, or even as——"

Gianettino's shining blade flew out of its sheath.

"For pity's sake, do not wound the air!" said the Baron of Marbach, with ironical composure. "Only consider, your presumptuous calumniator has already to wait a hundred years until he is born; and therefore I myself cannot induce my Marbachian offspring, either by anger or prayers, to place you in your best light. Therefore, fame stands written where victory stands written, and all incomprehensible things besides." He looked in deep thought upwards to the stars.

Gianettino let his beautiful blade sink slowly back again; but not before he had carefully wiped it with an Indian handkerchief, as something like rusting dew was sprinkled upon the noble steel.

"It is the fault of the changing climate!" he said, involuntarily explaining to the German lord.

With kind but grave salutation they parted from each other.

Chapter Second.

At the same hour of the night, alone, upon a watch-tower of Algiers, stood the chief of the horde of pirates, the so-much feared Hassan Aga.

With inward rage he looked out over the region round Cape Matifo, as if he would see with his naked eye the fleet of the Christians, which he knew was anchored in the bay. His angry spirit, like a grisly distorted monster, hovered about it with harpy wings and harpy claws. Then again, sinking back into his own breast, he refreshed himself there with the fearful thoughts of battle, which had made him so often, and for so long a time, a terror to the heretofore peaceful coasts.

But it seemed to him as if his own spiritual deformity glimmered against a mirror, a fiery flaming mirror. "Black upon a gold ground!" he muttered to himself. "Away! I have never been able to endure the colours. They are the most hateful to me in all the world! They are the colours of the Christian emperor's eagle! And woe is me! my soul floats like an eagle before my inward eyes, though far blacker than an eagle — oh, far blacker!" He looked wildly upwards to the firmament, murmuring — "Stars! I see you in multitudes; but where hides itself now the crescent — the sickle, the emblem of victory? Mahomet's crescent! where tarriest thou?"

And from the narrow passes of the rock, winding up between the wall of the fortress and the perpendicular rugged precipice, now overspread by the deepest shadows of night, like a ghastly echo sounded under the feet of the renegade — "Mahomet's crescent! where tarriest thou?"

Seized by a singularly convulsive, but else not unusual,

fit of shuddering, Hassan Aga cried, "Who sings there? Or rather, who howls there?"

A sudden, hoarse whisper, like the croaking of a raven, rushed up again as an answer, while the renegade could perceive nothing else than that it was spoken in the Arabic language; and a warning to be silent struck his ear about the tenth or twentieth word. The croaking creature now seemed to him under the shadow of the wall as a thing deformed, wound about with veils and thick drapery. Silently, but cautiously, with his sharp-bladed rapier in his right hand, he bent down far over the battlements. Still the figure of the veiled creature remained quite indistinct. He might have thought it a salamander stretched out by witchcraft to the size of a giant, but that now were widely extended long, dry, withered arms, the fingers armed with claws, waving through the night-air, as if forming an invisible web, wrought with thousands and thousands of threads. It appeared to Hassan Aga like a horrible magical net. Then the hoarse singing and howling began again, and the words of the song could be distinctly heard in the Arabic language:

"Crescent of Mahomet,
  Break through with magic might!
  Long wert thou standing
  In the heavens commanding;—
  Oh! cast from around thee
  The veils that enshroud thee,
Fling aside the pale dives, and vapour-like sylphs—
  Tarrying, hovering,
  Sorrowing, fluttering,
  Children of fleeting air;
  Fair as the blossoms white,
  White as the blossoms fair,
  Dew-clouds their veiling shroud,
  Dew-winds their whisperings,
  Children of dreamy night!
  Crescent of Mahomet,

Tear them with piercing breath;
Scatter the shadow elves,
Bid them go hide themselves;
Heed not their smiles and tears,
Coming like hopes and fears;
Break through with magic might,
　　Sickle of Death!
If they weep, 'tis but like the call
　　Of a young bird,
At spring-time by nightfall,
　　In flower-fields heard.
If they bleed, men but hear the sound
Of soft dews trickling round,—
Scatter with magic breath
The mists thou wearest;
　　In thy right hand thou bearest
Victory or death!
　　Crescent, appear!"

And inaudibly a thick shower of rain or dew overspread Hassan Aga's inquiring upturned brow, and the sickle of the moon, like the sickle of death, darted sharp and pale through the clouds, suddenly flying away on all sides. Hassan Aga could not but think of a mighty host driven asunder, of standards battered and torn to pieces in the wildest tumult and uproar of the battle.

But from the dizzy footpath at the bottom of the wall distinctly rose the croaking question: "Hassan Aga, dost thou still take me for a bewitched salamander? Or for an enchanted web? Or hast thou perceived at last, by the effect my magical song had on the firmament, what I *can* do? Know, proud Aga, here lurks one who is a powerful friend to thee."

"The lurking friend is not a very pleasing one!" said Hassan, turning away.

But then the voice croaked back, screeching with passion: "Renegade, as a sneaking reptile you crept into the avenging, destroying band of Mahomet—a traitor to your mother Christianity; viper, as they call you there, where you were a child, a most beloved child; now a cursed pirate beast—you, cursed by priests and women, and all who once prayed for you in your Christian churches."

"Silence, grisly wretch!" cried the horror-struck renegade, supporting himself, as he spoke, against the battlements of the tower, so that a dizziness of horror might not precipitate him over the rocky walls into the dark gulf below.

The croaking creature laughed almost unrestrainedly—like a glad and happy being she laughed: but the ghastly sounds of hell broke forth also from her execrable heart.

"Cease! cease!" cried Aga, each moment growing more dizzy; and for the first time in Algiers his command sounded through the unsubstantial space in vain and unheeded.

"Abominable mocker," he cried out at last, "who art thou? Answer! By Mahomet's sickle, I conjure thee! By his blood-dripping sickle, and by all the furies of hell, I conjure thee! Name thyself, thou she-devil!"

And suddenly stopping in her laughter, as when a trumpet in the clatter of the wildest musket-fire sounds the "halt" of the commander, the woman said, mockingly it is true, but nevertheless as if she were completely conquered: "For what reason have you not spoken with me before on such good and seemly grounds? I obey you willingly; it signifies little *how*. Attend, for you know me; at least you certainly know my name;" and suddenly shrieking out in a shrill tone, she cried: "I am the witch Baranaga! the moor-witch Baranaga! the black moor-witch Baranaga!" And gloomily the sea, and the stony rock, and the stranded shore re-echoed again and again, Baranaga! Baranaga! Baranaga! and the roused owls and bats fluttered out of the walls, and flew madly round the turbaued head of the renegade. But he said angrily to the witch:

"Away from hence, if life is dear to you. If you are caught, you shall burn to ashes on the wood-pile. Think you I have forgotten how, six years ago, you came creeping in from the desert, and croaked out just before the walls of Tunis the accursed foolery that this proud Christian emperor, Charles the Fifth, would take Tunis by storm?"

"And did he not truly and verily do so?" grinned the black witch.

"Yes, indeed!" murmured Hassan. "He did so because your howlings and curses had bewildered and disheartened the brave Musselmen of my companion in fate and arms, the great Barbarossa."

"Those were brave Musselmen," sneered the witch Baranaga, scornfully, "who allowed themselves to be bewildered and disheartened by the crack-brained, malicious howling of an old woman! Do you not think so, renegade?"

Hassan answered, "One thing I not only think—one thing I know quite certainly—my great brother in arms, Barbarossa, wished at that time to have you burnt for your uncalled-for prophecies."

"Oh, yes; he wished to!" murmured the witch—"there you are quite right; but could he? *Would* was there very far separate from *could*—even half the diameter of the earth apart; and so would it now prove to you if you still persevere in your murderous intentions.—Mark! Do you still see me? Farewell!" And she had slipped in between the stony cliffs and disappeared. Her wild singing howled up from below, distant and gloomy, like deep laughter from the hollow caves. But soon again gliding from a crevice in the wall, flourishing a blood-red burning torch in her black fist, which illumined her hideous features, that seemed to tremble before it, she said calmly: "Burn me now, if it pleases you, renegade; I bring you a consecrated torch for that purpose. But catch me first!"

Hassan was silent with the savage feeling of his helplessness against the sorceress.

Then the black witch began to dance wildly upon the narrow dizzy steps between the base of the wall and the perpendicular rock, and waved the torch in a thousand spiry circles about her dishevelled head.

"Down with you," murmured Hassan softly through his long beard, that was wildly floating in the rising night-wind—"Down with you over the hanging cliffs, with your accursed dances."

The witch stood silent and terrified. She must have partly heard the angry murmuring curse of Aga, however inaudibly he supposed that he had muttered it. Softly and slowly she now let the flames of the torch blow again in the calm breezes of the night, while she whispered to the renegade:

"So, so! will you curse me—me and my poor dances? You have danced with me willingly before now. I may have wished to dance with you oftener—but perhaps not to dance; for indeed I was also willing enough to talk with you. That you have noticed. Recollect when you were yet living in Livorno,—just then become a ship's ensign, after your first warlike attack upon a Venetian galley."

And with each word, her voice had become more sweet, more melodious still from the croaking that yet sounded in his ears; like the voice of a nightingale sorrowfully wailing, she added,

"Just now, when I laughed so gladly in child-like joy, then you harshly and peevishly scolded me, because I—a poor and now sorrowful and miserable being—because I in my way became for a little while more happy."

"It is not possible!" whispered the renegade with repressed tears. "How,—strange mystery—apparition of the night,—can you be—you—Rosetta of Livorno?"

And the sweet voice answered from the veil that closely covered her form: "Rosetta—yes—the fresh blooming maiden, whom you would fain have seduced by your persuasions. Already she stood on the silken rope-ladder, hesitating before her chamber-window, looking down undetermined upon you who, to give her encouragement, had half climbed up the aerial path,—already she even bent down towards you,—when at midnight from the neighbouring church was wafted the greeting of a church festival with a spiritual song, and, breaking into a flood of tears, Rosetta of Livorno sighed, 'O God, that song sounded also at the day of my confirmation. No, false seducer, I will not yield!'"

"Shew me your countenance, your dear countenance, O Rosetta!" whispered the renegade; and the veil rose from the head of the dark figure, and in the glimmering of the upraised torchlight a spring-like face bloomed on him, full of all child-like and happy joys, only somewhat paler than in those days of blooming spring and happy love.

"Rosetta, you are here!" exclaimed he convulsively, stretching out his arms towards her.

Then the veil again closed, and the former raven-voice once more croaked forth: "No, no! I am not Rosetta. No, I still remain myself, the witch Baranaga! the black moor-witch Baranaga!" And again unveiling herself, the sorceress opened her wildly distorted, hideous, black face to the view.

"It was only by dint of a little art in a mirror,—in the mirror of the full moon it might be still better obtained; but take that, if you please!" said she, laughing. "Do you remember at the time the little Rosetta spoke of her confirmation, and the song from the distant church sounded like the rippling waves of the sea, how you tumbled from the rope-ladder, and the servants of the house found you insensible upon the pavement, and woke you from your stupor by their contemptuous laughter, that the poor little ship's ensign had ventured to hang on a rope-ladder at the palace of the richest merchant of Livorno, and even at the chamber-window of his most beautiful daughter? And how you then angrily sprang up, and with your sword and poniard wounded four or half a dozen of the jesters, and then flew to a corsair that just crossed by the coast, and thus, poor dreamer, you were laughed into becoming a pagan Saracen? What have you to say in answer, Hassan Aga? Can the old black moor-witch do nothing else but curse and howl?"

"If you could tell me," said the renegade, "where you have stolen that sweet mirror-likeness of Rosetta, which a little while ago sparkled over your raven cheeks—"

"Oh, that is easy enough!" answered the witch; "I held my veil against the crescent moon in the direction of Livorno. Then I beheld, as it might be about three steps before me, Rosetta, strolling on the sea-shore, with her beautiful, most beloved husband, a renowned painter, who declared the wave was but a dim mirror for her charms; and as she bent carelessly over the flower-covered railings, willingly I would have snatched her away by a magical sentence, the idle little fool; but her husband, the fool, just then looked up with silent thanks to heaven—or to Him who dwells therein," murmured the witch fearfully; "and so, in his gratitude for his beautiful wife, my words died away. But I caught her image, reflected by the brilliancy of the moon on the waves, all damp and vapour-like, and laid it upon my black face with a wet cloth. But she had observed something, and was frightened. For this reason the little face looked somewhat paler than usual, and also because moonlight and the waves of the sea made it pale, and cold, and salt. In reality, the beautiful Rosetta blooms as bright and fresh as ever, only not for you, poor fool! Forget, therefore, every thing but the flame of war, which alone can render your life fresh and vigorous."

"And this flame of war—can you kindle it, monster?" asked the renegade. "Kindle it to fame and victory?"

"Yes, indeed can I, you fool!" cried the witch, angrily. "Already, for twice three hundred and sixty-five nights have I prophesied that the Christian emperor must come here to his own ruin, and to the glory of the crescent.

The people have already listened, full of hope; but you, you incredulous unbeliever, had still a bitter tooth upon me about Tunis, and would hear nothing from me—or you might have supposed, since I could prophesy ruin, I could prophesy also victory. And now has Charles the Fifth, the bravest soldier in Christendom, arrived. And now—" she sung,—

> "Storms will I brew for you,
> Clouds will I call for you;
> Men, for fear, pale shall grow,
> Even as maidens do.
> Lightning shall sparkle bright,
> And dark grow the night:
> Bound by a spell of might,
> Sea-nymphs shall dress for you
> Beds under waves of dew.
> Storm-songs draw near,
> Waves dance for fear,
> While they in wild embrace
> Drag you unto the caves
> Which are their dwelling-place,
> Beneath the briny waves."

"Good luck to the dancers!" exclaimed the almost-bewildered Hassan Aga. "But, horrible songstress of the storm, and waves, and clouds, will you to-morrow, at the dawn of day, acquaint my squadron that they should stand ranged in solemn order, upon the shores of Algiers, with the rest of the assembled people. For there is not a sailor-boy among them who would believe in what I might relate to them of you, so strange and like a dream is it!"

"I will come, and I will declare it! Rest satisfied: to-morrow, in the brightest light of the midday, I will come, and I will declare it," shouted the witch.

"But yet one condition!" said Hassan Aga; "that you never dare for the future, even for a single moment, to appear to me as Rosetta."

"You need not give yourself any trouble about that,"

croaked the old creature. "Once for all, I have had enough of that experiment. It lamed—almost lamed me to death. And know, friend renegade, death is no child's plaything; at least for such as we are—Hu!"

Trembling and shivering, she crawled into a hollow crevice of the rocks upon her hands and feet, more like a lizard than a human creature.

Chapter Third.

A CLEAR autumnal sky, free from clouds, shone the next morning on the landing of the Christian host. With joyful promise, the young sun looked down upon the beautifully-armed troops, playing on the bright silver cuirasses, on the brightly-polished barrels of the rifled guns, and on the golden-decorated hoods and helmets; while variegated plumes of feathers, like beds of flowers, were blown about in the refreshing breezes; and the standard-bearers and pikemen raised up and waved variously-coloured flags, like a festively-decked grove of weapons.

It is true, the Arabs of the desert—as they angrily watched the beautiful sight, like a swarming crowd of vultures, upon their swift slender steeds—threw up the dust beneath the neighbouring hills and on the sandy coasts. But the artillery of the ships and galleys had only to discharge a few thundering greetings, and the fleet horsemen disappeared again as suddenly as they had risen from their ocean of sand. It seemed that they were only come in order to put to the test the power of the landed Christian soldiers by the futility of their attack and the swiftness of their flight.

Without opposition, the clear rejoicing instruments of war sounded already like a triumphal procession. In half an hour the imperial squadron was moving on its way to the city of Algiers, the siege of which, in the different councils of war, it had been determined should be immediately undertaken.

"So we are here!" said the tall grey-headed Andrea Doria; "and thus far, I find no objection to such a noble, bold deed. But urge onwards. Forwards before the autumnal storms disturb us with their dissonant howlings."

The city, like an amphitheatre with the glittering cupolas of its magnificent mosques, and the kioskas stretching boldly up to heaven, interspersed with garden-bowers and groves of pomegranates, presented itself to their sight in full glory; and the nearer they approached it, the more embellished and variegated seemed the sea-shore by bright meadows and plantations, hedged with golden-coloured wire trellis-work. Behind this towered lofty aloe-trees, like a second hedge of blooming pillars; and still beyond could be seen beds of flowers, and noble fruit-trees, and most singular yet elegantly-formed alcoves. A more joyous certainty, at the pleasant sight, increased every moment in the heart of each tried warrior. Many merry words passed to and fro through the lines of the procession, particularly in the Italian corps. The Germans, though in a glad humour also, singing songs among themselves—now merry, now war-songs, now a sweet longing for home—on the whole proceeded a little more solemnly; but the most solemn, the most silent of all, were the noble, proud Spaniards. At the head of these now rode their far-famed captain, Fernando of Toledo, Duke of Alba, upon a high, raven-black, Andalusian steed, and, as he passed on with the train, quite motionless in his saddle,—haggard and solemnly grave, with his long beard flowing down over his chin, his commander's staff pressed close to his thigh,—he looked more like a monument upon the tomb of some glorious departed hero than a living soldier. Yet life—yes, strong and vigorous life—was perceptible in the sparkle of his large dark eyes, and in the low but commanding words and signs with which he called first to one and then another captain from his troop of foot-soldiers, and charged them to march close together to the front of the hill behind which the Arabs had disappeared.

But a very small part of the cavalry had yet landed. He called, therefore, only a few of his esquires around him, rather as swift messengers on immediate errands than for any particular use in the main squadron. Now he trotted on before with them to mark a station upon the hill, in which he thought he could best secure the imperial host from being molested by the swift sons of the desert.

His chosen troop of infantry, at a sign from him, were pressed into close lines—some light artillery in the middle—around which were a few scattered soldiers, all the rest keeping step in the sands of the African desert with as much order as if they marched on the shady parade at Madrid.

Meanwhile Gianettino Doria, riding near the Genoese foot-soldiers, some of his German horse-guards with him (the greater part were still in the ships), shared in the joy of the troops; and kindly inquired of the German trooper, Walprecht, already known to us from his last night's conversation on board their vessel:—" How now, brave soldier! what think you of our expedition?"

" It pleases me mightily, your grace, since we now feel the firm ground under the hoofs of the horses, instead of the unruly sea under the keel of our ship," answered the fresh, fair-headed youth. " I never consider myself a man, except I feel a horse under me. A dismounted horseman is only half a man."

" A centaur, I suppose!" said Gianettino, laughing.

And Walprecht answered, though with a misunderstanding of his words: " Yes, remain here.[1] But to think

[1] The similarity between the words *centauren ihr* and *dauern hier* make a play upon the words in German which it is impossible to express in English.

of that makes me regret many things. The rich people to whom belong the beautiful meadows, and the bright houses and castles in the city yonder, rising on the hill, may have led a pleasant life enough before we came. Neither into Germany, or into Genoa, have these happy people ever come to injure us. Therefore, I cannot tell—though at the same time my doubts do not in the least disturb my dutiful subordination—why we are come here to destroy their pleasures."

Gianettino Doria laughed, and seemed disinclined to carry the conversation farther. But a deeply sorrowful voice began the defence of the expedition that was ungiven on his part. From one of the golden-latticed groves proceeded sorrowful sighs; and the gloomy voice of a man was also distinctly heard in the Italian language:

"Oh, you who have come from the prosperous lands, where the sweet language sounds in which I heard you talk, and shout, and sing,—happy, beautifully armed companions of my home,—break to pieces, ruin those magnificent castles of the barbarians, and rescue your Christian brethren from the ill-usage and slavery of the Musselmen! Those whom you can no longer rescue, you can at least revenge! Behold me, for I am an example that shall urge you on!"

And, with a last agonising exertion, a tall thin man, of a deadly pale but noble countenance, his hair and beard dishevelled, as it is never seen but on imprisoned wild beasts, rose up from behind the golden trellis-work, firmly clinging to it, like ivy to a broken wall, bleeding from innumerable wounds between the mangling chains.

Gianettino Doria, with his esquire, looked on shuddering; while the sorrowful being called to them and the troops that were passing by:

"I am an Italian, like you. I was a happy vine-dresser on the sea-shore of Pausilipo. The sea-dogs, the barbarians, snatched me away—tore me from my wife and child. What is become of them, God knows, not I!

Fifteen years of misery have I lived here, in chains, like a wild animal in brutish labour, as an ox before the plough and wagon! The cry of your landing drove the family of my oppressor away from here; and I was too weary to follow the rest of their scourged beasts, slaves, and other animals to Algiers. The sweet little children of the house, like little Cupids, with sharp-pointed arrows, shot at me, as people often do in our country at ridiculous, strange figures painted on wood. Now rescue! now revenge!"

He sank down dying upon the trunk of an aloe, which, at a sign from Gianettino Doria, Walprecht had brought to ease him, so that his last breath might pass, along with his cries of rescue and revenge, undisturbed and unchecked into the hearts of his comrades.

When at length his voice was silent, Gianettino said to his squire, Walprecht: "What think you now?"

"Death or victory against these colonies of devils!" answered the young German; and his cheeks, a little while ago so youthful, had become pale, deathly pale, as the face of an old man agitated with the deepest passion.

Chapter Fourth.

THE Christian camp was pitched.

Some twenty thousand foot-soldiers, chosen from Duke Alba's band, were stationed on the hill, ranged in many deep files, as a protection against the Arabs.

Upon the left wing, which was stationed as a vanguard nearer to the city, the Spaniards were encamped, commanded by the vice-king of Sicily, Don Gonzago, Don Alvaro de Sandez, and the Duke of Camarino.

At the centre were posted the Germans; with them was the emperor himself. Five hundred gentlemen, as his body-guard, accompanied him, who, selected from the three great nations of the army, had each desired to be a sharer in so great an honour.

At the right wing were stationed the Italian troops, under Camillo, Colonna, Spinola, and Gianettino Doria.

Soon proceeded forth from the city the gloomy sound of trumpets, and kettle-drums, and other instruments mingled loudly together, and the wild battle-cry of the barbarians, giving evidence that the enemy were far too haughty to allow themselves to be surrounded without opposition, and much too proud to doubt in the least their victory over the infantry of the Christians, who were almost entirely destitute of cavalry.

A cloud of dust was raised above the gates, through which sparkled many shining weapons. Swift as the wind the Moorish and Arab riders drew on, hewing down the Spanish advance-guards, and those of the soldiers who had ventured out of the camp to seek the means of subsistence and other necessaries for the army. The shouting barbarians swarmed about the Christians, as if they expected to tread them to pieces under their horses' hoofs.

But having quickly discharged their first fire, the three warlike nations stood filed together in a close quadrangle, beginning their murderous attack with the harquebusses, muskets, and other weapons of artillery, and continuing it in cold blood, till the confused sally ended just as rashly and wildly as it had begun. Many dead riders, with their steeds, lay stretched out upon the plain,— silent witnesses of the enemy's defeat. The Saracen host, nevertheless, not pursued by the horsemen, had dragged almost all their wounded back to the city.

The Emperor Charles the Fifth, on his steed, still kept his place in the midst of the victorious troops that were again pressing into their camp; near him was the grey-headed Andrea Doria.

"Now, my noble, paternal friend," said the prince to him, full of martial ardour, "what think you of the first opening of the combat? Think you that Algiers will hold out to us a longer resistance than Tunis did six years ago?"

Andrea, his glance solemnly directed to the clouds, slowly answered: "Above yonder is it determined!"

And the pious emperor bowed low his helmeted head, encircled with a golden crown, in humble acquiescence, saying: "You know, father Doria, that not only what is sent down from the eternal throne above is good—it is most certainly the very best that could happen."

"My most honoured master," said the Doge of Genoa, his eyes sparkling with enthusiasm; "in the greatness of your thoughts you have oftentimes outflown me, but never more beautifully than now; for this time, I had only fixed my eyes and thoughts upon the visible firmament. Signs of an approaching storm seem to me to be rising in the air, and as yet scarcely a tenth part of your six thousand horsemen are disembarked, while of your heavy artillery not one single barrel is on shore; and the land-force is altogether without means of subsistence in these regions, which are cultivated with only useless vegetation, so that they depend entirely on supplies from the ships. Permit me, as your faithful admiral, to take my place again upon the ship, in order that I may hasten the disembarkation of the forces, as well as make preparations against the storm hanging over us. Meanwhile there will rage on shore another kind of storm. I hope again, at the right hour, to take my place of honour by the side of my imperial lord and protector."

"You are brave as you are wise," answered the emperor Charles with friendly respect; "and I tell you, father Andrea, why I depend so firmly upon the success of our noble undertaking: it is because God has placed at my side such a helper and adviser as yourself. Let us follow as God calls us. Where the spirit leads, there certainly is opened the true path for honour and victory."

The Doge of Genoa bent down gratefully to his imperial friend; then he walked slowly to the strand, deeply thinking and revolving great things in his widely-experienced heart.

Meanwhile the emperor Charles called the herald of the empire, and commanded the stately messenger, accompanied by a trumpeter, to proceed to Algiers, and to require a conference with the wild renegade, Hassan Aga.

"Here," said he, handing him a roll of parchment, "you have the generous conditions which I consent to grant the wretch, in case he yields, and gives up immediately the city and harbour; for if he agrees, it seems of such infinite value to spare the blood of subjects—of Christians. Believe me, valiant herald," added the emperor Charles with a moved voice, "to send you thus into that horde of robbers, and into the power of their apostate chief, gives me sorrow enough. God knows, I would willingly, and with all my heart, tread the dangerous path myself; but God knows also that I may not."

And the commissioned one, bowing with calm solemnity, said: "My imperial commander has called me a herald,[1] and I hope to prove myself worthy of the name, both in life and death."

And turning his horse towards the stronghold of the pirates, he rode forward with slow and stately step over the blood-sprinkled ground—a trumpeter before him, blowing at regular intervals, which, among civilised nations, is the customary greeting of a truce.

At the same time the emperor, having accomplished his duty as he desired, leapt from his saddle, and went— the last of all his soldiers—into his tent.

Chapter Fifth.

MEANWHILE Andrea Doria had reached the sea-shore, and was in the act of stepping into the boat which was to

[1] The word *herald* in German is *ehrenhold*, or *sweet-honour*.

conduct him to the admiral's ship, when he saw another boat near the land, out of which sprang Don Felix Carrero, nobly equipped: the young Spaniard approached the commander of the squadron with a respectful salutation.

He received him kindly, yet at the same time gravely, inquiring of him what weighty and most important event had occurred to call the commander of ten galleys upon shore.

Don Felix Carrero started at this greeting; but he soon recovered himself, and answered: "In the first place, I am not here without the knowledge of the Spanish captain, Don Mendoza; and in the second, my noble admiral probably asks me not so much, — ' Why so soon on land?' as, ' Why so late?' An hour ago did we not see from the admiral's ship its mighty leader depart? and do I not see even now your feet clad in rider's boots and knight's spurs? And, sire, your noble steed, from which you have just dismounted, shews plainly by its matted hair how vigorously it has struggled in this day's fight."

Andrea Doria looked on the fiery young Spaniard with a strange smile, wherein lay some slightly contemptuous superiority, which was, however, at the same time, softened by a most pleasing expression of paternal kindness. Then the rash Carrero involuntarily cast down his boldly flashing eyes.

After a short silence, Andrea Doria said: " Young comrade, half a century at least has passed since any one has called my eighty years' experience into question, as to why I did this, or why I left the other undone. Indeed, I had the good luck, even in the thirtieth year of my life, to arrive at some stability of judgment; and therefore I do not imagine that I shall now, before my perhaps very near passage into eternity, lose, just at the last, that most costly of all earthly goods. It is for this reason that your rebuke does not greatly disturb me, dear Don Felix Carrero; so much the less since it comes from you; for, indeed, not only do I love and honour your wonderful nation in general, but you in particular I love and honour above all others. Therefore listen, and judge. The admiral's place is often at the side of his commander-in-chief, partly to receive orders directly from him, and as directly give back information to him; to see with his own eyes the movements of the land-army, and to make resolutions beforehand suitable to any probable change of circumstances. Neither at this or at any other time could such reasons as these call the commander of the transport-ships from his post."

With some resentment upon his noble features, Don Felix answered: "Nevertheless, the commander of the transport-ships does not for this reason, thank Heaven, cease to be a Castilian knight, if the favouring stars have permitted him to be born as such, and if no unworthiness of his own has bereft him of that inestimable jewel. But a Castilian knight keeps his word; and I have given mine some time ago to that incomparable beauty, the Donna Lisandra,—I need only repeat her name to mark her as an object of respectful admiration to the whole world—yes, to her, who as my wedded bride has followed me hither with the noble courage of a Queen Zenobia, have I pledged my word, in three days at the longest after our arrival, to accompany her to the shore, at the west of the doomed barbarian city, that she may be a close witness of the deeds which I, upon this continent, in this imperishable and ever-famed warlike expedition, hope to accomplish. To choose out a place where I think I can with safety conduct the beautiful umpire of the army, under the protection of a few faithful followers, I have landed on the shore which, at a later time, I have determined either to redden with mine or the enemy's blood; for in the ranks of the foremost foot-squadrons, which was offered to me at the beginning of the battle, will I fight. Sorely I grieve that I have missed the engagement that has just taken place; yet I had to give some necessary orders for the unloading of the heavy artillery on board my galleys; now, all that can be finished by any one—"

"By any one?" answered Andrea Doria, shaking his head. "I hope you will be that one, Don Felix Carrero, for to you this important duty properly belongs; and that, at any rate, you will not leave the deck of your frigate, and the other galleys of which you have charge, till the whole of the valuable cargo entrusted to you stands safely on the shore. Then, possibly, it may be granted you, Don Felix Carrero, to satisfy your thirst for battle upon these African coasts. Till then, honour and duty forbid you to move one step from your galleys. And now allow yourself to be rowed back to them without losing a moment. No answer, I beg of you! Your admiral commands you, as you love your own honour and duty!"

With these words, the Genoese doge stepped into the boat.

Pale from noble indignation, Don Felix walked back to his, and leapt into it, turning the helm towards the deserted ship, without being able to utter one syllable from his lips, sealed with passion. The bark flew over the sea back again to Carrero's magnificent galley; upon the deck of which stood Signora Lisandra, clothed in a rich satin drapery of the deepest and most beautiful colours, holding in her wondrously beautiful arms a polished and ornamented lute; to its loudly awakened tones she sang the following words to her bridegroom:

> "Bravest captain, noble knight,
> Hast thou found a glorious spot
> Where thy love, thy bride may stand,
> By the battle harmed not,
> To behold the glorious fight?
> Haste! I long to go! I stand
> As for triumph decked, to see
> Mohammed's power in ruins laid,
> For thine and the Christians' victory!"

Felix felt not only the words but the music also rouse anew the rage that was burning in his soul; but softening his heart before the sounds of his lady's lute, he sang to her the following words:

> "A cold old man forbade our landing;
> He, proud ruler of the flood,
> A Neptune white, with snowy beard,
> On the Moorish borders stood.
> Noble lady, lay thou by
> The glorious signs of victory;
> Put off the glorious ornaments,
> Less bright how far than the form
>   that wears them!
> Lay thee down in gentle slumber,
> Servile tasks to me belong;
> Rest thy beauteous head in slumber,
> Till a noble stirring song
> Wakes thee from the world of dreams—
> Wakes thee to behold the fight."

And Donna Lisandra sang, in answer.

> "I will sleep, and I will dream,
> But adorned with noble pomp;
> For a solemn vow I made,
> Never more, were it a year—
> A hundred, or a thousand years,—
> My glorious gems to lay aside,
> When once I was apparelled thus,
> Till before Algiers' gates
> The eagle of our host should stand,
> And bid our conquering army halt!"

Chapter Sixth.

THE sun had already begun to sink to the west when the herald of the German empire, who had been sent to Algiers, again entered the presence of the Emperor Charles the Fifth. He sat in his magnificent tent, crowded with chiefs and captains, where, according to ancient custom, the herald struck his bright golden staff upon the ground with a long, widely-stretched arm, as if he were planting a young tree, and then began to speak thus: "Divine greeting, and divine prosperity from above, and my humble subject's duty, to my most gracious emperor, lord, and master! What I have to communicate to your imperial majesty from the pirate's stronghold of Algiers is bold insolence, diabolical madness, and obstinacy, to be bowed in no other way than by fire and sword. If it is not contrary to the will of your imperial majesty, I, the herald of the holy, glorious empire of Germany, stand ready to declare what I said and heard."

"Rise, and declare it to us, warily and with truth," said the emperor, kindly.

And the herald spoke as follows: "Arrived before the heathen robbers' nest, and at the call of the trumpet admitted to their presence with the apparent acknowledgment of an honourable herald, I still can only ascribe it to the protection of the Almighty Lord of all hosts that I arrived at the Mohammedan market-place (that they call the Bazaar) without being cut to pieces, and returned from it again in safety. The success of which marvellous return is considerably more to be wondered at than the success of the safe arrival. And yet this also seems far more like a divine miracle than an undertaking accomplished under mere human protection, though that be the highest, even the protection of the most mighty emperor himself. The whole way as we went through the city the rabble insulted us with coarse words, sometimes also cast stones, at the trumpeter as well as at me, which were but too well aimed; also from the windows and balconies of considerable houses were poured revilings and insulting words; and even by most gorgeously dressed persons—yes, I do not lie—were stones cast on us. My serious remonstrances were of no avail, but rather increased than decreased their insults. Notwithstanding, I finally arrived at the bazaar in safety, and found Hassan Aga, after the Turkish fashion, seated in state upon a throne formed of costly carpets and cushions, as our jugglers exhibit themselves in comedies, in coloured calico and gold paper. Hassan Aga himself received me very harshly, requiring to know why I was sent hither, and who had sent me, in such a supremely insolent manner, that I should not have dared to declare the same, if it had not been the express command of the most high emperor."

The Emperor Charles answered, smiling: "It is well, brave herald. We absolve you and ourselves from those uncourteous titles. What else may have proceeded from the mouth of the renegade? Proceed! I would hear Hassan Aga's final resolution."

"As for the rest," said the herald, "it may sound pardonable enough; for the renegade suddenly restrained his snarlings and menaces, as if to his poor lost soul there returned a memory of those better days, when he still would have paid honour to the blessed Christians, and with that also an awful feeling of innocent respect at the greeting of an imperial herald. But something sprang up out of the midst of the crowd like a she-wolf enchanted into a human form, dashing up and down between the people and the ranks of soldiers like a poisonous horse-fly, in a way that it was impossible to describe, or to give any adequate notion of. Thus far I can relate with certainty, that the people seemed mad at the howling witch as at the stinging of horse-flies, and the wicked renegade still more mad than any one. I and the bold trumpeter, in the firm belief that our last hour was come, encouraged each other with a few honourable words, to suffer as good Christians what might be inflicted on us by Heaven, and as stedfast German soldiers, to look joyfully on every thing, even in death. Then we prayed silently, fervently, and deeply, till dizziness overcame our brain; and the people seemed to be nothing more than mad puppets, swarming about in a mountebank's booth. But they became silent by degrees: it might be that in their wild frenzy they had raged till they were weary; or possibly the above marvellous apparition might have stopped them, feeling that it was permitted the tumult should go 'so far and no farther.' But the assembly grew ever more and more silent, almost like running water from a pond that is drying in the sun, which at first, swelled by torrents of rain, had overleapt its banks with a great rushing sound. Then at last (whether the above-mentioned witch remained or not, I was in too great confusion to ascertain) speech returned to Hassan Aga, and, in truth, in the most heathenish and coarse manner. But he nevertheless commanded that we should be dismissed, in order that I might inform my noble lord that he gave your imperial majesty his word that you would have no more occasion to rejoice in the present undertaking than heretofore the two bold Spaniards, Don Ugo de Moncade and Don Diego de Bera, could have boasted of theirs upon the same place of combat; and so they let us out, it is true, but not as became our dignity and office, accompanying us with hideous yells, and with stones that they cast upon us as we went. But we proceeded with calm, majestic steps, free from the least haste, as unbecoming the ambassadors of your noble majesty. And we comforted each other with the assurance, that He who drew us out of our first great peril would likewise continue to protect us; and truly with perfect right, for here I stand unharmed before your imperial majesty, the trumpeter also, my companion in misfortune and honour, stands behind me unharmed, and our good steeds likewise have met with no hurt in the insane tumult of that heathenish crowd."

The Emperor Charles the Fifth made a gracious inclination of his head towards the two ambassadors, and said, deeply moved: "I beg of you earnestly, faithful and worthy messengers, to refresh yourselves and be happy, after your well-withstood injuries and danger. Truly, not sparingly shall you be rewarded, if God continues my life and my kingly power."

Then rising from his lofty throne, his hand on his sword, he looked with sparkling eyes upon his chiefs and captains, as they stood around in motley groups. Each one, according to the order of his arms which he was accustomed to wear, like a clap of thunder, shouted the imperial words through the circle: "Algiers, the bold defier of all true people and united Christendom, must fall!"

"Fall!" was echoed again by many hundred voices.

"To your posts, my brave soldiers; they are known to you!" cried the emperor. "To-morrow shall the pirates' city be besieged from three mighty batteries; later, when all our heavy artillery is on land, we will attack with twelve. Not much longer shall this brood of heathens scoff at us, I, the emperor, promise you. To your posts!" he again shouted, in the tone of a commander, and left the tent.

Joyful at the noisy warlike rattle of the weapons, all pressed out of the imperial tent; while heavy rain poured down from the darkening night-clouds.

"It will lay the sand of the desert!" said many happy shouting voices, in the German, Spanish, and Italian languages.

Gianettino Doria, in the stately crowd, again met with Baron Marbach, the knight of the German order, and asked him, with his young heart swelling high,—" Now, baron, in what light do you view the world and our warlike expedition? Did you not join in the brave echo, when the emperor said, 'Algiers must fall!'—the *fall* that sounded as if from one mouth?"

"Fall? yes!" answered the baron, gloomily, just like another echo. "Fall! yes, indeed! But do you as certainly know who it is that shall fall?"

Chapter Seventh.

It was about mid-day, and high in the heavens would have sparkled the hot southern sun, only his glowing rays could not pierce through the dense grey covering of clouds which, like a wide and thick carpet, stretched over land and sea, streaming down endless torrents of rain upon Algiers and its environs, as far as the clearest eye could penetrate.

Actively did the soldiers of the Emperor Charles the Fifth work at the rising foundation of the three batteries whose flames were to pierce the stronghold of the pirates, and already from the distant hills sent forth a few solitary greetings of death over the heads of the workmen. But the sand of the ground, that was wetted quite through, caked together in huge lumps, and then again breaking asunder, checked and hindered the progress of the work; so that the workmen sank, now here, now there, up to their knees in the damp soil, or slipped out to try and reach a firmer footing. At every step, before and to the side, each person was obliged to hold firmly on his neighbour. The labour and trouble of this business overpowered the strength of almost all the soldiers, who worked at it in turn.

The young trooper out of Gianettino Doria's bodyguard, Walprecht, whom we have already made acquaintance with on board ship at the beginning of our history, now without his horse, and, instead of his sword, vigorously handling the spade, said joyfully to one of his fellow-soldiers, who was almost lying under his work:

" Now, Lupold, what would the merry wenches in Genoa, and our noble young ladies of the Maine and Rhine say, if they saw you — generally such a merry companion, and so active in the dance and sports — so overcome in a warlike business? Ah, Lupold, recover yourself, or I will tell them about it, I promise you, and make all your gestures so piteously absurd, that their laughter will not cease for a whole evening long."

"That foolish mirth," answered Lupold peevishly, sinking the spade into the ground, and exhausted, supporting himself upon it, in so far as the wet sand clinging about his feet would permit — "that foolish woman's mirth, and the wit from you, I would pardon from my heart, if it was come already, and I was well out of this dog's life."

"You!" said Walprecht, warningly, and for one moment also lingering in his work. "Bethink yourself, comrade! So easily vexed! Scarcely would the lowest German lancer murmur at such a cause; how much less, then, a trooper in the body-guard of the noble Gianettino Doria!"

But the other answered, still discontentedly, "Well, let it be so! Have you ever before in your life seen me discontented, when it was my business to break in or to train horses, or to curry them, or even to put a fine polisl on my saddling-tackle, and whatever else constitutes the duty of a good trooper? For as a trooper I was hired into the body-guard of my master, Gianettino Doria, and that with perfect love and desire; but not as a sapper That is verily only a boor's work, and I am a soldier, and moreover a horse-soldier."

"Where have the five hundred young gentlemen placed themselves, who serve his imperial majesty as horse-guards?" asked Walprecht.

"Well, but," returned Lupold, "they do it of their own accord; and though I hold them to be far richer and more noble, yet, as horse-guards, they are in no way better than you or I."

"But wait a moment. Who there, on your left, is working so diligently with his spade? Do you know him?" said Walprecht.

"A little," said the other. "He is an Italian nobleman out of that guard, and called Monte — no; what is he called? Monte-Cuc—yes, Cuc—Oh, heaven knows what he is called! but I know him very well, and that he is indeed a stout-hearted trooper."

"And," asked Walprecht, "who is he a little further on?"

"That is a Spaniard out of the same troop," was Lupold's answer; "a proud, bold swordsman, who would throw away all his fortune if a poor devil that he pitied asked him for it, but who would fight against a hundred devils from hell for a piece of buttered bread, if they tried to take it from him by force. He is a child of very considerable parents, and I think his name is Corduan—or some other such fine name. Yes, and truly, near him also digs the young nobleman, Gerd of Glemningen, another of the imperial horse-guards, whose father is the feoffee of my father. Now I understand why you asked me, Walprecht."

"Are you worse off than they are?" asked the other. "You allowed before that you were not so noble."

"But consider," stammered Lupold with confusion, trying to excuse himself—"these young noblemen do it quite unbidden, for their own will and pleasure; but such as we——"

Walprecht angrily interrupted him with these words: "Then, is not the command of a noble warrior more than the will and pleasure of a German trooper?"

"Forwards, comrade!" cried Lupold. "Work, in order that we may outdo the young noblemen!" And hastily and vigorously they both again placed their spades into the bulwarks, with their eagerness doubly making up for the time that they had lost in talking.

But there suddenly was heard a sharp fire from the right wing, where the Italians stood; also from the left wing, entrusted to the Spaniards. At the same time, the horde of pirates sent so powerful a discharge of shot against the centre, where the Germans were posted, that for a moment the rainy clouds, at least immediately over the combatants, seemed pressed together, and the sun shed his beams over the field of battle, but only faintly and gloomily. In this light—more horrible than the dim obscurity—was seen the Baron Marbach leaping towards them, or rather only trotting; for, however much he endeavoured to urge his horse to a swifter speed, the deep mire of the soaked ground, and also the fatigue of the former combat, prevented the otherwise faster motion of the noble animal. Wildly flew the white mantle of his German order about the knight, as well from his impatient movements as from the rising hurricane.

"He brings some news, but nothing of good!" passed in a whisper through the files of sappers. All looked as if paralysed towards the new-comer; while the falling of the shot right and left, particularly from the Italian side, gave evidence, by its direction, that the sallying enemy was advancing rapidly.

Then was distinctly heard the call of the baron: "Away with your hatchets and spades! To arms!—to arms! The dismounted riders back to their horses! All back to the centre of the army!—the heathens are there! They press hard upon both wings, but your emperor still hopes for victory from his collected Germans! Do you hear? Victory!—very soon will it be with you! But now back—back—speedily back! Leave your hatchets and spades! Quickly back to the head-quarters! Then again forwards to victory! The emperor relies upon his Germans!"

This call, full of animation, but certainly somewhat strange and disjointed, perhaps might have had upon other than German soldiers rather a confusing than an enlivening effect: here it proved far otherwise. Already the friendly sounds of their native language—which, in the army, composed of three nations, was but seldom heard by the German squadron—shed a joy over the otherwise unwelcome message; and, more than all, the sentence—"*The emperor relies upon his Germans!*'

Walprecht and Lupold, on their horses again, joined a party of other German troopers out of Andrea's body-guard, and Walprecht cried out joyfully: " Well, as it has turned out, it is all for the best that our master gave us this work to do, as now we are to fight once more, at the side of our German countrymen."

But Lupold answered, shaking his head: " At the side of our German countrymen! Dear brother, you were before more prudent than I was; but this time there is occasion for me to shake my head at you. In whose service and pay, then, are we?—yes, in whose oath? And hark at the thundering and the crackling in the foreign squadrons! Whose throat is the knife now piercing? and more—whose body-guards are we?"

"Thunder and Doria, you are right!" cried Walprecht. " Away with the spades!—out with the falchions! To the assistance of our bold young master, Gianettino!"

With these words they galloped over to the right, where the Italians were stationed.

There the combat raged wild and boisterous. The Moors and Arabs, accustomed to their strange African soil, and observing that the rain had wet the gunpowder, so that the arms of the Christians missed fire more often than discharged properly, pressed ever more fiercely forwards, flinging, with their peculiar strength and dexterity, spears and arrows into the enemy's files,—stones also of such fearful sharpness and weight, that every limb they struck was shattered or maimed. Even at the beginning of the combat, the barbarians, rushing on with their mighty falchions, had broken through the companies of the Italian foot-soldiers, and entirely hewn them down, as they stood, or rather slipped or sunk, upon the soaked and sandy ground.

Like a grove of pines crushed by a hurricane, or like a wildly-heaped funeral-pile, the mangled corpses lay one above another, staring horror into the hearts of their still living companions. It is true their files continued to hold together, though they were irretrievably weakened; but this resistance was owing less to their tactics and good discipline, than to the fear of falling alone into the hands of the victoriously-raging Moors and Arabs. The bold Italian chieftains, Camillo, Colonna, and Spinola, kept their men firm, to the utmost of their power, by the example of a noble contempt for death, and by now encouraging, now nobly-chiding acclamations. The retreat began slowly and orderly; but, nevertheless, it was a retreat. Vainly did the faithful German troopers seek in the crowd for their young lord and master, Gianettino Doria. They had caught sight of him for a moment among the three companies that were massacred; then he vanished and disappeared without the slightest trace.

All seemed lost here. But still, high upon his snowy-white Spaniard's steed, was seen the Emperor Charles the Fifth; his glittering two-bladed German knight-sword in his right hand, turning it right and left as it were a commander's staff; and it might well be seen, in the midst of such great danger, that a less sharp commander's sceptre would not protect the imperial master of the host.

Then it happened that two Italian foot-soldiers broke forth into a mutinous cry, shouting "Down to the sea! Away to the strand! Upon the ships alone is there any protection for us! Preservation for us from the fire of the pirates' shots! Away to the strand!"

And while the two ungovernable men shouted their mad words boldly and loudly, many thought it was a command from the officers — a command which in their hearts they were willing enough to obey — and numbers turned in the direction pointed out.

In vain did the captain of the company seek for the two mutineers to bring them to silence by threats. Become bolder at length by many occasional murmurs in their files, they stepped forth before the company, throwing away their muskets, and drawing their short swords, shouting, "Henceforth, comrades, *we* are your officers. Away to the ships! March!"

The enraged captain, thrusting his sword against the two frenzied men, unexpectedly found himself attacked from behind by one of their accomplices, and disarmed.

Already the squadron had set itself in motion towards the sea-shore. Then the Emperor Charles sprang up to it, accompanied only by a few of his noble body-guard (the other five hundred he had sent away through the field of battle, at various points, divided into little squadrons, to stop the retreat); and with an angry commanding voice, he cried:

"Halt! Where do you go?"

All stood a moment; but quickly encouraged by the boldness that had once broken loose, both the ringleaders (two of the lowest and most dissolute of the dregs of the people) answered him, "To the sea-shore, my lord! we are going down to the sea-shore. That is the only gate open to you for escape! We counsel you for the best!"

And they approached with quick steps, as if they would have seized the white horse of the emperor by the bridle, in order to lead his master with them after their own pleasure. Yet before his life-guards could prevent this insolent attack, the sharp commander's blade of the emperor struck both the mutineers, and they sank down in their blood. He who had been the captain of the company, panic-struck, sprang back again alone and timidly into the crowd.

But the emperor said, now halting straight before the first company, "Captain, there lies your blade at your feet. Take it up, and let it not be so improvidently wrested from you a second time. The worst pair out of your files have died an infinitely more noble death than they deserved; for death from a soldier's hand is a most undeserved crown of honour for a rebel. But the poison of mutiny has spread shame over the whole troop. You, captain, are also guilty; for without neglect of the gar dener, the garden is not overgrown with weeds. Up, altogether, to wipe away this stain from you—up! Halberdiers, prepare your weapons for the attack! Musketeers, load afresh! If henceforth, on this gloriously hard-fought day, the company remain nearest to the enemy, so shall they also, from henceforth, be the nearest to my heart. Drummer and fifer, do your part! The treason is washed away from the company of the Captain Tibaldo. To the enemy, and forwards! March!"

And forwards pressed, in perfect order, the troop, inspired strangely by the words of the emperor. With firm steps and flourishing of drums, they proceeded on their way, followed by those of the company who were nearest them; and thus their revived courage spread through the united Italian squadron. And then, as it often happened in bygone days—and the old Romans, trying to explain it, said that the wing of their heathen goddess Victory was turned—then pressed a fearful apprehension into the soul of the Mohammedans, not over-courageous even now, that their as yet dormant adversaries had gained an unknown something; an apprehension which even the careless gambler is not a stranger to if the so-called *fortune* turns over from him to his adversary; how much more to be felt, then, in a noble combat, where fortune also is an inspiration!

But vainly may verbal or written words endeavour to express that which is inexpressible. Enough that it has existed.

The medley of the Moors and Arabs recoiled. The squadron of the Italians took a firm and joyful stand.

"Now away to my Germans!" cried the Emperor Charles, and calling to his noble body-guard to re-assemble about him, he trotted after the firmly-ordered centre where the Germans were pressed together like an unconquerable wall of fortification.

Opposite were innumerable strong troops of the enemy on horse and foot; but beyond reach of the artillery, and without having as yet joined in the attack. The firm halting of the German squadron seemed to astonish them, or had brought them to the determination rather to tarry until the Spaniards and Italians at the wings should be entirely discomfited, in order then, with their full unweakened force from all sides, to fall on their enemy in the centre. Only a few cannon-shots fell here and there, seldomest from the side of the Germans; for they rightly determined to save the small quantity of powder already landed, to use at the most decisive moment.

As they saw the winged file of their master approach, they cried out joyfully and with a voice of thunder, "Long live our most gracious emperor Charles the Fifth!" and the whole battle-crowd, perceiving the approach of their noble commander, took up the word and shouted it again and again.

Kindly thanking and greeting them, the emperor rode slowly to the first rank, often repeating the words, "To you, my brave Germans, I grant to-day a chief part of the victory! Now go forwards, with my most high person immediately at your head!"

Joyously flamed the noble German blue eyes, and brightly glowed the fresh German countenances; and as the general now rode before their front, the captains of the German files, forming a circle around him, thundered still more loudly out of the troops to heaven, "Long live our most gracious emperor Charles the Fifth!"

The heathen adversaries seemed to tremble at this sound, as if it were already a shout of victory. At least there was evident a strange moving to and fro in their squadron, without any distinct or definite intention; also quick assembling of their leaders and then separating again, and numerous swift riders hurrying away to both wings of their host.

The Emperor Charles looked at them a long time with the sharp and eager glance of a commander. Then he despatched some of his noble body-guard to the strand, entrusting them with a sealed paper for the admiral Andrea Doria, with the command of the strictest haste, and the knowledge by what signal they could immediately call in a boat from the admiral's ship to their relief. The messengers sprang away, using their utmost strength to vie in speed with the Arab messengers.

Brightly smiling, the Emperor Charles for some moments looked through the circle on the surrounding colonels, then turning his eyes upon the Baron of Marbach, he said, " Well, now, my experienced knight of the German oroer; you are by no means always friendly to my hopes, but—I know it—much more often accustomed to chide than to encourage; what think you of the present position of affairs?"

" I admire the high gifts of the commander, and the wise knowledge of war that my imperial lord possesses," answered Marbach, bowing gravely, but with eyes glowing with enthusiasm.

" Do you, then, understand me and my measures so perfectly?" smiled the emperor, with an almost imperceptible tincture of disdain.

And the knight returned, suddenly icy-cold, with a firmer voice: " I hope so indeed—with certainty: yes."

" Now let me hear them, lord of Marbach," said the emperor.

Casting a look round, the baron asked, " Before all these witnesses?"

" There are none among them from whom I hold more secrets than from you," was the calm reply.

And the German lord, deeply wounded in his inmost heart, yet on that account—as from a mortal wound—growing more cool outwardly, only that his large eyes sparkled like stars through a thunder-cloud, said, " Well, my great emperor, seeing that the time of the year, weather, and the soil of the ground, are against his bold undertaking, his most noble friend (but sometimes also his most noble enemy), the Baron Marbach, hopes that ne has subdued his own great heart, and has just sent a command to the admiral, Andrea Doria, for the re-embarkation of the army. The collected German corps is sufficient to cover the retreat of the Italian and Spanish squadrons, and has already inspired the barbarians with sufficient respect to be able worthily to follow, as a rearguard, without too great a hazard."

"It seems, my baron," said the emperor, "that you see the objects as they present themselves in strangely-polished mirrors—quite correctly as far as they go, but only just shewing the head. Not with a command of re-embarkation are my messengers despatched to the great admiral; but rather for the disembarkation of all the artillery, all the horses, and all the means of subsistence destined for the land-army. Also, not for a rearguard will I employ my German squadron, but rather for a vanguard in the general attack, which shall begin, I intend, as soon as the body-guards that are despatched to the left wing bring me information how it fares with my Spanish squadrons."

"And if the answer is returned, that they fare badly?" asked the Baron Marbach, drily.

"Then shall the attack of the Germans be somewhat modified, but only still more bold," returned the emperor; adding, with a louder voice, "for mark you, brave colonels and captains, Algiers will your emperor vanquish, or before Algiers will he die!"

A deep silence at these words overspread the assembly — a warlike, noble silence, in which gravely mingled apprehensions of death, as well as proud and beautiful hopes of victory.

It was broken by the voice of one who called in haste, "Where is the emperor? I bring a message for the emperor! A message of victory I bring!" Then within the circle, quickly flying open for him, leading his nimble Polish steed close before the emperor, entered the young Baron of Lichtenstein, one of the emperor's noble guards; and his cheeks glowing with joy and thoughts of battle, he said, " In a good hour has my imperial lord dismissed me. I was witness to a splendid deed of victory. The bold Spaniards stood on the plain, assaulted by the whole of the heathen force, which had thrown itself between them and the high position of the great Duke Alba. He meanwhile had enough to do to repel the Arabs, who seemed to rise up out of the sand, whirling from thence horrible pillars into the air; so that neither from him nor from the left wing of the chief corps could any resistance be expected. Then Don Alvaro de Sandez seized the standard —the standard of St. Jago de Compostella—and cried aloud, 'Give our saints and me into the power of those heathenish devils, or crush them to pieces! San Jago and I will venture into hell, in the name of God and of all the saints!' And all followed that heard or even saw him, as he waved the banner, on his horse which far overtopped the crowd; and the bold vice-king of Sicily, like a sunbeam, hastening through the ranks, led after him those who tarried. You may still hear their flourishes.— Forward, without delay!"

" To the attack, noble knights!" cried the emperor. "To-day will the banner of the cross yet triumph upon the walls of Algiers!"

And while the colonels and chiefs left the circle, each springing to his squadron, the Emperor Charles the Fifth, towering in the midst and visible to all, raised his high glittering sword of the cross, and turning to heaven, cried out to the neighbouring German corps with his powerful commander's voice, " In the name of God, forwards: march!" And as they pressed on closer towards him, he cried to them with a serene victory-declaring countenance, " My friends, soon shall the enemy vomit upon us more horrible flames, the more fearful the nearer we press to the abominable dragon's nest. But turn not at their rage. Victory is decreed to us! In God's cause you combat! for the glory of your old and glorious nation! for the good and the honour of united Christendom!"

Forwards then went the squadron with a triumphal step, the emperor in front; opposite them the heathen corps began immediately to turn and give way. The Italians courageously backed up the Germans; and from the left wing, already quite near the walls of the city, sounded loudly the victorious call of the Spaniards and the flourish of their trumpets.

Chapter Eighth.

FROM Don Felix Carrero's magnificent galley, he and his beautiful beloved looked down upon the warlike contest now going forward on shore—Donna Lisandra still arrayed in her glittering ornaments: Don Felix sparkling in his chosen decorated weapons; the silver target on his arm; at his side the great Spanish rapier, with a beautifully-carved golden hilt; and sparkling out of his richly-embroidered girdle the smaller short sword, with a diamond-cut hilt, which he generally used with his left hand, and called Daga.

A busy crowd of men moved around the two tall silent figures. For a short time ago, the great admiral, Andrea Doria, on receiving the imperial message, had given the signal for the disembarkation of all the land-artillery, horses, stores of powder, and for all the provision destined for the army. Don Felix, who had been keeping every thing in readiness for the landing of the cannon committed to his charge, now joyfully saw how quickly the work went on in all the galleys over which he had the command, hoping to feel himself soon disburdened from the interdict which still held his battle-dreaming soul far from the African strand, already besprinkled with the blood of heroes and heathens; but, full of proud melancholy, the glorious Lisandra stood at his side, till she at last, not being able longer to restrain her indignant feelings, broke out in these words:—

"O Felix! the inferior gods, to whom a higher power seems to have left the management of our human fate—elements, accidents, whirlpools of time, and whatever else they may be called—are hurtful to you and to me. It may be, because your great father too boldly challenged them at your cradle, in calling you Felix, the happy; so may they now hazard their wild power to transform you to Infelix, the unhappy."

"They may," returned the noble, proud youth, while he looked smiling upon his wonderfully beautiful beloved, and then upon his glittering sword, that had already oftentimes been sprinkled with glory. "Till now," he added calmly—"till now, at any rate, their trouble has not been particularly rewarded."

"Oh," said Lisandra, "I know very well that gifts and joys are destined for you, Felix, which none of those malicious hobgoblins—indeed, they are only deserving of this name, not that of gods—may venture to intermeddle with—my love, Felix, and your heroic courage. But the garlands of this courage should deck you, and not a single charm out of them should be lost, if all went right in this world. Yet look!—only look how the attack against Algiers presses forwards, like the all-absorbing waves of the sea! Oh, you shall experience it, my knight! Yet before we land—yet before the business of this day, this disembarkation of the artillery, is accomplished, that glorious contest will be decided, and will have enveloped us, with ever flowing-on waves, in the dark night of forgetfulness."

"The lady has rightly spoken," said a tawny, weather-beaten boatswain, from the coast of Majorca, while, misunderstanding Lisandra's words, he suddenly stopped, as he walked to and fro before them; "only too rightly has the lady spoken," he said again, while, shaking his head, he now looked up to the firmament, now down over the sea. "Dark night! Do you not see, Don Carrero, how they already begin to gather, the approaching stormy clouds, on the firmament that was a little while ago so sunny, so serene? Do you not mark the flowing-on enveloping waves, how they begin to raise their heads, ever more foamy? Those are the signs of an approaching fearful tempest, particularly fearful on this strand, and at this time of the year. God preserve us! the business of the disembarkation must soon have an end, at least for a while. Would to God we were upon a higher sea! There at least a storm can be partly warded off, when a man understands his handiwork, like you and me, signor. But here—God preserve us! for many of us the last hour draws near."

Crossing himself solemnly, he passed them. Lisandra, with searching glances, in which there was ever mingled more proud hope than timid fear, looking at her loved one, felt nevertheless, with inward trembling, that the answer which the air and sea returned to her silent question was not a joyful one. And at the same time came another still more fearfully warning answer. The speaking-trumpet from Andrea Doria's admiral-ship thundered through the dark and lowering air—"Discontinue the disembarking! All power is useless against the rising storm!"

The captain sent as a signal down to the distant frigates the same ill-boding message — "Halt with the disembarking!—the storm comes!" And the storm whistled and howled, and the day became as night, and frightful claps of thunder broke over land and sea, and the waves dug loose in the deepest abyss of the sea the anchor of the ship, and rocked madly about, with invisible gigantic arms, ships, and barks, and galleys; shattering barks to pieces against the ships and galleys; and striking galleys and ships against each other in an equally ruinous crash of destruction.

"Are we lost?" sounded Lisandra's voice as clearly as it could through the tumult, into the ear of her beloved.

But he, not hearing her in the bellowing of the storm and tumult on board ship, could only press her to his heart with his left arm, thereby signifying, " Even in death we are one!" holding at the same time the captain's pipe with his right hand to his lips, crying out a signal-call, through the howling of the elements, to the many neighbouring vessels that were already going down and being wrecked.

Chapter Ninth.

THE storm of the firmament had driven the storm of war back from the almost conquered ramparts of Algiers. In piercing lightning and in rattling thunder, the angry heaven seemed to open over those who had considered themselves as its warriors, and created a far higher and holier sort of fear and despondency than mere earthly danger was able to awaken in these otherwise bold and valiant hearts. The European squadron retreated on all sides, and the Emperor Charles, formerly braving every threatening danger, convinced that to him it was decreed to plant the banner of the cross over the ruins of this robber's stronghold, leading as a commander, and fighting in the tumult as a common soldier — the Emperor Charles felt awful shudders of mighty thoughts pass through his great soul.

" Thou Almighty in heaven and earth! Thou willest not this work."

And so he ceased from the attempt of stopping the fugitives, and encouraging them anew to the attack. Thoughtfully he rode after the retreating troops, unpursued by the enemy; he himself was the last to reach the camp.

But within the walls of the fortress the heathens wildly rejoiced, as though mad with their unexpected triumph, and with praises shouted the name of their sorceress, Baranaga, to the sulphureous stormy clouds, which they imagined had been drawn together by the demoniacal art of this magical woman; and between the shouts they clattered their tin vessels deafeningly, and shook the bells on their light lances, adorned with half-moons, and blew out of their shapeless trumpets and horns a hellish dissonance.

The renegade, Hassan Aga, in abhorrence at this distracted tumult and crowd, stood alone on the battlements of the tower — where we have already once before described him — that here he might refresh his wild heart with the defeat of his enemies, which he hoped to see perfectly from this high station. Yet soon the clouds of rain came between him and the wished-for sight; soon the shade of clouds lay over the Christian host; and soon also his ally, the wild stormwind, raged with such terrible violence, that he feared being precipitated over the battlements, and fixed his spear into the mossy joints of the stone floor, striving thus to keep himself firm.

Meanwhile, it seemed to him as though he heard a mournful voice sighing through the air — "Be faithful! — be faithful!"

Already in dreams he had heard that call before; involuntarily it recurred to him;—yes, hundreds of times in dreams he had heard those words, and in fright and sorrow had awaked out of his slumber. Once he had heard them in reality, while he was yet a boy, when his dying mother was weeping in her last pangs, full of bitter prophesying anticipations of the danger of her darling's future apostacy.

Now, as he strove to keep his body firm by his spear, rusty with blood, he also strove to keep firm his agitated mind by haughty pride.

"Pshaw!" muttered he between his teeth. "My mother sleeps soundly in her bed, three ells deep. I myself saw her let down into the earth; I myself heard the clods of earth rattle against her coffin, and wept over it like a boy, as vainly as though I were now to howl in emulation with the storm. No, my mother sleeps under the high raised bed, decked with turf, and made firm by the stroke of the spade. It was a night-owl, who mistook this stormy, dark evening hour for midnight—perplexed, foolish owl's hooting—nothing more."

Then rose before him, out of the midst of the building, a dark, mysterious creature, and danced in wild evolutions up and down before him.

"Ha!" exclaimed the renegade, with suddenly awakened horror, "what are you? For an owl you are too gigantically large; and you cannot be the shade of my softly sleeping mother, you unearthly creature!" added he, with a milder voice.

And the ghastly appearance stood and croaked: "I am Baranaga—the witch Baranaga—and require my reward for the storm, raised by my art, that has put your strong enemies under your feet."

But the renegade replied: "You have not caused this tempest, black witch; you could not. That could only *One* do; and with Him such as you can make no covenant."

"If He is so powerful," murmured the black witch, with a hellish grin, "why did you not remain faithful to Him?"

"Alas!" sighed the renegade out of the fearful anguish of his soul. All other sound was denied him in that horrible time. It was as though a dream had carried him back for a moment to the paradise-playing years of childhood, on a hill blooming and pleasant, when suddenly the ground at his feet sank away, an unearthly sea of naphtha, with hissing tongues, whizzing and jumping up, surrounded him; and a black spirit stood near the trembling one, and exclaimed, "That is hell!"

"Save thyself! save thyself!" sighed a sorrowful voice near him

But the witch snarled, laughing: "I do not flinch or retire for mere words; and you—whatever you may have in your trembling and tumultuous soul, poor apostate—you have as yet only given me mere words. I will have payment—my payment."

The renegade, with an effort collecting all his strength, said: " Well, demand the payment, and take it; and let me be for ever freed from you."

" That can by no means happen," said the witch. " Willing or not willing, we are now yoked to one and the same master—to the blood-furrowing plough. But to name the price: that is not my custom. You must propose something."

" If a thousand zechin content you," said the renegade, " take them—they are yours."

But the witch answered, wildly laughing, " Fool! you might at least have begun with a hundred thousand zechin, then there might have been a little more chance of making a bargain. But do not trouble yourself about your zechins: I would not have them if you were to offer me a million. I require what will be neither hardship nor pleasure to you—only the finger of a babe that has been born into the light of Algiers within the last month. You shudder! But why? It is not necessary that you yourself cut off the little finger. If you only say 'yes' to my request, I shall have the little finger brought here, by certain mysterious spells, quite of itself. No suspicion of it either shall fall upon you. Yet more, you may hoard your heap of zechin, offered to me as a reward, which never need be paid, as a prize for the animal or race of demons which tore away or bit off the little finger of the child. But now, before the moon again grows bright, we must be more familiar, my friend. For mark me——"

She seemed as though she would whisper something in his ear, and bent over nearer to him, with her black withered arms extended.

But he, as in dreamy horror, struck her from him with convulsive force; and she flew lightly as a ball over the battlements of the tower, then dashed heavily as lead on the cliff, and cracked like a fallen thunderbolt over the rocky ground. And the frightful being howled: " Hu! hu! You have killed your love! You have broken all her bones! For I am Rosetta! Rosetta! It was only to have seen through that provoking disguise; and you, weak coward, have horribly crushed me in."

The voice failed, as that of a dying person; and Hassan Aga leant hesitatingly over the battlement of the tower.

With the last horrible gasp, she uttered a fearful curse; and then, in a wild howl, her unhappy spirit passed away.

Yet Hassan Aga, breathing more calmly, said: "Oh! no, no! the curse of the sorceress, truly that told me certainly that she was not Rosetta. Rosetta wanders quietly and sweetly by the side of her noble love, on the blooming, sunny Italian shore; protected and guarded from me, and all other phantoms of the desolate night,—protected, guarded; Rosetta!"

And a sweeter slumber than the unfortunate Hassan had known for many, many years fell on him, as he lay behind the battlements of the tower on the sprouting grass between the stones. He heard no more of the wild cries of victory, and the clattering of the tins and trumpets, with which the crowds of barbarians were still raging through the city in mad jubilee.

Chapter Tenth.

THE same hour passed much more solemnly in the Christian camp—if, indeed, it could be called a camp—deluged by rain, and storm-floods, and raging waves of the sea,—a desolate plain, where, a little before, bright tents and well-made fortifications had begun to be erected, and which now only stood like boggy ruins, inhabited, or rather restlessly haunted, by wandering spirits.

Next to the sea-shore, as near as the dashing salt waves

would allow of, were assembled a little group of dismounted German knights, belonging to the body-guard of the nephew of the noble Doge of Genoa, Gianettino Doria.

Many princes and captains, full of earnest consideration and in weighty business, passed to and fro, warning the little troop not to give themselves up so uselessly to the possible danger of the sea-waves, which rose higher every moment.

But the same answer was always returned,—" We will search land and sea for our young knight and master, Gianettino Doria. We have till now learnt nothing. Here he left us, and here he must again appear. And so we fear neither the sand of the shore, nor the foam of the sea."

To such answers no further question was made; and every one was too much engaged with his own affairs, and his own immediate duty, to repeat in this time of confusion the injunction that had been given them.

So the bold German body-guard remained almost undisturbed, faithfully and sorrowfully listening and looking over the sea and plains as far as the stormy clouds, and showers of rain and sea-foam, would allow them. Sometimes the name of their dear lost master sounded through the howling of the storm, ever without answer; sometimes one strolled right or left along the strand; but all came back without intelligence.

The setting sun, as it approached the horizon of the sea, broke through the clouds; and his last rays, like blood-red arrows, illuminated the tossing ocean, covered with numberless broken ruins of ships.

And as the faithful troop directed their glances with renewed perseverance over the waste of water, Walprecht, our well-known young trooper, suddenly exclaimed, full of sorrow: " Look yonder! But perhaps it is only a heathen ghost of the wild god Neptune, as I have seen in Italian statues. He must have a noble troop of horses when he goes swimming forth into the sea. Ah, would that these were nothing more than Neptune's steeds! But no, no! they are really and truly noble horses, cast into the waves out of the wrecks of the ships! See! there a hundred—it may be five hundred! Certainly they have not fishes' tails, as Neptune's distorted beasts; for then they would stand much higher above the mad waves than now. Oh, those beautiful, delicately-formed horses' heads! not clumsy, broad, and fishy, as Neptune's horses! no! beautiful, high, noble heads! proudly maned necks, sorrowfully bent, perhaps, in the uselessly struggling pains of death! Dear companions in war, strive no more! your endeavours to save yourselves are vain! Ah! that would be no use, even if they could understand me. Ah! but to rescue one noble champion from the clutch of death, before he grasps him! Ah! who can help? Only to save one out of the lordly troop!"

Quickly he cast round his daring blue eyes, to discover if there was not some possibility of doing so. Finding none, he said: "I can look no longer, from sorrow." And he veiled himself closely in his mantle, and turned away.

The others, in their kindly feelings, for the most part, did the same; when one of them again looked at the sorrowful spectacle.

Lupold, Walprecht's bold companion, asked: "Do they still swim, the poor noble creatures?"

"Yes, still!" was the mournful answer.

"It is better," sighed Lupold, "that such noble animals seek not to shew their necessity by complaints or calls for help; otherwise the heart must burst in our breast."

Then the clouds thickly gathered again over the disappearing sun, and higher swelled the waves in the increasing darkness; and soon the unfortunate struggling horses were lost from sight, and soon they sank into their moist, sedgy, watery graves.

Now came some soldiers from the shore, walking

slowly through the damp upturned sand; on a bier, made of their spears, bearing the body of one dead, or severely wounded, thickly enveloped in mantles.

"O God!" said the troopers, softly and sorrowfully, one to another; "then they have at last certainly found our prince, Gianettino, and are bringing him to us—but how?"

But one of them answered: "No, this is not our Gianettino Doria. Of him, unfortunately, we have no trace. It is another of our noble comrades that we bring, the German nobleman, Baron of Marbach, mortally wounded. Give room, and your mantles for covering for his couch and tent, and your spears for tent-poles; we will let him rest as well as we can, as it may be the last time, on this inimical and desolate strand."

In pious brotherly zeal they soon did as their comrades had desired.

The lord of Marbach rested, still and pale, as under a canopy, his eyes closed, an earnest hero-smile around his lips. His light breathing gave warning that the high soaring spirit had not yet left his wounded and fainting body.

As they all stood round the noble death-bed, some of them softly praying, after the good old German custom, some striving to lighten the last struggles of the knight by their diligent care, a loud voice sounded over the heads of the warriors,—"Blessed are those who depart from this world."

It seemed to the astonished people as though an angel had descended from the heavenly halls to guide thither the brave, faithful soul; and the same thought came into the mind of the dying knight; he cast up his large beaming eyes, and murmured, gazing up into the clouds inquiringly, "Who blessed me?"

"A mortal man, as thou art!" returned the voice.

And all now perceived that it was the Emperor Charles the Fifth, who, on a high horse, halted near the circle, and recognised, with his eagle, loving glance, who it was that there on the bloody ground was breathing out his bold true life.

"Marbach! brave Marbach!" said the emperor, deeply moved.

And the baron, with a heavenly smile, answered: "Welcome! That is balsam in the death-hour."

"You speak awful words, dear Marbach," said the emperor.

And Marbach said: "Yes, truly; to me also it appears in no way of small importance. To few, very few men is it permitted to be so nobly cared for; and to be dismissed, as your majesty has just dismissed me, with a truly imperial gift from the imperial service, and even from life itself."

And raising himself up with a strength which the beholders expected not to see in him, he looked eagerly round the circle, exclaiming—" Have you heard it? the emperor has called me the 'brave Marbach!'"

"Who calls you other than brave must lie," said Charles the Fifth. "But no knight dares lie, and still less a Christian emperor."

Marbach looked round thoughtfully, with an absent mind: "If besides other wounds, I did not also bear with me a death-wound in my almost bald pate," he began after a while, brightly smiling, "perhaps I should express myself better; but, dear comrades, you must accept the intention. It is a beautiful thing, my friends, when a soldier risks his life joyfully in battle, in assault, in retreat, in pursuit, or whatever else he may have to do. But it is much more beautiful, when a soldier, of brave heart and valiant arm, also possesses a prudent foreseeing soul, even in the hour of action offering counsel, and practising the noble art of war with all wisdom. Comrades, in both kinds of duty I hope to have done what was possible for me ; and I feel that what was possible was not altogether trifling. But there remains yet another duty for a soldier, which is the most beautiful of all: trust in God,—and from that flows fresh hope and vigour of life through all ranks of the army. To you, dear friends and brethren, I must faithfully and sorrowfully confess, that in my otherwise honourable career I have often failed in this most beautiful duty. It was to me then—howbeit, I only see it clearly in the death-hour; for God knows in life I ever did what seemed to me reasonable and for the good of the army—it happened to me often that my own imagined superior wisdom stood in my way, towering as the mountain Atlas, so that I neither over it or round it could see what others had imagined to be great or beautiful. If it had not been conceived by me, it was to me as though it was not there; and how prejudicially this has worked on many otherwise brave fellows, and so to the whole army, Heaven only knows; how prejudicially it has worked to myself, I know, next to Heaven, the best—or rather the worst. If you look into the history of the world, contemptuously rejecting what is therein, your own soul in your bosom will also soon be deformed by the mournful spectacle. Soon your head and limbs will feel lamed, and what beams from your eyes will no more be your own inborn fiery spirit, but a sorrowful transformed thing."

He stopped, and then smiling, added: "I can truly call it by no better term, and in so doing I speak my own sentence; out of our languid eyes looks a pale, grievous, melancholy, wise-acting little monkey! and, alas! I have acted much and often with such wise folly."

"You have also often and much helped with firm and earnest opposition, valiant Marbach!" said the emperor; "and when you helped not, it was the fault of him who did not take your warnings, and not yours."

"Oh!" said the knight Marbach gently, and kindly shaking his wounded head, "I have a very mild confessor, and a still more generous one. Truly, I have never failed in warning, and that is a good thing, when one does not let the die out of one's own hands. Whether the instruments of fate roll over the earth, or whether they lie firmly fixed, we must say the best we can of things that have already happened; valiantly forbearing all the criticism and especial examination of 'what any one had!' or 'any one has!' trusting and confiding in God for the present and the future. But I——"

With a light shaking of his head, as though blaming himself, the Baron of Marbach grew speechless on his death-bed. A dark troubled shade fell over his hitherto friendly and true-hearted features.

But the noble knight returned to himself again. Smiling, almost laughing, he once more raised himself up, and said: "Now, you have truly heard the confession of the departing Marbach, perhaps a more than usually candid confession; at least to many prudent men it may appear so. But during my life I have been a greater lover of plain words than of disguises; and, more than this, my great emperor has absolved me. Receive, then, all of you, ye brothers in arms, Marbach's parting blessing! Far from every one of you be murmurings of wisdom that has come too late, and after-handed prudence! Far from the lowest of the foot-soldiers and esquires! for it is as bad for the lowest in the army to trespass as the highest—I mean, for himself and before God. It is certain that from the summit the pestilential air is wafted more destructively down into the valleys, than from the valleys up into the heights; and so that God more particularly considers complaints and murmurs in high places. There are many below the imperial dignity who might receive my words as a wholesome medicine. My blessing be with you, comrades, and with——"

He sank back, his countenance growing bright in the slumber of death; and the Emperor Charles, when the last breath of the dying one was over, said, with moistening eyes—"Thy dear soul is with God, brave Marbach!"

Chapter Eleventh.

MIDNIGHT was past, yet still the fleet pressed onwards, veiled in the horrible darkness of the sea-storm, and threatened by many dangers, partly from the separation of the ships one from the other, partly by wrecks on the hostile, inhospitable shore.

Leaning against the mast of his admiral's ship stood the great Andrea Doria, his large speaking-trumpet in his hand; from time to time he raised it to his mouth, and the thundering word of command sounded over the storm and waves. Some of the captains gave the answering-signal from their pipes, but not all. Many of them were for ever silent, and had disappeared with their ships, naval instruments, and lading. Some might have considered it their duty to save the ships entrusted to them from the dangerous harbour, by running them for a while into the Bay of Busia, which lay not far from here. Andrea Doria, remembering this, called through his trumpet: "I proclaim, for the third and last time — no one leaves the landing-place without my command. If we live, we live with the emperor; if we die, we die with the emperor, in God's name!"

And lowering the trumpet, he repeated softly to himself, "in God's name!" Then murmured more softly, his lips scarcely moving between his snow-white beard — " Many, oh, many have I seen sorrowfully perish in this fearful hour! And that dearest one, whom I have not seen perish, has vanished without a trace in this dark gloomy night of universal sorrow. Oh, that I could mourn over the corpse of my dear Gianettino! But no! such happiness is not allowed thee, forsaken old man! Thou gazest inquiringly in vain through the veil of thy sorrow, and no intelligence canst thou receive; and the horrible possibility of the pangs of death, or the yet more horrible life of slavery of thy loved one, pierces thy very brain as a spark from hell. Unhappy one, what now shall save thee from despair?"

Then suddenly shuddering before the most fearful of all maddening words, the old man collected all his strength. Looking towards heaven, and folding his strong hands, he said: "What saves thee? God. The little stars shine brightly yonder, though the clouds hide them from our sight. Why not the more glorious eternal sun?"

Then he said, after some thought, earnestly shaking his head: "Fool that I am — so to prattle in my fond old age in the antechamber, when the Most Holy is accessible to me. His royal ears are open every hour. Yes, Lord of lords, I seize, I embrace my heavenly right. To Thee will I speak! only and alone to Thee!"

His lips were silent, his eyes spoke to heaven.

Then there came near to the admiral's ship from the African shore a light boat, wildly dancing upon the waters, now raised on the foamy summit of the highest waves, now again disappearing in the gloomy deep green valleys of the salt waters. Yet it appeared again, and in it the forms of two men—one sitting at the stern, deeply shrouded, like a motionless, veiled statue; the other eagerly holding the rudder, while his white hair and beard wildly and strangely flew about in the storm.

At this strange spectacle there arose a low yet angry whispering among the sailors of the admiral's ship.

"That is the goblin," murmured one to the other, "the water-goblin whom the sorceress Baranaga — you have heard the Algerine prisoners who were sent on board of us boast of her—the goblin she has conjured up from the depths of the sea to destroy us! Do you see how jeeringly he slips in and out among our broken vessels?"

"Let us destroy the creature, for the fun!" said a second. "If we all at once directed our cross-bows and fire-arms at him——"

"Oho!" broke in a third. "Do you think it is possible to shoot a goblin?"

"No," answered the other; "yet I thought even he would be frightened, and that would be some satisfaction. But which of the two may the goblin be? Or are they both goblins?"

The one who had spoken first now said authoritatively: "No, no. The veiled one is a soul whose body has been lost in the storm, and the goblin now carries it about in this boasting way as a sign of victory. But the one with the wild white beard and hair—only look how firmly and eagerly he swings the rudder—he is the chief goblin of the waves, and the learned call him Charon!"

"And you are the chief goblin of fools!" exclaimed a strong man's voice from the boat. "But as to myself, I am Ruperto Sansogno, steersman of the galley of the Prince Gianettino Doria, and he whom you presently shall help me to take from the boat into the admiral's ship is the noble, brave Gianettino Doria himself, preserved from a thousand dangers."

"Gianettino Doria! he lives—he lives!" cried the sailors with loud shouts of joy; and while some of them hastened round to help the young prince from the boat to the ship, others hastened to their admiral to cause him by their message of joy to weep no longer.

Andrea Doria still leant against the mast, his large eyes directed heavenwards; he kindly motioned them away with his hand, and said, with a scarcely perceptible inclination of his head: "Yes, yes, I know it all! I thank you, good people, I have seen it all." And then he murmured more softly: "O ye ministering angels, bear my thanks before the throne of the Eternal!"

Meanwhile Gianettino had quickly cast aside the veiling mantle, and sprung on to the admiral's ship, carefully assisting with his firm, youthful hand the old steersman, Ruperto Sansogno, not leaving him until he stood beside him on the deck. Then he hastened to the feet of his uncle, where he sank on both knees before the grey-headed old man, covering his face with his mantle.

Andrea Doria caressingly bent over him, and asked, "Are you wounded, my dear son?"

"I am not wounded," answered the voice of the youth gloomily from his thick mantle.

"Hide nothing from me, dear nephew," said the old man. "If you were mortally wounded, I should never cease thanking the all-merciful God that I again hold you in my arms. Compared with the dark, uncertain disappearance of him whom I loved above all men, whom I looked upon as the blooming heir of my fame, my power, and my treasures — Gianettino, compared with that most horrible disappearance, it would be heavenly joy to see you softly and happily die in my arms, under my protection, and with my blessing. Dearest Gianettino, hide nothing from me."

"I am not wounded," groaned the youth, still in the same position. "Would that I were wounded! To return from such a night without wounds seems only the herald of a yet more miserable fate."

"Strange boy!" returned the old man, kindly, shaking his venerable head. "Surely you have fought with me often enough before now to know that wounds do not always fall to the lot of the bravest. Many a one keeps himself in the background, as far from danger as he can, and returns purple-sprinkled from the field of battle against his will; and the brave strives not after wounds — it is indifferent to him whether they come or not — he strives after victory. Rise, my brave Gianettino; unveil your dear features."

And Gianettino, loosing his uncle's purple mantle, tremblingly rose, saying these words: "I pray you, my great foster-father, let no one in this moment see my countenance but you. You see it is deluged with hot tears, and I cannot restrain them. A stranger might deem it a womanly weakness. Uncle, you will not do so. You know the blood of Doria. You know I am not altogether unworthy that it should flow in my veins.

But so noble a Christian armada as this is by land and sea, commanded by such heroes as the Emperor Charles the Fifth and my great uncle, to meet with such a fearful and destructive issue—oh, uncle, one image of sorrow after another, of every various and horrible kind, crowds upon my afflicted heart in strange, fearful confusion!"

He covered his flowing eyes with both hands, and was silent. Sorrow had penetrated his soul; his swelling heart wept in every pulse.

Not only the great Andrea Doria's purple mantle, but his uncle's arms now tenderly surrounded the weeping youth. They both slowly walked to the admiral's chamber, where a lamp, swinging by a golden chain, cast a wonderful light, now pale as moonlight, now glowing red.

Then Andrea placed his nephew close to him on a couch, and said: "Gianettino, I also once lived in the land of youth. That you will say is plain enough, and could not be otherwise. But it is not so. There are men, Gianettino, who have never been young, in spite of the calendar. Youth to such people is only a Fata-morgana breath. But I can assure you, Gianettino, that I was once really and truly young; and therefore my heart, after beating for eighty years, has still a sympathy with the joys and sorrows of youth—a loving, answering sympathy. Relate to me, dear rescued youth, what has happened to you during the last fearful, sorrowful hours. I pray you, turn not away from your physician. I shall be able to offer you comfort; I am sure of that, in God's mercy."

The youth raised his head that was sunk sorrowfully to the ground, shaking back from his lofty brow the thick black hair, wet with the dew of heaven and sea-foam, and seizing his uncle with both his hands, he looked at the old man like a deeply sorrowing child who has been half comforted.

"Say on!" repeated the old man, in a gently commanding tone, and with earnest, approving gestures, his large dark eyes flaming still more solemnly; and the youth began:

"At the first onslaught of those demoniacal enemies, our Italian battalion was pushed back to the yielding, slippery quicksands, and I saw myself cut off from all my companions, surrounded by raging swarms of Arabs and Moors. The descending rain and the darkening clouds might partly have led to this result, but it was yet more owing to the fierceness of the battle, and the angry ferocity of my own nature. I sprang from my horse and seized a banner, exclaiming to two or three of the nearest of my companions, 'After me, upon the enemy!' They followed nobly. Peace be with their brave souls! They all fell under the lances and scimitars of the heathens. I thoughtlessly hastened with quick steps over the deceitful ground, hearing unexpected cries of fury from the destroying Arabs behind the sand-hills, at my companions' flank. The muskets miscarried, soaked by the continual rain. It was far more from the prodigious numbers of the enemy than from their skill that our brave Genoese were overpowered, after a bloody but short resistance. You may be sure that I wished to have been with them, but there was a wild swarm of enemies between us, and prevented the attempt. I can die bravely alone, thought I, fixing my banner as firmly as I could in the sand, and holding it with my left hand, while with my right I grasped my good sword, ready to protect the honourable signal.

"God knows what the rabble of heathens took me for when I was in this position, alone in the midst of them! I only know, that whoever approached me retreated in a sort of wild terror. But ever before my eyes raged the host of enemies. How was I to regain our squadrons, command them to halt, and again lead them to danger, encouraging them by example and words?

"Behind the sand-hills, the rolling sea carried on a mad sport with the sand. Yet I thought my only hope was to work my way down to the shore; and resolved to fulfil my duty as captain, I climbed, or rather slid down, carrying the banner with me. Yet I soon thought I had stepped into my grave, so treacherous was the ground beneath my feet, so fearfully and awfully the waves rolled over my head, like towering grave-clothes, and at every ebb spreading over me a shower of sand. Sinking down under so many strange horrors, I still remember what dreamy words escaped my lips: 'Here graves are easily and quickly made!' I shuddered at my own words. Then consciousness left me.

"I was aroused by the agonising cry of a sweet woman's voice. With an effort I half-raised myself from my damp, sandy grave, and saw the wreck of one of our ships floating to the land, and standing on it—by the light of the awful, almost continuous lightning—I saw a beautiful, magnificently-dressed woman, and a knight kneeling at her feet, who strove to hold her firmly; but whether she fell into the waves, or whether she rose to heaven with her beautiful garments extending as angel-wings, my reeling senses could not inform me. Again lethargy came over me. Powerless and exhausted, I sank back into my damp, sandy bed. 'Only hold fast the banner!' was my last thought, and I grasped it in my arms with a strong convulsive effort.

"Then something thundered in my ear, 'Loose it, you Christian corpse! you half-stiffened Christian corpse, loose it, or, for sport's sake, I will hew your obstinate hands from your body!' In anguish I felt the banner nearly wrested from my arms, and roused all my strength to protect this sign of honour. When I unclosed my eyes, I saw before me the black face of a Moor frightfully grinning; his clutch had already loosened one of my arms, the other still firmly grasped the pole of the banner. 'Assist me, ye saints!' I cried, and repulsed my grim enemy with all my strength. But he, laughing in mockery, had already drawn his scimitar to accomplish his threats. I still held fast; when a huge wave rose, covering and overwhelming us both. With a shriek the heathen loosed me, and flew up the sandy hill. I still held fast, but in vain!—the waves dashed, and wrenched the pole out of my hands, in mighty sport, tearing away the swelling flag, whilst I, nearly buried, could only half raise myself up. Away floated the banner into the immeasurable sea; my head grew dizzy. But still proud in my misery, I looked up the hill to the fugitive Moor, exclaiming, 'You, grisly wretch, have not the banner, thank heaven! I resign it with a willing heart to the waters of my God!'

"The black infidel looked in the flashes of the lightning like a spirit of the desert, peering down from the sand-hill not very far from me! In better days I might have reached him with a firm arrow from my cross-bow. He ran, and sprang on to a neighbouring hill, on which knelt, surrounded by the moonlight now streaming through the clouds, an angel-beautiful woman, she who had been cast on the shore from the storm of the wreck, but no longer under the protection of the knight who knelt by her side. No; by her stood, instead, that ghastly Moor, swinging his scimitar over her, howling wildly: 'Die, you jewel-dressed doll! The jewels are for me—death for you!'

"Uncle, you may imagine how I extricated myself from the sandy grave, which before had quite enclosed me. You may imagine how I hastened up the hill with my last strength, crying, 'Stop, accursed Moor! Here comes one who is a braver object for your death-blade!' I knew that my sword was left behind in my sandy grave. What did that signify? I still had sufficient strength to sacrifice my own life for the threatened angel. Alas, how fatally slow were my wearied steps! Still looking on the threatened figure, I discovered, O uncle, that it was Donna Lisandra, the beautiful bride of the brave Spaniard Don Felix Carrero, who had followed her lover hither, boldly hoping to see him win a crown of victory, if not a regal crown; and so was she dressed in bridal magnificence for the triumphal victory of her loved one; now, some hours ago——"

Gianettino sank back, speechless, more like one dead than living; then he added, in a feeble, mournful voice:

"Yes, now, she is dead! The Moor's scimitar pierced through her tender breast; such a deed was fit only for a night like this. Is it not true that she still murmured, praying for her life—that she cried, 'Oh, woe is me, I was too proud! Oh, woe is me, life is sweet! Oh, let me live, if it were only to be the ornament of a seraglio!' And yet the scimitar of the infidel cut off her lovely tender life; and I, uncle, was forced to see it, and climbed the hill only a moment too late to tear from the wolf the fair gentle doe. Alas!"

And again innumerable tears flowed from the eyes of the youth, stifling his voice.

Andrea Doria asked, with difficulty restraining his emotion, "Did the Moor stand to fight with you when you had climbed the hill, my son? For, weaponless and exhausted as you were, I know you would have attacked him."

"Ha!" cried the youth, aroused again by angry remembrances; "close to the beautiful murdered one he cowered to plunder her ornaments. As I approached him, commanding him to stop, he grinned at me sideways as a tiger over his prey, without pausing from his detestable task; then he mocked my defenceless condition, saying, with a sneer, 'Hunter without arms, sailor without rudder, painter without pencil! Such as you have not much power to command obedience. Would you see how I release this little doll from her polished jewels? But when I am ready, if you are still here, I will kill you. Do you hear?'

"But I found my dagger in my girdle, and swung it threateningly over the monster. Then, with an angry leap, he rushed wildly upon me, brandishing his scimitar

I slung the dagger; it struck him in the forehead. The wretch staggered back like a horrible unicorn; the sabre glittered in his hand, he fell over the declivity, and lay at the bottom crushed to death.

"But I knelt down by the beautiful dead lady; yet no — not yet quite dead; a gentle breath still came from her bleeding breast. I looked up to see if there were any means of help. Near me stood a noble warrior, his hair and garments dripping with sea-water, and murmuring in a bitter voice: 'Sweet crown of most beautiful women! Of sweet women the most beautiful crown! Was it for this I carried you from the wreck to the shore, and sank back into the wave rejoicing that you at least would be saved as an ornament for the whole world? And now you lie slaughtered, making your couch float with your noble blood—such costly purple as the mightiest king dares not wear, the purple blood of your own sweet life and strength!'

"And then recognising me, he took my hand caressingly and said: 'I saw you with your bold right arm take vengeance on the robber. Scarcely had I struggled upon the land than you avengingly struck the tiger; the dying tiger fell by me, and expired at my feet. Ah, Doria, why have you robbed me of my revenge—of my last gleam of happiness upon earth! O Gianettino, the tiger had not ruined you—but me!'

"He said these last words almost angrily; and, I gradually recognising him, exclaimed, full of melancholy, 'In what a sorrowful moment are you come, Don Felix!' But he returned, gloomily, 'Infelix! That is my name for the few short moments I have yet to live in this dark, bloody vale of pilgrimage called the world. But those black Moors shall feel to the very last the revenging arm of Infelix.'

"And so he tore his sword from its sheath, and hastened down the hill, where raged thick crowds of the enemy. I would have followed him, and groped after the sabre which had glimmered in the darkness in the hand of the dying Moor, when there sounded in the distance the battle-cry of the unhappy youth :—'Infelix!'

"But a silvery voice near me murmured, 'Felix!' It was Donna Lisandra, returning once more to this earthly existence at the call of sweet true love. When I knelt near her, asking whether I could lessen her pains, she murmured very softly, but with the sweetest accents: 'My pains are nearly over, kind friend. I swim in a sea of purple blood, but its waves sing to me heavenly lullaby-songs; and soon, very soon, shall I be landed on the ever-green and ever-blooming shore. But tell me, did I dream when I thought I saw standing near me a black, hateful devil, and then a flaming angel? It is true the angel was in wrath; but these glorious princes of heaven are sometimes angry when in combat with this sinful world or the horrible abyss. Or was it my sweet bridegroom — was it Felix?'

"'Infelix!' sounded again the war-cry from the battle amid the clattering of swords. But she exclaimed, in wonderful emotion: 'No, Felix; still Felix you remain to me, my own loved bridegroom. Felix, the happy — look, the gates of victory turn on their silver hinges; the purple hangings are agitated, lightened by the eternal bright radiance — you Felix, and I Felicia, for ever!'

"She sank back smiling, and thus she died: still murmuring with her last voice, 'Felicia.' Yet it was like a voice of triumph. The clattering of swords was silent. Felix Carrero must have perished in the fierce battle; or rather, must have flown to heaven. I would have followed him, and seized the Moor's sabre, ready to rush destructively with it on the heads of his companions for the last struggle, when there sounded, it seemed to me, out of the foamy sea: 'Gianettino, Doria's Gianettino! Your great uncle, the deserted hero, waits for you; bitterly he calls for his Gianettino.'

"I stood as though benumbed and enchanted; soon I

thought it was a phantom of your soul, blessing me, and calling me with a heartfelt cry; that it was your spirit, freed from its body in honourable battle, which came to conduct me home to the eternal halls! A form with white hair appeared on the strand, as though rising from the waves;—was it a sea-god's threatening image?— whatever it might be, I exclaimed to it, 'Here! who seeks Doria?—Gianettino Doria is here!' And he landed, and laid aside his boat, and came up the hill, and spoke to me words of earnest meaning, pressing me with prayers and entreaties to come away from that scene of horrible destruction; it was Ruperto Sansogno, the steersman of my galley, who faithfully and bravely had sought me in the sea and storm, and has preserved your nephew, dear father Andrea."

They embraced one another full of unspeakable love and sorrow; and the tears of the old man rolled down as fast as those of the youth. Yet Andrea Doria, remembering the beautiful duty of gratitude, opened the cabin-door, calling—

"Ruperto Sansogno, brave preserver of my brave nephew! come hither."

At the same time the fresh young beams of morning burst into the cabin. And the old man Ruperto Sansogno was seen nimbly approaching, surrounded by the glowing light—almost like a bright and awakened soul separated from its earthly life.

Andrea Doria spread his arms to embrace him; the morning's glow shone round him also.

Yet Ruperto remained standing, shaking his head, and looking sorrowfully at his commander.

"What is the matter, my friend?" said Andrea. "You have saved what is dearest to me in the world; my whole soul is full of gratitude. What appears to you so wonderful, so blamable in me, that you stare at me, shaking your head?"

The old steersman could only gradually bring out these

words: "Tears! in the eyes of the great Andrea Doria —tears!"

And the brave man, looking up to heaven, while still some large tears rolled from his glowing eyes on to his snow-white beard, said: "Yes, truly, many, very many things must have happened to make Andrea Doria, in his eighty-second year, learn to weep, after for half a century having sailed over and almost ruled the seas."

Chapter Twelfth.

THE Emperor Charles the Fifth sat on the strand, the waves of the sea gradually growing more peaceful in the first beams of morning; his earnest hero-eyes now directed to the desolation which the wide sea offered to the mournful commander, now to the sand-fields on the African coast.

Instead of a throne, he was now seated on a blood-sprinkled cuirass, which had been loosened from the body of some slaughtered man. Instead of a canopy, there floated over him some rent banners, which his faithful and noble attendants had zealously collected from the bloody field, in order to shelter his imperial head from the beams of the rising sun.

Of these brave attendants at least a third part had found their death on the field of battle. The rest stood round their emperor; the horses of those who still possessed any were ready bridled—yet men and horses were alike sunk into gloomy lassitude; the rich, but now torn mantles wildly floated in the wind, saturated with rain; the plumes of feathers, formerly so proudly waving, hung down from the helmets; the horses' heads were sunk sadly towards the ground, and on the ground was fixed the melancholy gaze of their riders.

The deep silence was interrupted by the emperor's chief cook, a hearty, merry, fat old man, born in the imperial city of Vienna—who came in this universal depression, as if to recall the image of some former feast-day; walking with the help of a broken spear, but yet announcing, with bright smiles; "Your imperial majesty, a morning meal is prepared—certainly only a spare one. An old faithful servant must implore the imperial majesty's extreme lenity for once for an extremely scanty meal. But little is better than nothing. Will it please your imperial majesty to eat?"

A peculiar smile passed over the features of the emperor; he signed to the master-cook that he should leave him.

But the faithful servant was not to be so easily dismissed.

"May your imperial majesty graciously pardon me," he began; "meat and drink keep body and soul together. That is a principle and maxim, to which the whole history of the world serves as an incontrovertible proof. Your imperial majesty is head and heart of this our powerful armada. Only let your imperial majesty properly eat and drink; then, no doubt, the whole affair will again be prosperous."

"Ah, yes," said the emperor, with sorrowful, conscious kindness; "that is the way with all men. If a thing will not move from its place, every one thinks that those means have not been tried which he knows best how to use—the soldier his arms, the husbandman his spade, the merchant his goods, the learned his pen, the cook his soup-ladle. And yet," he added thoughtfully, "that is for the most part the principle on which human undertakings are accomplished. Every one is properly satisfied with his own tools, and the whole is preserved. Now, good master cook, consider, if the sword cannot in every case accomplish every thing, so neither can the soup-ladle in every case accomplish every thing. If you could prepare a breakfast for all my poor soldiers, I would go to table as willingly as the happy prosperous householders in the imperial city of Vienna. But do not desire the householder, when he is travelling with his family in a foreign land, having lost all his money—whether by his own fault or not—do not desire him to take the only spare place at the well-spread table, while there is no room, not even a fallen crumb of bread, for his little ones. He cannot satisfy himself while the others hunger. You might say in return, good master cook, as you seem inclined to, Of what use will it be to the hungry family for their father to remain hungry? I do not know any logical way of answering you. But, good master cook, it is not so; the emperor cannot eat while his soldiers fast—go."

And the good servant went away, sorrowfully shrugging his shoulders. But he gave vent to his grief in a speech to his faithful companions, and many of the noble attendants and others who stood round the emperor Charles the Fifth did the same.

And thence gradually spread a stream of comfort and strength through all the squadrons, which perhaps could not have been dispensed by the richest distribution of bodily refreshments. Even before this, no tongue had murmured against this obstinacy of the emperor for undertaking this campaign at so unseasonable a time of year, nor against his firm perseverance in the enterprise after it was once begun. But now it seemed as though it were granted to the bright spirit of the knight Marbach, as a reward for his pious confession, to look down upon the noble spectacle of an army in such unspeakable outward misery, and within free from all murmurs and complaints.

Yet the less these brave soldiers blamed their great commander, the more the imperial commander blamed himself. Truly only his own great soul perceived the tragical mystery. Yet many sorrowful reflections of it might be seen on the countenances of those who watched him sitting motionless on that bloody cuirass, a waving canopy of torn banners hanging over him. Sometimes a swelling sigh burst from his noble heart, as though he longed for and ardently desired sympathy, in order thus to soften a part of his indwelling misery.

Then there came a noble attendant announcing to the emperor,

"Admiral Andrea Doria is come to land, and approaches, wishing to appear before the imperial majesty."

"Thank God!" was the only answer of the Emperor Charles.

As though loosened from a mighty load, he quickly sprang from his seat, eagerly going to meet the old man. Seizing his hand, and bowing his head before him, with tears in his eyes, he said, without any restraint, so that many might hear him, "Dear father, my disobedience to you brings me this heavy punishment."

Deeply moved, the old prince of the sea answered:— "My gracious emperor has already often honoured me with the name of father, permitting me to call him son; so it was when we were in the harbour of Majorca, and I warned you to desist from this at present too bold enterprise. But your answer was, 'Two and twenty years' power for me, and two and eighty years' life for you, is enough to content father and son, and make them satisfied to die.' Well now, my imperial son, let your noble words bear fruit for us both in this solemn hour. If we must perish on these barbarous shores, let this little word be the memorial of us both, 'Vixi.' Truly we have lived, and it shall not soil the memory of the Emperor Charles the Fifth, nor that of his Admiral Andrea Doria, if in this moment the last sleep comes over us. But let us work as long as it is day. And see, the Lord God has caused to rise over us the sun of a new day. What does my imperial master resolve on in this distress?"

But the emperor led the venerable old man away to his tent. There, without witness, turning to his fatherly counsellor and friend, he said, "Question against question, dear father. In how far is the embarkation of the remainder of the army still possible?"

"My imperial son and commander shall himself judge," said Andrea. "I will begin my dutiful report as clearly as my confusion, which has not yet subsided, will allow me. Of the twenty-two galleys equipt by me, eight at least are sunk; probably two more. I have the sorrowful certainty of the destruction of four other galleys. Of the ships, eight at least are sunk in the waves, or entirely wrecked on the strand. Of all the troops on board these vessels, not a hundred living souls are saved; therefore my imperial commander will not blame his sailors. For the fifty years that I have ploughed the salt waves, now as the friend of old ocean, now as his opponent, I have never witnessed such a tempest, either in the threatening flaming scourge of heaven above, or yet in the horrible storm of the sea beneath, as in the dreadful hours that have just past. But what is certainly a crime in the captains is, their running their ships into the port of Busia; thinking more of the preservation of their ships than the danger of the naval army, or even of the mightiest temporal prince in Christendom. Yet I have already sent after them some light sails to call them back with all earnestness to the fulfilment of their highest duty. What still remain of my galleys wait the imperial command, and shall be severed plank from plank before they retreat from this shore, until your imperial majesty, yourself on board, in the height and plenitude of your power, shall give signal to raise the anchor. And in my absence from the fleet, I have a pledge for the punctual obedience of the rest of the ships, in the presence of my nephew, Gianettino Doria."

"Gianettino!" exclaimed the emperor, with quick joyful sympathy; "he lives?—his German life-guard look anxiously for him. You have him again safe and sound?"

"God has returned him to me for the approaching Christmas joy, I think," said Andrea Doria, casting a beaming glance to heaven.

"And, father," said the emperor, "God's mercy has also restored to me a younger brother. Certainly, of such

Christmas joy I did not think as we sailed hither. It will be to me only the dearer, after returning from such threatening dangers. Scarcely the broad heaven could compass the idle hopes and vain magnificence with which I sailed here; and now in deep humility I have to praise God for restoring to me one innocent endangered head. Alas!" he added, with the deepest melancholy, "how many shall I have yet to mourn! How can we save the rest, dear father? What is our safest plan?"

"Would your imperial majesty come on board the ships?" asked Andrea.

"Not imperial majesty," returned Charles the Fifth, humbly raising his eyes. "Every thing is written above; yet we here below must counsel how it is to be done. What is the most considerable obstacle, admiral?"

"Next to the diminished number of transport-ships," said the admiral Andrea, "the worst will be want of provisions. Even if no threatening autumn-storm descends from heaven upon us, our provision will not last for the voyage home. A great part of the ships now become a booty for the sea were laden with food."

The emperor, after considering some moments, said with decision, "The horses must serve for food! All the rest of the horses of the whole army—slay them, cook them, and bring them on board in pieces. O dear father Andrea, this time offer no objection. A hundred and fifty of the noblest horses are landed for my stud— they shall be sacrificed first. Yet yesterday my beautiful white horse bore me so nobly from the battle—he shall be the first of my horses to suffer. When there is a hill to climb, it is well to have reached the summit. Good night, my beautiful true white steed! Good night!"

"Rather, good morning," said Andrea Doria, sadly. "Does not your imperial majesty see how the young day softly rises out of the waves?"

"Ah, yes. For eternity or for time? It will be proved, father Andrea Doria," said the emperor.

Chapter Thirteenth.

THE command was issued to kill all the horses of the army. Our young friend, the German trooper Walprecht, had led his beloved brown horse a little from the rest to sacrifice him behind a sand-hill, near to the now again mirror-like smooth surface of the sea. Here he stood by the side of his good horse, and spoke to him the following words: "What I have yet for you, good friend, is a bold well-aimed sword-thrust straight into your true brave heart, that your death may not be more painful than it need be. And, first, I have some fodder for you, comrade, though only a miserable piece of bread, wet through and through with rain."

And as the good animal joyfully received the long-needed nourishment, and sometimes laying his head gratefully, caressingly upon his rider's shoulder, the thought of what was impending, and drew nearer every moment, was almost too much for the faithful trooper's heart. "Good steed," said Walprecht, "if you could only understand that the wonderfully-beautiful white horse of the imperial majesty has not in the least a better fate—no, a great deal worse, for you die by your honourable rider's hand; yet the emperor has not time enough to kill his noble horse with his own knightly hand. And well—in the name of God, and according to the imperial majesty's express command—"

He placed himself a sword's length from his horse, and bared his good blade. But the noble steed, invigorated by the food, and thinking it was a mock-fight, which sometimes his merry master sought to teach him, reared up on his hind legs, and eagerly sprung forwards.

"Ah! do you think you are playing?" loudly exclaimed Walprecht; and with a sudden blow he plunged his sword into the horse's heart. He pranced higher, and then fell over with clashing violence, and lay, stiff, stretched, and motionless on the ground.

"Well fought, my poor frolicksome boy!" exclaimed the rider, bitterly. And weeping he sat down by his faithful companion, now looking at his bloody sword, now at his slaughtered horse.

Meantime there came from the strand, walking with quick steps, the great Andrea Doria: near him a noble Genoese, to whom the old man was eagerly imparting his commissions. "Now, I pray you, signor, repeat to me—but let us continue our way, we have no useless moment to spare—repeat to me the chief heads of my instructions."

The noble, with humble inclination of the head, began: "Every thing is to be made ready for the shipping of the land-troops. In your excellency's name the word of command immediately goes forth by call of trumpets to all the ships, that by their honour and duty, by the danger of their chief, no captain or pilot shall turn the keel from the shore before receiving a full and complete lading. If the storm which threatens to rise from the south-west break ever so heavily, it will not release any one from this holiest duty. But above all, that your excellency's remaining galleys give the firmest example, and that they should rather be dashed to pieces, and wrecked on the strand, than that one should put out to sea before the intelligence sounds through your trumpet, 'The emperor is on board.' And it is irrevocably determined that his majesty and his guard will not leave the shore until the last squadron is shipped. Your excellency remains attendant on the emperor's person."

"Just so, my brave signor," said Andrea; "and therefore quickly to boat, and to the admiral's ship."

Now as the quick-winged oars of the boat divided the waves, the old admiral exclaimed from the depths of his loving soul, "And a father's greeting and a father's blessing to my dear nephew, Gianettino Doria."

But as the name Gianettino Doria sounded through the

air, the trooper Walprecht raised himself from his seat near his bloody horse, and humbly presenting himself before Andrea, he said, "Forgive me, illustrious prince and admiral; is it only in the confusion of sorrow that you call for my noble young Signor Gianettino through winds and waves? Truly, after all that has happened here, the best, even his imperial majesty himself, need not be ashamed of being a little perplexed. Or is it possible"—the youth's strong voice faltered with little expectation—"that you have really good news of my young master? Bloody and wet with rain as I am, yet you can easily see that I belong to the German horse-guard of your illustrious nephew."

"Truly I see you are a brave fellow," returned old Andrea, kindly; "and very lately I have heard my nephew say, 'If I had not commanded my bold German troopers to the fortifications, but had kept them with me, they would never have deserted me in the greatest necessity; and who knows whether I had not yet been able to give the battle a favourable turn? No one should divide himself from his guard, when God has granted him so valuable a one as mine.' So spoke my bold nephew Gianettino."

"My noble prince," exclaimed Walprecht, "in the same words you give me joy and sorrow. Honourably has Prince Gianettino spoken of us; but he has been betrayed into danger far from us. For God's sake, Excellenza, does he live? Is he wounded? Is he bleeding to death?"

"He is on board my admiral's ship unwounded," answered Andrea. "God has wonderfully preserved him to you and to me during the past wild night."

"We praise thee, Lord God," said Walprecht, with deep emotion, bending one knee to the ground, his head and hands raised beseechingly towards heaven; yet soon turning to his slaughtered horse, he said, "Now, sleep in peace, good brown steed; when I killed you, in obedience to the imperial majesty's command, I thought the last thing I loved upon earth died with you. For Signor Gianettino I imagined was dead—he lives. Peace be with

you! Not that I shall not many times weep for you—
sometimes when, at evening, the world seems dull and
dreary. But if I must necessarily doom one of you two,
without being able to sacrifice my own blood for you, then
' Live, Signore Gianettino!' "

The venerable admiral remained standing listening,
pleased at this strange discourse of the trooper, and now
said kindly, " Let it be my care, brave German, that you
come to your young master in the next boat that leaves
the shore; he will have great joy in greeting you."

" I hope so, noble sir," answered Walprecht; " yet
especial joy if I may accompany him back to his great
uncle. Permit me, Excellenza, to call my comrades around
you. That is my service before the embarkation; then I
shall know my young lord and master again, and joyfully
appear before him. Only let me accompany you—do not
send me away, Excellenza. A good old man such as you
cannot be so harsh to such as me; and if you could, I
would not leave you any more than the lion did the footsteps of the Archduke Henry, following him like a faithful
dog, as the old song relates, from Palestine to Brunswick.
Resolve and take me willingly!"

" In God's name, dear youth!" said the doge Andrea
Doria; " very few men on the earth have pleased me, but
you are one of those."

Chapter Fourteenth.

IN the halls of the divan in Algiers, on richly-ornamented
cushions, after the Persian fashion, sat the terrible renegade Hassan Aga. Since his slumber on the platform of
the tower where his people had found him, and from which
they carefully waked him as from a fainting fit, he had
been more fearful of himself than of others—more fearful
his friends than his enemies.

With dull staring pride, his black eyes turned now upon himself, and now flashed in strange angry glances upon the warriors who surrounded him, as though he would say, "Who in this circle desires a bloody death? Let him venture to address me!"

But this threat appeared to be quite unnecessary; for on the sunken brows of all present nothing else was to be read than stupid fear, which, however much their inward rage might torment and vex them, still predominated. All were speechless. Hassan Aga also was silent—only sometimes his scorn-pressed lips opened through his monstrous beard with the angry question, "Is there no supplicating messenger from the Christian emperor before the gates?"

When a dumb denial was returned him for answer, he murmured, half audibly, "Yet he must—must—certainly must." And again he sank into fearful silence. He seemed like one vanquished, in whose soul raged the fury of the most hopeless despair.

Message after message came that the army of the Franks was preparing to embark. Many a vigorous Musselman's arm grasped the sabre; many glowing Musselmen's eyes were turned inquiringly to the high seat of their commander. But he either silently shook his head, or said, "They dare not move from their place. The Emperor Charles the Fifth must first crave permission. Before my throne he must first pray mercy for himself and the ruins of his army. Attend! here come the deputies—perhaps he himself."

After some such burst of arrogant pride, or the returns of short messages from the gate and halls, all was again silent.

At last a messenger announced that they had found without, on the rocky stone before the walls, the mangled corpse of the Moorish sorceress Baranaga—or rather, the crushed remains of it.

A shudder passed through the assembly.

But the renegade severely and coldly asked, "Who

T

has gone beyond the gates without my command? Who has unbarred the gates without my permission?"

"Sire," stammered the frightened messenger, "your friend and relation Mulu Abdul wished to make an excursion with twenty Arabs. The gate-keeper held that for a sufficient reason to unbar the gates."

The renegade motioned him to be silent. Turning to the guard of black slaves, who stood behind him with drawn sabres, he twice touched his neck with his hand, and said, " Mulu Abdul; the door-keeper."

And four blacks hastened out noiselessly. Then he turned to the messenger and said, "Come not before me again with such senseless news. And above all, come as seldom as possible. From this day your stupid head stands but insecurely on your slavish shoulders."

Trembling with fear the threatened man hastened from the saloon.

Then Hassan Aga, deeply breathing, said to the assembly: "Now my breast is lighter. Now I feel my old strength in me, which nothing can resist. For this Mulu Abdul was to me what none of you are—no, not ten of you together. Go, one of you. I may not see their two heads; but they shall be hung for a warning over the rashly unbarred gate. So now I am well again, and kindly as before. No one before me has cause to fear. Weak, enchanted dreams clouded my head in the night, and pressed into my heart—childish dreams of my past life. There stood before me a foolish Christian maiden, formerly beloved by me, who eagerly beckoned to me, as, in my dreams, I seized my sabre to begin a second attack upon her emperor. 'Maiden,' said I, contemptuously, in my dream, 'is, then, this old Frank emperor thy brother or thy lover?' Then she chanted an old Christian hymn, which I have often formerly heard sung in the Italian churches. Then it seemed as though gradually all the Christian voices in the whole earth, and under the earth, and over the earth, all joined in one wonderfully, and to me fearfully, loud-swelling chorus. If you, my good people, had not then awoke me, I should have died from that thundering harmony. But it has left me dizzy and confused. But ha!—no supplicating messenger from that proud Christian emperor?"

A deep silence within and without the hall gave answer in the negative.

Then the renegade again rising up in the wildest anger sprang from the cushions of his throne, as the enraged tiger from his lair, exclaiming, "Out, out! we ourselves will force an answer from the vanquished! But now it is too late for any attempt on their part. Too late for negotiations and prayers. Fire their ships; make their bodies drunk with their own hostile blood—out!"

A swelling cry of triumph from around answered the newly-awakened demon of anger; and now his companions again recognised him as their old commander.

Then, in wild certainty of triumph, out streamed the Saracen hordes—Moors, Turks, and Arabs—over the bazaar, in horrible thirst for slaughter, each one prepared to slay the conquered Christian warriors.

Hassan Aga, on a foaming red horse, sprang to their head, and pressed through the gates after his host, that he might feast his eyes on the conquered enemies, and order and arrange every thing for their entire destruction.

"Hurra! hurra! worms crawling beneath my feet," sometimes his followers heard him shout in angry triumph.

The wonderful Moorish battlements and defences of the dazzling gate Babazon opened before the enraged leader. The renegade wildly bowed over his horse's neck; and on both sides pressing the spurs before the saddle-girths, seemed as though he would dash through the gate as the storm-wind, when suddenly his red horse started and pranced into the air; and scarcely could the hardy rider save himself from falling from his saddle.

Astonished at so unusual a spectacle, his eager followers suddenly stopped his way. But Hassan Aga urged his horse forwards; he sprang up suddenly wildly prancing, so that it seemed horse and rider must have fallen one over the other if they went one inch further.

Then slowly and circumspectly the boldest of the whole band of Arabian horse—Emir Saïd—rode up to Aga, speaking softly—" Flower of Saracen chivalry! what storm-wind, or what inimical mist presses on your bold soul, that you have so entirely forgotten the beautiful and honourable art of horsemanship?"

Permitting his foaming steed to rest a moment, while the bewildered animal still snorted and dashed the ground with his forefeet, the renegade himself grown wild, answered: "Saïd Emir, is it of my horsemanship that you should complain, or of the sudden fury of the mad horse that bears me?"

"Sire," said the emir, "at first, certainly, your red horse started in a strange manner on his course, and then stood staring wildly round him. Then, as often as he obediently sprang forward, I clearly saw how you tore him back by the reins, then tugged him forward, and then again tore him back, so that your hands and feet have been in opposition; that is enough to drive the quietest horse to madness. Press both your spurs sharply, and loosen the reins, and may my head fall if the noble horse does now bear you away like a storm-cloud—a spirit of the air."

"Do you think so, emir?" said the renegade, with a strangely weakened voice—"do you think so? but I think differently. In my angry thirst for battle, I did not see at first what scared and terrified my steed; but when the war-horse started and pranced, then I looked, and my own soul grew mad and wild. Do you see nothing in the gate, Emir Saïd? Do you not see something which, with strange juggling tricks, bars this wide-opened gate? Now it looks like a spider weaving bloody threads, now like a horrible salamander woven and imprisoned within the spider-web. Hu! it is the detestable soul of the crushed sorceress, Baranaga. And look! in the brightly adorned angle of the arch of the gate, under the gallery-roof—there, where like moonlight gleams the pale Rosetta! Do you not see her beautiful, tender, pale, blooming rose-form beckoning to me, and calling—'Back! unfortunate one!—back! Every thing may yet be well with you! Unfortunate one! once so dear to me. Back! —oh, back!' Wise Arab Saïd, do you see and hear nothing of all this?"

In earnest denial, Saïd Emir shook his venerable head, yet added, with a solemn voice—"Though another may not see it, yet it cannot be said that it is not there. If such spirits are visible to you, Aga—above all, if they are distinct in the depths of your soul—act according to your knowledge and conscience. I cannot say yes or no."

And Hassan Aga turned his horse round towards the troops, and thundered—" Halt!" and his messengers speedily rushed to the gates, commanding, under pain of death, a quiet retreat; the gates were closed, and deathlike silence lay over the but even now warlike, rejoicing city of Algiers.

Chapter Fifteenth.

THE Emperor Charles the Fifth stood on the African sea-shore, watching, like a guardian-angel, the embarkation of his troops; in a solemn attitude, he leaned upon his drawn sword. At his side was the most trusted of his soul of all the Spanish princes, Don Alvaro de Sandez; behind him, ranged in a warlike half-circle, stood in health and vigour what yet remained of the troops of his noble guards.

Yet nearer the strand was the noble hero, Andrea Doria, surrounded by Gianettino's horse-guards, but now dismounted, carefully arranging them for the next embarkation, giving and receiving signals, and commanding them on board the boats.

With sorrowful steps, as is usual in time of retreat, the troops moved over the strand; and here, perhaps, among all the soldiers of the land-armada, there was not one who had not lost what was especially dear and precious to him on this blood and tear-drunken coast. From one or other indistinct sound there was raised a false alarm, that the enemy was breaking out of the city for a last attack on their retreat; and this produced, if not disorder, yet too great a haste, and too great a crowding together of squadrons on the shore. But the discretion of the commander and captains, supported by the bravery and firm discipline of the soldiers, prevented this threatening evil from an outbreak. The majestic presence of the emperor had a mighty effect on all.

Whoever glanced on that tall solemn heroic form, with golden-crowned helm and dazzling cross-sword, felt himself penetrated with all the majesty of war. Unconsciously he raised his head prouder and higher, fell into the step of the noble and solemn march, and eagerly grasped his weapons as though at some festive procession.

So the Italians passed over; and now the Germans began to move off. The Spaniards on the left wing, under their great Duke Alba, still turned a front towards the robber's nest, to guard against pursuit. But now, in the almost unclouded light of noon-day, there was no movement to be seen in Algiers; the Moorish city, but now re-echoing with violent shouts, lay as though entombed, or buried in enchanted slumber.

The Emperor Charles turned to Don Alvaro de Sandez, and smiling said, so as to be heard by those standing around: "One might scarcely trust these barbarians, except for their concise proverb—'Golden bridges to the flying enemy.' If, indeed," added he, with a prouder attitude, demeanour, and voice, " a warlike, honourable retreat, so forced by the elements, must be designated by the name of flight."

Now also the Spanish battalion began to move away. Only with one little remaining band, the great archduke stood marshalled on the extreme left wing, these brave men, holding their honourable posts, keeping watch to the last over the city of their destructive foes.

The retreating cavalcade of Spaniards came towards the emperor, who approached Don Alvaro, and in a low voice, only to be heard by him, said: "I cannot and would not hide it from you, noble Sandez. He alone who reads the heart knows how dear to me all the squadrons are that are entrusted to my sceptre; but the Spaniards are particularly dear to me. The Italian lives in a quick, witty, boldly crafty, bright existence, which sometimes wonderfully breaks loose, but often more wonderfully conceals itself in apparent lassitude and rest. They change according to their chameleon impulses; in each moment they are what they are thoroughly. They are rebels thoroughly, when once the evil spirit of mutiny penetrates their sharp, finely-formed soul. Look at these Germans! The sparks rest in the flint—the fire-work bursts out at the sound of steel; yet, though the stone may sparkle, stone remains ever stone, immovable, true, and firm. As men are able to soften and melt even the diamond — though by dragon's fire and dragon's blood — so these rocks of men faint with want of food, and become frantically mad with too much wine. Now, only look at our Spaniards! They are the soldiers of the soldiers! Earnest in enjoyment, joyfully strong in endurance; rendering obedience, because it is their pride to obey. With them one might conquer the world—if the elements did not oppose the mighty thought," added he, while his bold swelling voice sank again to an unconscious melancholy.

Then approached him the great Fernando Toledo, archduke of Alba, with a proud step, feeling himself stronger, now that the sacrificing of his noble horse had given him an opportunity of shewing that heroic power dwelt within his noble heart. Therefore, his commander's staff in his right hand, bowing in respectful salutation before the imperial majesty, he said: "It is time to announce to the mighty lord of two hemispheres, that the moment for the embarkation of the king's person is arrived."

Yet the emperor returned, earnestly: "Your announcement, archduke, is a mistake, and to me a very incomprehensible one; for I see some troops still standing firmly on the shore behind me, and truly they appear to me those under your especial command. Call them forward, and begin their embarkation; then the moment for mine will be declared to me—but from One above; not from the soul or lips of a subject."

He cast up sparkling to heaven those beautiful heroic eyes which had been sunk in melancholy.

The Archduke Alba answered, strangely yet heartily smiling: "Now may your imperial majesty yourself perceive how so many false and evil tongues—I know it— have slandered me to my noble prince, as a man of proud, lofty, irritable, and perhaps disobedient and obstinate nature. Some of these faults might have otherwise appeared, at an answer so little gracious, returned at this moment to my dutiful announcement; but God rules in heaven, and princes upon earth."

"God my master in heaven knows," said the emperor, kindly, "that my words would least of all offend my most faithful and most powerful commander on the earth, Archduke Alba; but it has been decided by me, and not without the advice of my subjects, that I do not leave this unhappy shore as long as one troop of my army remains here. With my bold body-guard, I must stay the last on this African shore—or stay for ever. The body as well as the soul belongs entirely to God."

"My emperor's noble soul is always elevated with high thoughts," said Archduke Alba. "Were thousands of your troops remaining, I must speak. Those who are the first in dignity, must also stand nobly to the last in threatening danger. Now but seven hundred of the chosen old Spaniards are with me; all the rest are on board. Let the imperial monarch allow me and my soldiers to be his rear-guard—we all desire it."

"The emperor must shew that he also is a true soldier," returned Charles the Fifth, kindly. "If, noble duke, you would not longer delay my embarkation, you will not lose a moment in leading your remaining troops to the ship."

Full of melancholy, the Archduke Alba bowed; and raising his staff of command, he beckoned to his brave troop—"Forwards, march!"

The brave files advanced; and Charles the Fifth murmured in their commander's ear: "I gratefully permit you, my noble Alba, to remain on shore when these brave men shall be embarked, until I lead you, with my noble guards, to the galley which shall bear me."

"My emperor knows how to pardon imperially," returned Archduke Alba, and humbly and gratefully kissed the monarch's hand.

At the same time the seven hundred Spaniards moved off with joyful steps, shouting loudly, but solemnly and earnestly, as if singing in chorus,—

> "Viva el nuestro emperador!
> Mueren por el sus soldados!"
>
> Long live our emperor!
> For him his soldiers die!

Chapter Sixteenth.

In clear sunshine, on the sea-waves, now agitated by favourable breezes, the imperial fleet sailed from the African shore. Charles the Fifth, as he had decreed, with his body-guard, and great Alba, and the noble Alvaro de Sandez, were the last to embark. The command of the imperial galley was, for the present, given to the Doge of Genoa, Admiral Andrea Doria; so that this boat was honoured with bearing more heroes than are often found together in so small a compass.

Three hours had their voyage lasted, and still the bright blue heaven beamed over the clear green sea.

"The firmament clothes itself in the colour of faith, and the sea in the colour of hope," said Don Alvaro, joyfully, to his thoughtful commander, who sat on the deck under a canopy of sails. "The elements are again reconciled to your majesty."

"Do you think so?" returned the Emperor Charles. "To me it does not appear so. But truly it may be a sort of bodily ailment, for I know nothing about it really, which persuades me that a fearful threatening storm lurks under this apparent peacefulness. When we have so lately felt the ground of the firm land of Africa melt and sink under our feet, it is no wonder that mortal nature does not place very firm trust in the changeable sea. But here comes one who understands it better, not only than either you or I, but than all living men, whether on land or sea. Admiral Doria, old ruler of the waters, what think you of the heaven and of the sea?"

Brightly, but with deep earnestness, the old Andrea returned: "If I am the ruler of the waters, my most gracious master, in the waves but lately I have found very rebellious subjects; and if all signs do not deceive me, in spite of their smooth surface, under their deep hollows they are now murmuring even worse conspiracies and insurrections than before. May it be that they have not such evil designs, and they are mounting up there only to gaze more clearly at the clouds, more animated by sorrow than presumption! If you have anticipated an approaching sea-storm, most gracious emperor, you are not deceived; and above all things, I rejoice that you have the old sailor

Andrea for your boatman and guide through the approaching tumult of winds and waves, which must burst out in less than half an hour. The signals have been given; every ship in the fleet has answered them; here on board every thing is prepared for a strife with the elements.[1] Now come what God will."

And soon the sea and heaven confirmed his prophetic warning. The waves, at first only audible to his listening sense, now howled in cries of death to every ear and heart. The clouds, at first playing as light, gentle messengers of joy, like white doves or silver lambs, now pressed closer and closer together, weaving a grey tapestry before the sun, who, instead of his golden arrows of joy, only darted blood-red spear-rays through the ever-blackening clouds; and the beautiful crystal-clear firmament was changed into threatening, sulphureous blue; and the peaceful green sea raised itself in more horrible, more foamy grave-crowns, and ever in madder frenzy bellowed its waves, and ever bolder whistled the icy wind. Now loudly crashed a grim, rattling thunderbolt; and as sometimes the threatening battle bursts out at the report of the artillery, so now broke out the war of the elements. Woe to the ships who met it!

Yet still the admiral Andrea Doria preserved his accustomed bearing, strong and firm.

"To the bay of Utika!" he thundered through the trumpet, and his voice sounded over the tossing of the sea and howling of the storm. "To the bay of Utika, those who have still command over their vessels! those who have not, if possible, to the open sea!"

"To the bay of Utika?" said the emperor, thoughtfully to himself. "How strange a command! Yet, if we go not there, we shall certainly be lost; and if we anchor in Utika——"

He was silent for a time, doubtfully shaking his head;

[1] "Guerra agli elementi!"—*war of the elements*—the Italian sailors are still accustomed to cry at the breaking-out of a storm.

then, with an earnest glance to the stormy and thundering heaven, he exclaimed aloud: "If Thou willest it, Thou Almighty One, and what Thou willest, we heartily submit to."

He loosened the buckle which clasped the golden crown of his steel helmet to his corslet and cuirass, laid his weapons down by the side of his ermine-covered seat, and breathing more freely, looked out with his large dark eyes into the still increasing storm.

Then suddenly, in eager haste, sounded Andrea Doria's cry: "Galley to the leeward! with all strength, quick to the leeward!"

And scarcely had the order gone forth when the fearful cause revealed itself: a large transport-ship, with its deck thickly covered with troops, driving sideways, without mast or rudder, must have run against the emperor's galley, if they had persisted in its course.

"It is they!" exclaimed the great archduke, who stood behind the emperor's seat, in such a voice of anguish as, perhaps, had never before proceeded from his firm noble bosom. "They are my seven hundred remaining Castilians! O my heroic squadron, must I see you perish, without sharing your destruction?"

"Destruction!" repeated the emperor, shuddering. "Must this faithful band perish? Admiral Doria!" he called out, "is there no deliverance to be hoped, Admiral Doria?"

But the old captain approached the emperor's seat, and bowing down, said, inaudibly to the others: "They are lost! the ship already begins to sink!"

In that fearful moment, the soldiers on board the sinking wreck, perceiving how near they were to the emperor's galley, shouted the war-cry, loudly swelling, as before, on the strand:

"Viva el nuestro emperador!
Mueren por el sus soldados!"

Then they brandished their weapons on high, and clashed them together as in joyful salutation.

Then the ruined ship, suddenly and quick as an arrow, sank down; and the noble band of those who had shouted vanished; and the mighty structure which bore them vanished; and the foamy waves rolled on without a trace.

The emperor covered his face with his purple mantle. Then again looking up to Andrea, he said: "Did you hear the parting shout of that band of heroes, Father Doria?"

"Yes, clearly," returned he, with firm determination. "Also I, and many other bold warriors, I hope, will one day part from life with the same salutation:

"Long live our emperor!
For him his soldiers die!"

But the Emperor Charles added sorrowfully, shaking his head: "It may also be rendered—

'*Through* him his soldiers die.'

And in this enterprise, so obstinately begun and persevered in by me, it certainly might so be said—yes, through me my soldiers die!"

Deeply sighing, he arose from his seat, took the crowned helm, which lay near him, held it for a time with both hands towards heaven, and then walking with quick step to the edge of the vessel, determinately threw the imperial ornament into the sea. Then he walked back and threw himself on his couch, pleased, as though after some wearisome but well-wrought work.

A low murmuring passed through the circle of lords and princes who surrounded him.

Meanwhile Andrea Doria, sorrowfully bending over him, said softly, in a tone of the tenderest reproach: "How now, my imperial son and master? despair in a spirit such as yours?"

But the emperor returned aloud: "Despair? no!

My trusting soul knows nothing of that. What I do now I may not declare at this moment to any one; but patience and trust; soon the time will come when it shall be declared to the whole world."

Chapter Seventeenth.

TRADITION tells of holy pledges, by the offering of which the rage of the storm is abated and the waves of the ocean are appeased. And so they now appeared to be satisfied when the crown of the Emperor Charles the Fifth had sunk into the sea; at least it became calmer around the galley which bore the emperor.

Some hours after, the great Andrea Doria, now rather to be called captain than admiral, anchored in the bay of Utika his nobly freighted vessel, and the disembarkation was accomplished without obstacle.

As the troops landed, the Emperor Charles sent them forward to the castle that for many years had been furnished with a Spanish garrison, there to rest and to refresh themselves. He had determined not to move from the shore until all of the ship-squadron that had escaped from this unfortunate voyage were landed.

The imperial guard hastened to seek some shelter for their master; they could find nothing better than a small, decayed, ruined Roman building, which though it scarcely diminished the howling storm, yet kept off on one side the pelting rain. The roof of that formerly hospitable little dwelling had long ago broken in over the carefully arranged, now jutting out, stones of the hearth. The Emperor Charles silently took his seat thereon; and before him, on the rubbish, leant his naked sword-blade, which in this place looked less like a weapon than a grave-cross. The emperor appeared to think so, as he sat with his eyes firmly fixed on it; only sometimes sorrowfully yet eagerly gazing out into the bay and sea, where floated the sails of the dismembered fleet like white sea-birds, some approaching the hospitable shore, others driven by the storms out into the trackless, measureless, hostile ocean.

On a projecting wall, next the door of the little house, the great Andrea Doria had found a resting-place. Near him stood leaning against the wall Archduke Alba, supporting himself by his mighty rapier like a cherub posted before some holy edifice, with shield-like protection: behind the emperor stood Don Alvaro de Sandez in a solemn, earnest attitude, as though he waited on his noble lord and master in the magnificent chambers of the palace.

Then a young Italian life-guard came before the entrance of the ruin, saying, with graceful inclination, "Will my invincible emperor please to remain a while in the narrow shelter which we have procured for him? There is a better being prepared at a farm not far distant, which, though not worthy of so noble a guest, is, however, more suitable than the mossy halls of this ancient and ruined abode."

The emperor returned with a bitter smile, shaking his head, "Invincible! that seems to me a name that is past. Ask Hassan Aga and the people of Algiers what they think of the title."

But the young Italian said gaily, "If it please your imperial majesty to discover the author of our late misfortune, it does not seem to me the right road would lead to Algiers; I should rather seek a sure direction and guide to the halls of Æolus, or the grotto of Neptune."

"Ah, young man," said the Emperor Charles, with a brighter countenance; "you Italians all bear some poetical nature with you: but perhaps you have quite devoted yourself to the beautiful lore of the Muses?"

"No, pardon me, gracious master," was the answer; "if I commune with the Muses, it is as the birds in the wood do—unconsciously, and less guided by my will than happy leisure."

"Those are not the worst sort of poets," said the emperor. "Your name?"

"Taddeo Guarini, at your imperial majesty's command."

"Guarini!" repeated the emperor; "a relation of the famous pastoral poet Guarini?"

"His art does not bloom in my soul," answered the youth; "but his kindred blood flows through my veins."

"It is a beautiful thing, this gift of the Muses," said the emperor, turning to Alvaro Sandez; " on so wild and desolate a shore, so far from all transplanted flowers, they yet wave and breathe their soft air around us." Then he said to the young Italian, "O Guarini, your kindred muse, the inventor of the pastoral Idyll, must have taught you that a Roman emperor could find no where better rest and shelter than in an old Roman hearth. Go, my brave youth, and tell your companions that the Emperor Charles the Fifth has found a resting-place."

Astonished, the young Italian went out, and the monarch spoke to the three faithful friends around him.

"Here in Utika, perhaps in this same hearth, Rome's last citizen, the great Cato, rested for the last time, when it was clear to him that a Divine Will had destroyed the right for which he had been striving his whole life. There was no place left him on this changeable earth. Now, when a Roman emperor comes to Utika, truly it is a mighty coincidence in the whole history of the world."

"1 do not understand my great emperor," said Alvaro Sandez, deeply moved.

"God keep such bad thoughts far from my noble master!" exclaimed Alba, eagerly.

Andrea Doria said peacefully but very solemnly, "The last citizen of Rome was a heathen; my afflicted emperor is, thank God, a Christian."

And the Emperor Charles enlivened, looked round and said, "It is a coincidence, a strange coincidence, however little my three brave companions may perceive it; and it will be clearly acknowledged in after-days. But listen now, you three dear faithful men, and faithfully bear witness of me,—the tempter shall never disturb my soul with heathenish thoughts of Cato's self-chosen death. But what you may have missed on me since the sea-storm, the crown-decked helm, is quite different: the helm is not my head. That divinely bestowed crown is very great, yet it is not my divinely bestowed soul, and does not affect it. Therefore when a Divine command, deep within, in the mysterious and the most holy haunts of my soul, where no glance can penetrate but the all-seeing eye of God, when the command is heard: 'Thou standest on the brink! The weight of the imperial crown will henceforth destroy thy eternal salvation!'"

He was silent; moved with a momentary shuddering, his eyes fixed as in questioning inquiry on the cross-form of his sword.

The three men around him were silent, as though petrified. And ever and anon the lessening storm cast its organ-notes over land and sea. Then in quick joyful steps approached the ruined edifice the young trooper Walprecht, from Gianettino's German life-guard. Quite regardless of the others, he came to Andrea Doria, who sate nearest to the entrance, announcing, in a soldier's manner, "Your noble nephew Doria is come to land, Excellenza; and see, one can count in the whole fifteen galleys now riding in the bay! The storm is abating fast; in an hour's time one might float the safest of the boats; in six hours time two or three others, and in twelve hours the whole number."

"Thanks, brave fellow!" said the noble old man, joyfully. "Your master's youthful vigour, imparted to me through your fresh spirit, refreshes me wonderfully."

"I do not quite understand you, Excellenza," answered Walprecht; "but, at any rate, I am glad you are merry, or joyful, or at least cheering up; for truly, what can a man do better than be cheerful? especially so long as the storm is not passed, and he will pass for a man; afterwards he may sit in a corner beating his arms together, and lament what has happened to him during the hustle; he then may weep a little, as I shall some time for my good brown horse; but as yet, nothing of this! hark how the weather-gods are still making music over our heads."

"Quite right, brave fellow!" said Andrea, despatching him with some message to Gianettino; and the bold German walked briskly away,.without being conscious of the presence of his emperor.

Then the Emperor Charles the Fifth rose solemnly from his seat on the hearth, saying, "Hark how the weather-gods are still making music over our heads! Did not the hearty German trooper say so?"

Andrea Doria assented.

"And," continued the emperor, "the youth also said, that as long as the storm is not over, it does not become any one to sit melancholy in a corner, beating his arms together, especially if he would be deemed a man. Yes, truly, Charles the Fifth has hitherto lived as a man, and in the last part of his life he will not cease to demean himself like a man. The storm still roars, not only here but in the political world, and Europe requires a crowned head in such a scene. Bold Alba, you look at me astonished; yet more astonished you may be hereafter. Do you wonder that the words of a common trooper should make such an impression in your emperor's soul? My friend, a bird flies over the empty desolate wilderness, and lets fall two little seeds out of his beak: in two hundred years a wood is grown that otherwise would not have been there. Or would you have it quicker? A scarcely visible ball of snow rolls down from the summit of the snow-mountain. Look three hours after: an overwhelming glacier forces brooks and streams out of their course, and destroys huts and cottages, leaving no trace behind. But nothing in the world moves and acts so quickly or so powerfully as the mind of man. Do not consider me vacillating — my determination is not changed; my Alba should have known me. But now the Gallic cock will jeer and banter without rest so soon as he hears of our misfortune. The first galley ready to sail, to Genoa, Father Andrea; from thence a quick messenger to Milan, to our stadtholder, Marques del Guasto! The next that puts to sea, to Carthagena, with letters to our royal infant Don Philip; another to Naples, which will take the vice-king on board in case he lives and is here; otherwise it will take you, Archduke Alba, and so will require no letter. The others must be quickly written, so up to the castle. And if there are no pens to write with — as certainly they are seldom supplied with such things — a strong finger must serve, which is also an instrument of the Eternal Lord."

Eagerly he caught up his sword that leant against the ruined wall, and what had appeared as a still and solemn grave-token, sparkled now in the emperor's hand like a meteor-flame that should shine over the world.

"God be praised!" exclaimed the Archduke Alba; "now is our great emperor himself again, and many enemies shall yet know it in many a noble fight. Yes, even those robber-hordes, who now rejoice in noise and riot in their heathenish feast, because the storms and sea have prevented my emperor's great purpose. We will one day return again to that renegade Hassan Aga, with revenging sword-flame, and plant the Christian banners of victory over the ruins of Algiers."

"What think you of it, Father Andrea?" asked the emperor, looking to Doria.

"As God wills," answered the grey-headed old man, turning his eyes to heaven. "The ways of the Lord are mysterious below; the purposes of the Most High are accomplished in a way we know not."

The emperor bent humbly; then he said, "My knightly Don Alvaro Sandez, what think you?"

"Your majesty knows that we have old heroic histories," returned the Castilian, "which now are begun to be laughed at, because much that is incomprehensible is mingled with true occurrences. Every one criticises them according to his pleasure; but to me there appears in all of them a spirit which is quite worthy of questioning; and also to the humble, earnest, pious questioner, many a clear beautiful answer is imparted. Among other such things, I have conceived that for every undertaking there is only one knight appointed for the victor, while all others, however bold they may otherwise be, in that enterprise are overcome, and must be overcome. Algiers seems to me such an adventure, and your majesty not the chosen knight for it."

"You speak truly, dear Sandez," said the emperor; "I feel it echoed in the depth of my life and being; and truly if I ever was the knight chosen to take Algiers, I am so no longer. My too-great confidence in my own power and pride that God has granted me the direction of so many warlike people, has been taught me by my Eternal Master in a voice of thunder. In after-days He will raise a bolder knight for this taking of Algiers, who will have more trust in God than in his own strength. For the victory must at last be accomplished to the glory and prosperity of Christians, who are now so shamefully oppressed there."

"Amen," said Father Andrea.

And the emperor, with his three followers, walked towards the Castle of Utika.

What afterwards happened belongs not to this story, but to the history of the world.

Head-Master Rhenfried.

"SHUT the door, Margery, my dear," said her old grandfather, "and bolt it too very carefully. Our young gentlemen-students are about to jubilate in the streets tonight, as our neighbour Schwertfeger informs me; and it may be better for quiet people who occupy

the ground-floor, like us, to be something upon our guard. Meanwhile I will look to the window-shutters; it is already getting quite dark, and it is high time to light a candle."

"But how will our old lodger find his way in, then, grandfather?" said the little maiden; "you know he is still out among the pine-trees, and wandering about the old heathen monuments and tombs."

"Let him rummage there as long as he pleases, child; we cannot hinder him. And he may please, likewise, to wait awhile before the door when he comes; for, to say the truth, I do not like his ways at all; and I am sorry that I ever promised the professor, on taking the house, not to turn the strange lodger out of doors."

"Oh, grandfather! it was surely hard enough upon poor Mr. Professor to be obliged to leave his nice family house, all owing to his wicked creditors; and it vexes me to think of it. For Mr. Professor always looks so kind and pleasant, and not so old as the other professors; then he can tell so many fine stories of by-gone times, which, though they almost make one's hair stand on end, are very pretty to hear. And as to the strange lodger, he is perhaps much better in his heart than he sometimes appears to me."

"May be so, child; but I wish I had stayed in my own little house. Whenever I go past it, I feel a kind of sinking at my heart; it was much pleasanter there."

"Yet I think you used to complain and groan more there than you do here, grandfather."

"How can you make that out, Margery? You know I only removed just to please good Mr. Professor. I wish from my heart he had continued to live here instead of us; at all events, he would have paid no house-rent: yet he would not listen to the idea for a moment. But now, my dear, let us think of the door! see that it is made quite fast!"

Little Margery did as her grandfather bade her; she turned the key three times in the lock, slipped the bolts as far as they would go; and then both seated themselves, with a feeling of quiet and security, snugly round their little hearth.

"Shall I go on reading where I left off, grandpapa?" said the pretty child with a smile. The good-natured old man nodded assent, at the same time taking out of his portfolio his lead-pencil, paper, and ruler, at his accustomed hour, in order to draw designs, which he afterwards exhibited for the instruction of the young artisans, as headmaster of the joiners' trade.

Margery having by this time seated herself opposite to him, began to turn over the leaves of a huge richly bound folio in parchment, and proceeded to read as follows:

"And it likewise once happened in the famed city of the sea, at Venice, that a gondolier, whose occupation there is to row backwards and forwards in boats, hung with black, upon the canals, had taken into his service a stranger, for his rower, of uncommon size and strength. Neither the gondolier, nor any one else, could learn whence the lusty varlet had last come, nor where was his native place. Some there were, more deeply read, who observing that this huge hireling was deprived of the use of speech, though he could drink well, and hail passengers politely enough, imagined that he must be some great animal metamorphosed through the wondrous power of some sorcerer into the human shape; and that from his strength and docility he was most likely formed out of an elephant.

"Be that, however, as it may, the gondolier was well satisfied with his journeyman, who, if he devoured a good deal of food, also went through as much labour; and he troubled his head very little with inquiring into his descent and country, leaving all such conjectures to the solution of the learned.

"In this proceeding, however, he could not be justified, as no Christian master and householder ought to engage any servants, whose faith, good character, and conduct, are not sufficiently known to him, since he must remain accountable both to God and man for the demeanour of such domestics, or other hired persons."

Here the old man sighed deeply, and leaned down his head, white with age, upon his hand. Margery stopped, and looked at him with surprise. He then recovered himself, and forcing a smile observed, "Well, my love, read on: I want nothing. I was only thinking how much better it had been, if—but go on, Margery, my dear." And Margery thus proceeded:

"About the same period there happened to pass that way a famous necromancer, who applied to the said gondolier for three able-bodied boatmen, in order to make a long and quick passage by night. The gondolier thought he was rendering him a great service by letting him have his dumb rower for one of the hands, which he calculated at the rate of five others. This he seemed to shew by the speed with which his gondola began to skim the waves. But just at midnight there was heard, from the vicinity of the route it was then going, a most hideous uproar, in which the voice of the great sorcerer was most loud, and resounded far over the waters. A few of the boldest young men hastened with torches and arms towards the spot. Soon they saw the form of the huge rower conspicuous on the deck, engaged in sinking his own vessel, and stamping it deeper and deeper into the waves below; at the same time he seemed to be playing at ball with the sorcerer, and at a single blow struck off his head, after which boat and boatman both sank together into the deep.

"On the following morning the shattered limbs of the necromancer were found scattered in different places, washed up by the waves. What appeared still more remarkable was, the discovery of a dead elephant lying, apparently drowned, upon the sea-shore, a few miles distant from the city. But whence the strange monster could have been brought, or by what means, no one knew.

"It was surmised, however, by many, that the same necromancer had, by his infernal art, metamorphosed the huge animal into the human form, and employed it in this way, at Venice, for the purpose of effecting some of his diabolical schemes;— that at this time he must, for once, have miscalculated the exact hour and planet under which he was operating; and had, unluckily for himself, been deceived by the evil spirits with whom he was tampering, so that, in ascending the gondola, he did not even recognise the enchanted beast, as oftentimes, indeed, happens to such practitioners in the black arts before attaining their end. Others, again, wished to infer that the magician had only assumed the strange ancient-looking form in which he appeared, and was in reality a very handsome young man, deeply smitten with a passion for the lovely consort of the doge;— that, moreover, he had sent the huge elephantine rower before him, in order to assist in the abduction of the noble duchess, or, at all events, to stir up some wild insurrection in the city and in the state-council of the Republic favourable to his views. As it has been stated, however, he, in this instance, fell a victim to his own want of foresight in directing the potency of his own fatal arts.

"Hence we may learn" . . . . .

Just at these words Margery was interrupted by a tremendous uproar in the street. She cast an anxious glance towards the windows, and at length whispered, "Ah, grandfather, I fear the young gentlemen students are even more wild than usual to-night!"

"It is only according to custom," said the old man with a smile; "and birds of a feather will flock together, as the saying goes. So give no more heed to it, love, than to the blustering of a storm towards spring, and go on quietly with the book."

Margery was once more applying herself with all diligence to the exact line and word, when suddenly there came three such thundering blows against the window-shutters, that the fine old vellum book slipped out of her hand, and she hid her face in the cushion of the arm-chair, which rattled, along with all the furniture in the room.

But not so the worthy head-master; for hastening close under the window, he exclaimed, in the same strong clear tone in which he gave the word of command when serving *à la militaire* in his youth, " Who has the boldness to disturb a free citizen in his own house? Let the wanton young blade give his name from the outside, and we shall soon see if he be as valiant as he would make us believe. As to this house, let him know it is the residence of Head-Master Rhenfried—Philibert Rhenfried, President of the Honourable Joiners' Company, belonging to this town and country. What say ye?"

A low anxious wailing was heard on the outside, very strongly distinguished through all the violent mirth and uproar of the collegians, and gradually dying away along with the same in the distance.

" What was that?" inquired both the grandfather and the child at the same moment, with a look of surprise.

The students meanwhile made a fresh movement, and formed in a grand square in the mark. Torches were seen waving in the air, mingled with no few cudgels; and it is said that a number were observed to be sharpening their hangers upon the stones. Apparently they had pronounced their *pereat* upon many an unlucky professor's pate; and in particular upon his who had so greatly won little Margaret's regard. For though he was accustomed to banter in a friendly way with some of these wild spirits of the gown, he was very severe and unrelenting in cases of excessive wickedness and extravagance on their part, insomuch that they hardly knew how to deal with him. However, they were in hopes, at least, of terrifying him out of the vexatious censorship which he had assumed; and they were the more emboldened by the efforts of a new collegian, named Marcellin, who had been residing during some weeks, while on a tour, in the town, and ingratiated himself extremely with the whole fraternity by his superior courage and dexterity. Though a good deal older than the usual run of them, he it was who schemed and executed the most mad and juvenile tricks, while at the same time he won equal admiration by his superior abilities and acquirements. He had also conceived a great dislike to poor Margery's favourite, the Professor Nordenholm; hated to hear him named; could never be prevailed upon to call on him as on the other professors; and felt infinitely delighted at the idea of beholding the rod, which was now hanging over him *in terrorem*, descend upon his professional shoulders.

Their whole force marched forthwith, until they formed a junction before the said Nordenholm's house; and there they set up a shout for Marcellin. Marcellin! echoed from a hundred voices; but it was in vain—no Marcellin made his appearance.

At length he was seen sinking quite pale and breathless, with difficulty supporting himself upon his sword-stick, out of the crowd about him. Some of the senior natives approached him with looks of eager and terrific inquiry, while the light of their torches glared strangely upon his livid and distorted features. "What!" cried he, scornfully, as they gathered round him, "do you think this either wellbred or right to dog me in so scandalous a style to the very steps of a strange old master-joiner, one whom I may not so much as call by name; and would you delude me by maintaining that this is the family house of the hated Professor Nordenholm?"

"Of a truth," replied one of the students, in no goodhumoured tone, "the head-master resides in Nordenholm's family house; but who, as you so outrageously insist, has offered to dog your steps thither? and, moreover, how happen you to know any thing respecting Nordenholm's residence? you who detested to hear him named, and gave yourself no sort of concern about him! all this appears to me somewhat strange."

Marcellin's pride took alarm; but at the word 'strange,'

he seemed greatly confused, and replied in a hurried, unconnected manner. This only plunged both parties deeper into the brawl; and shortly, in his excessive choler, he challenged two of the natives to meet him with sword and pistols on the ensuing morning.

After fierce words on both sides, they separated, and went in different directions, without attempting to resume any of their former schemes, and without a single *pereat* executed on any professional head.

Nordenholm watched their retreat through his half-closed windows, barricadoed with huge tomes, and burst into bitter laughter as he recalled to mind a similar convulsion, which was, years before, followed by the loss of his sweetest earthly enjoyments.

Meanwhile the head-master and Margaret had ceased to read, and were sitting nearer each other, quite still and contemplative.

" No, read no more to-night, child," said the old man, " the evening seems to have set in so strangely ; and then the history you began to read was so very extraordinary, who knows but still more wild and incredible accounts may follow it; better bring your spinning-wheel to the table, and then if you should happen to call to mind one of your prettiest ditties, sing it for me, my dear."

Margery smiled and nodded her head, at the same time beginning to spin in right earnest ; but no pretty song rose up in her trembling little heart. She seemed rather to anticipate, from her looks, though the streets were again quiet, that there was yet something strangely unusual and dismal in the approaching night ; and this weighed heavier and heavier on her mind. Nor were her forebodings without reason ; for just then they heard heavy footsteps pacing backwards and forwards in the room above them, the same which was occupied by the old lodger, who had not yet returned home, and of which he always carried the key about him, being extremely jealous of any one entering it in his absence. At times, too, they thought they heard a fearful sobbing and sighing, almost like that of a man dying of great pain. Margaret raised up her hands, as if directing her grandfather to the spot, but said not a word; while he went and took down his old broadsword hanging on the wall, then prayed a few moments within himself, and lastly went towards the door.

"Dearest grandfather, my own best grandpapa," whispered Margaret, "take me with you, then! for whatever terrible there may be, it cannot be half so agonising as I should imagine, were I to be left here in the little study by myself—all alone, with such dreadful thoughts. Oh yes, you must take me along with you!"

And after a few moments, while the old man had been engaged in trimming the lamp for his lantern, and putting out the candle which they were before burning, he motioned to the timid girl to accompany him, and lighted her on the way. But she clung fast to him; and they began to ascend the stairs together. As they proceeded up the narrow stone steps, and along the creaking landing, they continued to hear more plainly the same strange moaning and whimpering from the lodger's chamber. They were now standing before the door, and could perceive there was a light burning within, apparent through the key-hole. "In God's name," cried old Master Rhenfried, "what kind of being is within there, and in what manner engaged?"

The door flew suddenly open—wide open; and "Huzzah! hulloh! who disturbs, who affrights me?" was repeated from a voice within, so horribly wild and mad, that Master Rhenfried involuntarily stepped back, and the child fell upon her knees behind him muttering her prayers.

In the middle of the chamber stood arrayed in a blood-red mantle the strange lodger, and he trembled greatly. After a short pause, he said in a low, hollow voice, "See! take your rent for one half-year. It is upon the table; there, take it away, for it fell due the week before."

"I shall not receive it to-day for all that," replied the

old master, with a firmly recovered and determined tone of voice; "but I both will and must know what it is that so dreadfully agitates you, and by what means you gained access into my fast-locked and bolted dwelling!"

"What I moan and what I sigh for?" half-sobbed and laughed the offended lodger. "Eh! surely the spirits that haunt the gallows have a right to do that; and why not he who regularly and orderly pays for his own lodging? How did I gain access here, you say?—Eh! what kind of questions are these?—why, the house-door was standing wide open when I came; upon my honour I can assure you of this."

"For all that," said Master Rhenfried, "I have earnestly to entreat of you to leave these lodgings to-morrow morning; for truly I am not accustomed to live with people whose doors fly off their hinges when they just approach them; I will never live with them any more."

"But I do not happen to be of the same opinion," said the strange lodger, in a contemptuous tone; "I laugh at the idea of going out; you know you are bound over to the former landlord to suffer me to remain. So there is your rent; pick it up; it is all there."

The old master, glancing sideways at the glittering gold, observed, "Hand to hand; I can receive nothing more from you; I see you have brought such curious old doubloons, all marked Venice, and I know not what date they may bear. I believe, too, I have said before-time that I am no exchange-broker, and have no dealings in strange obsolete coins, though I were to gain ten times the amount by them."

"Here, however," cried the lodger, laughing, "are no Venetian doubloons. They are old Saxon gold coins, which your forefathers have been acquainted with these thousand years. And if you sottish folk no longer prize them, yet the former master here, the wonderfully wise Nordenholm, may surely contrive to exchange them. Now pray leave me alone, or take what is due to you!"

And as old Master Rhenfried was turning reluctantly away, the strange lodger slammed-to the door with such violence as to blow out their light. Slow and sad did the grandfather and daughter descend the stairs, and along the landing which sounded dismally to their footsteps, until they again reached the snug little study, and felt as if a burden were suddenly removed from their mind. They lighted and trimmed their lamp, and Master Rhenfried shouted aloud for the maid-servant, to go instantly with a message for Professor Nordenholm, entreating him to come thither without loss of time. Should he be gone to rest, he must nevertheless get up, and hasten as fast as possible, to converse on some very important business.

In a short while the professor made his appearance, pale and terrified. "You have sent for me on account of the lodger, have you not?" he inquired in a low voice: "well, I might have guessed how it would be! but let our pretty little Margaret go to bed. I have much strange matter for your private ear, and our conference may be prolonged far beyond midnight."

The head-master expressed his assent, and bade the servant go along with Margaret, and both retire to rest. Margery looked a little anxiously round her, but observing that her good old grandfather, as well as the professor, was going to keep watch, she thought it would be better to try and forget her fears in sleep; so, without a word, she bade them both a sweet good night. Soon she fell into a soft slumber, and lost all recollection of the fearful occurrences of that dismal night; they had no longer power over her gentle spirit, for the smile that played upon her lips betokened innocent and angelic rest.

Meanwhile the professor and Master Rhenfried were in earnest communion together, seated near one another at the little round table. After a long pause, the former in a low and fearful tone thus resumed the discourse:—"I ought in the outset, my dear Rhenfried, to remind you of a great calamity which happened to you, though I am also aware, that so singular a period of your excellent life should, if possible, be wrapped in an impenetrable veil of oblivion; but it is all of no use now. I loved your lost daughter, who disappeared ten years ago; and if she did not return my affection, there was a time when she seemed to receive it with a degree of sweet complacency and friendship. The cause of the beloved girl's loss, so inexpressibly distressing to my feelings, remains still as unaccountable to me as I suppose it does to you."

The old man made a sign for him to say no more, and seemed to be absorbed in deep meditation within himself. At length he said, "No! that dreadful occurrence is not such a complete mystery as you seem to think, though more severely felt, my dear sir, than any similar affliction that perhaps ever befel me. Yet, when I take all into consideration—your known integrity, your present sincerity, your kind attachment to my granddaughter, and the confidence she seems to feel in you—I feel I can no longer withhold mine; I feel that you fully merit it, and I will state every circumstance I know relating to the fate of my poor unfortunate girl.

"It may now be rather more than twelve years ago when there came to my house, where till then I had resided so quietly and pleasantly with my little girls;—there came, I say, one day, a handsome young man, who expressed a wish to see my workshop; and after examining my models, &c. very attentively, he began to talk about an apprenticeship. As you may imagine, I at first treated the matter as mere jest, and then rejected it as a piece of uncalled-for mockery on his part, warmly entreating him not to think of amusing himself at my expense. Still the young gentleman insisted he intended neither jest nor insult: he was much attached to turning and joiners' work of all kinds, and he had resolved to become thoroughly acquainted with it in all its branches, under the care and tuition of a skilful master. He hoped he had succeeded in finding an instructor, and he was resolved, with my permission, never to relinquish his design, until he had made himself fairly master of all that it was in my power to teach. Like a madman as I was, I gave my consent, though I knew literally nothing either as to who he was, or whence he came; nor even whether he had any testimonials with him. I shewed him every thing in my shop; drew up an agreement, as if the devil possessed me, and called him, at his own request, by the name of Ludibert Wendelstern."

"Ludibert!" said Nordenholm mournfully, — "alas, there is a Ludibert occurs, likewise, in my own history. But go on, go on, dear master! Was he, then, the man who deprived you of your angelic daughter?"

"He — he! no other on earth!" replied the old man, his face growing darker and darker as he spoke. "Right well did the cunning deceiver know how to apply himsel. to my noble art; never had I an apprentice half so skilful, for he possessed fine talents, and in more branches thar ɔne. He could play the flute beautifully, and could sing as well; while with his rapier he was a perfect master."

Nordenholm earnestly signified his assent; and the olɑ man continued, without noticing it.

"During our leisure hours he amused himself with instructing the rest of the apprentices and their companions in the noble science of defence; and having myself been a soldier, fond of the sword-exercise, it afforded me no slight pleasure to witness their feats with the foil. On all occasions the young master exhibited the greatest politeness and good breeding in his conduct, and daily established himself more firmly in my good graces. This continued for the space of two years; when suddenly the scales fell from my deluded eyes, and I stood lost in astonishment and dismay. The young students had engaged in a similar piece of work to that we have witnessed this evening; and one of those who returned no more that night to supper, and was never afterwards seen, was Ludibert Wendelstern. On the ensuing morning I found a paper lying in my daughter Agnes' chamber; but she was gone—gone for ever."

The old man here rose, and unlocking a small cupboard, took out two letters, which he handed to the professor, who, recognising the hand of his beloved Agnes, began to read, though almost blinded by the tears that came into his eyes.

"A happy destiny calls me away from you, my dear father; but I know you would never have yielded me your consent. Farewell, then, and take comfort; for I feel quite assured we shall soon meet again, when you will congratulate me a thousand, thousand times on the happiness which will soon be mine."

"That," said the old master, "was indeed a poor prophecy," and he drew his hand across his eyes, as if in pain: "she was far too confident, and that ever brings failure and disappointment along with it for wretched mortals such as we are. There is only one thing certain;—but that is quite certain; wherefore the Lord be praised."

He took his cap from his reverend white head, held it between his folded hands, and prayed within himself. Afterwards he continued, with more cheerful resignation:—
"During four years I could learn nothing respecting her; but at the expiration of that period, one fine morning, an infant of about four years old was found wrapped delicately up, and laid at my door. It was Margaret; and the following note was attached to its arm, which I will endeavour to read to you:—

"I have been lawfully united at the altar with my beloved Ludibert; and the sweet pledge of our affection, which I herewith commit to your care, was born in honourable wedlock. If you would not wish to curse and to kill me, I beseech you to preserve the dear infant for me, until I come to claim her; till when her existence must remain a mystery. My noble consort maintains me in great wealth and splendour; yet, oh, best and dearest fa-·

ther, you cannot believe what abundance of wishful tears I shed—what sighs I pour, once more to cross our sweet home's threshold; and which I am fondly trusting soon to do. Oh, think often of your absent, but faithful, fondly-loving

AGNES."

" In the basket that contained the child was a large sum of gold and silver, with precious stones. This, however, I deposited as the donation of some stranger for the use of St. Ursula's hospital. But I deliberated not a moment in announcing that the young child was my granddaughter, the offspring of the marriage of my daughter with the stranger. And now, God be praised, our good city is pleased to give full credit to any assertion from the lips of head-master Philibert Rhenfried: so far my good name helped me; and I troubled myself no farther with any needless inquiries. I have brought up her little girl to the best of my knowledge of what is good and right; and so, by Heaven's mercy, she has gone on improving, doubtless, under its wise dispensations, to the fulfilment of God's purposes on earth."

Nordenholm here pressed the old man's hand, and leaning down his head, wept bitterly. After a long sad pause he then said: "Alas, my good master, I see how much you suffer; but your sufferings are not barbed with the stings of guilt, therefore do you bear them freely and boldly. But woe, alas! I feel no sweet confidence in the same freedom. I have my misgivings, though I have nothing dreadful to reproach myself with. There is something weighs at my heart, which seems to grow heavier and heavier as the night proceeds.

" The cause of this first arose on occasion of the forementioned festival, when I was young and happy,—alas, doubly happy! for I then flattered myself with delightful hopes of winning your daughter's love,—and came along with other students to enjoy ourselves here.

" After our rounds, we held jubilee in a grand decorated hall, where we were joined by a mask arrayed in very splendid apparel. We had once, and only once, before observed the same man make his appearance, and concluded that he was one of our merry company who had some especial piece of mirth in view. This time the unknown made his obeisance, and, with very humble voice, petitioned for leave to propose a question for the consideration of our society. Receiving our unanimous consent, he began:—' It is a question of honour and of duty; whether a lover have a right to carry off his beloved, when he is persuaded that he can maintain her in all due and lawful honour and worthiness; and is equally persuaded that her happiness and his own can be accomplished by no other means.' He paused; and the voices on both sides rose loud on the ear; though the greater part was in favour of a mad assent to such a proposition, many of the students being pretty well heated with wine, and full of adventurous spirit, eager for exploits. I, even I! good master, joined in the wild and wicked votes that carried the question; but it was the first truly blamable act of my life. Even now, within this last half-hour, I have heard from your own lips how very lamentably I may have assisted, by such a vote, by supporting such a proposal, in striking at my own sweetest hopes of happiness on earth."

He hid his face in his hands and was silent. The old master laid his hand gently upon his bowed head, and while he pronounced his forgiveness, also gave his blessing: his repentance was enough. Nordenholm then rose with renewed hope and strength, and thus continued:—

"It seemed, at the same moment, as if I was carried away by a strange impulse of wilful rioting and folly, quite foreign to my usual calm and moderate feelings of enjoyment on such occasions. It appeared as if I no longer recognised myself; I wished to be foremost in the mad career we were pursuing, every where ambitious to give a spur to the follies of the hour; and in all companies striving to lead the revels, in singing, dancing, drinking, or rioting. Shortly I heard reports that the stranger was exerting himself very strenuously among our colleagues to obtain some of the most bold and adventurous hands for the purpose of carrying into effect the identical exploit which had gained our unanimous applause; and that he spared no powers of oratory, no influence, to gain his point. My rude and boisterous mirth seemed to offend his more genteel and delicate bearing; and soon we had words together. Then he tore the mask from his face, and we beheld a perfectly strange, but beautiful youth, with a smile of scorn upon his features, which could not, however, impair their noble symmetry and lively expression. 'My name is Ludibert,' he cried, approaching me nearer; 'for that of my family, it is noble, princely; but I shall not mention it to you. Enough that I now cite you to appear and decide our difference in honourable combat; enough that I so far condescend.'

"The proposal was as quickly accepted; every thing was prepared; I met him with perfect ease and confidence, for I was the unrivalled master of our ring; and stripped to our shirts, with single rapiers, we set to. Almost at the first pass, I was overpowered by the irresistible vigour of my rival's arm: I could not even stand my guard; but was instantly struck senseless and bleeding to the ground, a part of his weapon sticking in my breast.

"Many weeks afterwards, on my return of consciousness, my first inquiries were respecting Agnes; and the tale of her abduction then saluted my ears. I could learn nothing of the time and place; while my ideas on the subject were so mingled with the occurrences of that dreadful night, that I could only feel remorse for the mad disposition which I had indulged, and confess myself unworthy of the happiness that once appeared in store for me.

"But alas, good sir, my cup was not yet full. There was a favourite subject I don't much like to mention, which I once pursued for the sake of poetical embellishment—the research after strange old charms and other magical influences; and this my despair respecting the fate of Agnes now led me to employ, for the purpose of discovering whither the beloved girl had disappeared. Ah, my worthy master, fix not your eyes so sternly, so reproachfully, upon me, much less turn away your sympathy from my sorrows; for know, God be praised, I have never either denied or misapplied what is holy by any instigation or pursuit of mine." At the same time he stretched out his right hand in token of such assurance, which the good master with a look of compassion accepted, and motioned to him to proceed; as he did in the following words:—

"I knew that it had been conceived possible, through a fit conjunction of times and circumstances, so to fabricate a magical mirror, that it shall retain the moon's beams in such a manner as to exhibit, by secret reflection on the surface, every thing that passes on the earth's sphere in succession, according as such magic mirror shall be directed and applied. This wonderful piece of mechanism I succeeded, with infinite labour and great expense, in procuring: and once in the garden of this your, but formerly my, house, I began, when the moon was shining clear in the heavens and at the full, about the eleventh hour of night, to try my secret experiment. That my own apparition would be seen, in case my image fell upon my glass, seen even from the farthest corner of the earth, I was well aware; but my whole soul was so intent upon learning the fate and residence of Agnes, that I could dwell upon nothing else.

"It now seemed as if some assistant being were directing my hand in the motions of the mirror, which fortunately had been placed aright. At first only small strange forms cast their reflections over the surface of the mirror; when at length, in the direction of the south, there arose one so enchantingly sweet and lovely before my eyes!— Oh my good master! father! she sat looking so beautiful and angelic amidst the soft bower" . . . .

"I see your eyes sparkle with delight!" interrupted

the old man, in a tone of displeasure; "you ought rather to take shame and sorrow to yourself for having dared to dabble in any forbidden species of witchcraft, than to display the least feeling of exultation. Let me hear you describe what follows with a becoming degree of seriousness and regret;—what farther appeared?"

With the humility of a repentant offender, the professor cast his eyes upon the ground, and in a lower tone said, "It was indeed Agnes! she was handsomely attired, and was seen sitting beside Ludibert, who was reading to her, and conversing with her in an earnest manner. I concealed my features cautiously, at a distance, to prevent them from falling upon the mirror. Next, you yourself, sir, suddenly appeared in the garden; and on the mirror's surface the pale and sorrowful cast of your features was plainly visible. Seized with alarm, lest you too should catch sight of Agnes, I ran to the glass, beheld my own distorted features reflected there; and bursting into a thousand fragments, the wonderful instrument fell from my trembling grasp."

"I know it all, as well as if it happened to-day," said the white-headed Rhenfried; "yet amidst all the images that floated before my eyes I could distinguish no one; clouds of heart-sprung tears concealed them from view. For at that time I had not fully resigned myself to the will of God: I lay weeping upon my bed, but suddenly I heard a light whispering, as if it had said in my ear, 'Rise, unhappy father; in Nordenholm's house it is known what is become of thy daughter.' I obeyed, and doubtless it was no good spirit, which had so whispered to me in my chamber. Then when I came and found you labouring under such excessive terror, you know well that I retired without speaking a single word, and never more alluded to the appalling and mysterious subject. Long afterwards, however, a heavy weight seemed to oppress my soul; from which you may learn, my poor deluded friend, how very critical and dangerous a pursuit it is, that can involve in its forbidden operations even the peace of the innocent, who would willingly resist its incantations to their last breath."

Meanwhile they again began to hear the voice of the strange lodger above stairs, mingled with sobs and sighs, and wild fierce laughter, even louder than before.

" Good God !" cried the professor, in much alarm ;— " suppose the horrid noises were to awaken the child !" Already he had raised his hand with threatening gesture towards the room above; when instantly checking himself, he sank down upon his knees and said : " Help! help me to pray! good master; that will avail us much better here." Both then prayed, and all grew still.

When they had again seated themselves at the table, the old master first spoke:

" Assuredly, Mr. Professor, you must have disturbed my mind by some other means besides those used with the magical mirror. You had better at once speak boldly out, and confess how it is that this strange unhappy lodger continues here; he is in some way connected with your proceedings."

" So indeed it is," replied Nordenholm. "For having learned that my Agnes was to be sought for somewhere in the south, I instantly collected the scattered remnants of my fortune, in order to seek her in those parts. The better to further my views, and gain access to various classes of society, I assumed the title of doctor and professor. While I was absent, you were presented with little Margaret, whom you found at your own door; but it was my fate, alas, to encounter many less fair and pleasing sights, cruel and frightful adventures, which bore me, like a whirlpool, into the gulf.

" I had journeyed as far as the city of Venice. There I heard mention of a certain sorcerer, who knew how to unravel all mysteries upon earth ; and as I found all my inquiries after my lost Agnes were fruitless, I formed an acquaintance with him ; and he is the very same strange being whom we just now heard crying out and lamenting over our head. On consulting him, he declared that he must have some fixed abode, where he might prepare his conjurations; and that having first provided him with a floor in my own house, he would attend to my wishes. When he got possession, however, he did not keep his word; pretending that the image of Agnes appeared only dimly floating before his eyes. Moreover, I heard it currently reported at Venice, that this was merely the apparition of a real sorcerer who had flourished centuries ago; and, owing to some want of foresight in his art, had fallen a sudden victim, and had never since been enabled to enjoy the least repose."

"Just Heavens! that I feared," exclaimed Rhenfried. "Margaret has this very evening read me his dreadful history aloud! Come what may, however, no time is to be lost; we must rid the house of him, at all events." Having said this, the old master proceeded once more to trim his lantern; took his good sword under his arm, and strode boldly out of the room. Nordenholm ventured not to oppose him, but followed at a distance, trembling with doubt and terror, up the steps and along the sounding staircase until they reached the strange lodger's room.

The grey-headed host knocked smartly at the door; it began to open very slowly, but not as if moved by a human hand; for the fearful guest was seated quite at the other end of the chamber upon the ground, wrapped in a red mantle, several household implements scattered round him, and a dull blue fire flickering, and casting its fitful shadows upon the opposite walls.

The strange lodger cast a keen glance at the intruders, with a smile of scorn upon his lips; and as they continued to gaze upon him, more fierce and fiery glances shot from his sunken eyes.

"Give yourselves no trouble!" he shouted, in a hollow voice; "I well know your object, and what you want here; but nothing will come of it, at least during your lives; and it is a question even whether Master Philibert's grand-children will make me quit. For I am of a very tenacious nature, and apt to tarry long at a place."

The professor here sighed deeply from the bottom of his soul. The red mantle tried to force a laugh, but in this he could not rightly succeed; though he said in triumph, "One of you, I well know, is burdened with heavy thoughts. Of that at least I am certain!"

"For me," replied old Master Philibert, very calmly, —"for me, I feel still more certain that I am not the person. Yea, and I know something yet more—that you will not venture to stay in this house another quarter of an hour; for I hereby conjure you, in pure and lively faith, with the fear of God before my eyes, confiding in Him only, to depart from hence out of this house, and never to cross its threshold more. What is more, you shall decamp forthwith, secretly and quietly, without offering to disturb a single Christian soul within these walls, without any knocking, rumbling, or roaring of any kind. Now!—avaunt! —are you going? or will you have me to appeal to more strong and terrible adjurations in the name of the Lord? Will you wait and rue your folly, or be gone?"

At these last words, with quick, horrible, and threatening gestures, the lodger gathered up his strange furniture, and hiding them under his red mantle, he hastened towards the door, fiercely murmuring as he went by, "Thou cunning old professor—thou arch-deceiver—not a word in my defence against that savage greybeard, dumb villain as thou art! I will away from these walls; but, then, what woe—what woe—yet—yet!"

His voice continued to utter this close in their ears after he himself had disappeared. With the careful eye of a prudent householder and father, Master Rhenfried examined all parts of the room with his lantern, in order to ascertain that nothing of an unhallowed or diabolical kind had been left in the haunted room. He could discover nothing, except that upon the little table there remained the same old gold coins, counted out in payment of the strange lodger's rent.

"Hem!" said the master, thinking awhile to himself, "an honest spirit in his way; yet I must not venture to take possession of the gold; though, again, it is doubtless a Godsend, which ought not to be buried without turning to use, nor misapplied; I will convey it, then, to St. Ursula's hospital. Morning is already glimmering through the window-shutters; I think we will awaken little Margaret, and take her along with us; for the child is always eager, and even quite fond of walking that way; none so pleasant, she thinks, when I go along with her."

Very soon, then, the professor and Master Rhenfried were proceeding on their route, conducting the pretty Margery carefully between them, along the beautiful avenue of lime-trees which leads with gentle ascent to the front of the hospital. The little girl laughed and jested in so artless and engaging a manner, as to lighten up the sad contemplative features of her companions with occasional smiles. They met one of the women of the establishment; and clasping her little hands, Margery addressed her in the most friendly voice:—"Ah, lady Sibyl! ah, lady Sibyl! thou that art wont to bring me always such sweet fruit, and gett'st nothing but a pat on the cheek in return. Good morning, a very good morning, lady Sibyl."

Just at that moment was heard a confused uproar on the opposite side to where they stood, and a group of students made their appearance carrying a bier, apparently with some wounded person, to seek assistance at the hospital. Lady Sibylla, at this sight, breaking loose from the child, hastened to her post; the two friends followed her thoughtfully, while Margery hid herself anxiously behind a rose-bush.

The bier was now let down, the students gathered round in a circle, while the woman began cautiously to examine the person's wounds. They all made way, how-

ever, for the professor and Master Rhenfried with marks
of great respect; and one of them began to whisper to them
how the strange student, Marcellin, had engaged with and
disarmed one of the senior students, and then confessed
an injustice of which he had been guilty on the previous
evening, upon which a complete reconciliation took place.
"So it might have been, likewise, with the second quarrel,"
continued the relater, "or at least nothing fatal would
perhaps have happened, when suddenly—no one knew
whence—an old strange-looking man, clad in a red mantle,
stood in the midst of us all, murmuring some unintelligible
words, and looking highly displeased at us. The combatants seemed to fight more and more furiously. In a moment the stranger, stooping down, filled his hands with
sand, which he cast repeatedly with the speed of light in
thick clouds between the rivals, at the same time loudly
laughing, ' Hail to you, old master! well a day! have I
played you a trick? Now for Venice; now thou hast got
it well—woe—woe!'

"We heard him say these words, though he was gone,
nobody seemed to know how. Lost in astonishment, we
at length turned our eyes to the combatants, who both lay
bleeding upon the ground; the senior was dead, and Marcellin we have here brought along with us in the situation
you see. Their companions have made their escape: and
we, though less guilty, are come forward willingly to deliver ourselves up to whatever punishment may be thought
due."

The professor and Rhenfried, not without evident reluctance and shuddering, drew nigh the bier; pale and
bloody, Marcellin raised himself up; he knew Nordenholm, moaned, and then exclaimed in rage, "Thou black
sorcerer—abandoned sorcerer—I vowed to do it; I saw thy
hateful visage when you conjured up the image of my sweet
wife's father, all sorrowful and bathed in tears. Then sat
she in her bower, near Naples—in the soft moon-shine—
know you it—know you it not well? In an agony of

remorse she turned away from me, and thenceforth our bonds of love were broken asunder .... Nay, I have never since once beheld her any where on this wide and desolate earth. Then hastened I hither, to have my revenge on thee: and here I must sadly die. And yet now were all obstacles overcome; and the sweet saint was again mine, the partner of my ducal power and splendour—she for whose sake I became a vile apprentice—and God knows what worse—yea, I had led her home—had her mine own in all the pride of love and splendour .... But now she is far away, and I am dying—dying, another victim of thy hateful infernal arts."

A murmur was heard among the students, "The fever is mounting into his head;" others, however, were more doubtful, and hazarded a variety of conflicting conjectures. Master Rhenfried looked round him with a free and noble air ; he then took his cap off his fine grey head, and spoke in a clear but mild tone, "To the very respectable young students, and any other spectators who may wish to put questions on this affair, I here stake my life and honour that Professor Nordenholm is wholly innocent of causing this young man's death."

The murmurs became still, all moved respectfully in token of assent to the worthy old man, and they began to advance excuses, and canvass the professor's conduct in a more favourable manner. He himself, however, appeared unconscious of what was passing around him; he stood the very picture of grief, the hot bitter tears coursing each other down his cheeks.

Master Rhenfried meanwhile bent over the dying man, and with gentle firmness said, "You will soon appear in the presence of the great God, my dear sir; and now you see before you the face of that man whom you have the most deeply betrayed and injured, even deprived of his last sweetest hopes on earth. But God be praised—I know, I confess, Him who purchased us with His blood, bore all our sins, and has paid the price even for yours. So take comfort, dear sir; I forgive you from the bottom of my soul; and if you depart with feelings of penitence and reconciliation, you may likewise meet with still greater compassion — pardon — rest in that eternal state to which you are now hastening. With whatever of evil and deceit, Ludibert, you assumed the name of Wendelstern on earth, you may yet, through this your sorrow and ruth, retain your name, and become a bright star[1] in heaven, high above all your earthly pomp and state; in a sphere where all may unite in the enjoyment of the same heavenly blessedness and delights. Go, then, dear Ludibert, with a meek and reconciled spirit, in humble hope that thou mayest yet wake mid the light of a happier morn."

The supposed Marcellin, now the unhappy Ludibert, stretched forth his hands to the good master, and mildly turning his eyes to the spot where stood the late hated Nordenholm, a friendly smile played upon his features; he pressed his hand, bowed down his head upon it, and died.

Now, too, it was first observed, that the female attendant had fallen into a swoon by the side of the bier. The old man gently raised up her head, and held her until she came to herself; when, refusing all farther assistance, with feeble step, and drawing her hood and cloak closer around her, she proceeded towards the hospital. The students again raised the bier, and in perfect silence bore the deceased slowly along towards an ancient half-dilapidated church at a short distance; while Nordenholm, not a little consoled after seeing Ludibert's peaceful departure, with his usual promptness and decision pointed out to them, in few words, when they had set down the bier at the church-door, all that was necessary to be observed on such an occasion, and how they might best clear up their conduct by shunning not, and by disguising nothing from, the civil power.

[1] In German, *Stern*.

The students bowing respectfully and returning their unanimous thanks, while they at the same time condoled with him, then took their leave, shewing, by the sorrow of their countenances, how much their hearts were made better.

Meanwhile the spital woman had beckoned the aged Rhenfried to accompany her; and stopped, as she was entering the hospital, under the vaulted entrance, where she began to enter into earnest discourse with him. Seeing the professor approaching, the old master beckoned to him, and said, "Here, friend, this good woman wishes to communicate something to us; let us hear her."

She then threw back her veil and hood; and there stood before them the long-lost and lamented Agnes, saintly pale indeed, and bearing the traces of deep suffering, but whose features were not to be mistaken by the eye of a father and of a lover. In the same serious and lofty frame of mind, produced by what had so recently happened, all three seemed now to regard earthly sorrows and earthly wishes with a spirit of serene and cheerful patience; and whatever the future might have in store for them, either to part with or bear, they were already prepared for, and saw as it were approaching along the vista of coming years.

Little Margaret, who had laid herself to sleep beside the rose-bush, overpowered with the last night's anxieties and fatigue, now came skipping towards them, and playfully caressing the weeping Agnes, said, "How beautiful you look this morning, dear lady Sibylla, now you have thrown aside your black cap and hood; but you must not cry—women never cry!" But her delight knew no bounds when she learned that the lady was going home to live with her, and was to have the room of the strange old lodger for her own, who was never coming back any more.

This, too, she found to be all true; she was quite enraptured at the change: and under the delicate and incessant guardianship and attentions lavished upon her by the three friends, pretty Margery grew and flourished, until she bloomed in full beauty, one of the most fair and lovely flowers in the rich garland of Germany's gentle women.

www.ingramcontent.com/pod-product-compliance
Lightning Source LLC
Chambersburg PA
CBHW030748230426
43667CB00007B/890